The Woollen Industry of
South-west England

**Origins of Industry**

The Woollen
Industry
of
South-west
England

*by Kenneth G. Ponting*

An industrial, economic and
technical survey

Augustus M. Kelley · Publishers
*NEW YORK 1971*

© 1971, Kenneth G. Ponting
ISBN 0 678 07751 7
Library of Congress Catalog Card Number
77–78616

*Published in the United States by*
Augustus M. Kelley · Publishers
*New York, New York 10010*

# Contents

# Illustrations

CONTINUED OVERLEAF

*Acknowledgements to the illustrations*
The illustrations other than listed, are from the author's collection:
A. Adams 20, 23; Aero Pictorial Limited 10; Mrs. L. Holloway 55; Kenneth Hudson 8, 11, 14, 16, 17, 18, 19, 22, 46; K. Rogers 15; National Buildings Record 4, 5, 6, 7; National Portrait Gallery 53; Science Museum 39, 41, 42, 53; Tolson Memorial Museum 48; W.I.R.A. 35, 36, 37, 38, 40.

# *Preface*

MUCH HAS BEEN WRITTEN ABOUT THE history of the wool textile trade in the West of England, but most of it has been in the form of individual studies and it was thought that a general picture is needed. Increasingly the effort and work of economic historians are based on special studies. The nature of the documents that they have to use, and in particular the great number of them, make any other approach impossible. This can lead to outstanding work. One has only to instance Dr Ramsay's brilliant book on the Wiltshire woollen trade in the sixteenth and seventeenth centuries to see what can be done.

Given the great amount of published information and the even greater amount of unpublished documents that are now known to exist, it is perhaps over-bold to attempt a general picture, but it is hoped that the excuse will be allowed that this is written by one engaged in the trade with practical experience of cloth-making. This approach is, perhaps, permissible because processes in wool textile manufacture have not greatly changed, and the problems of the purchase of the raw material and the final selling of the cloth remain much as they have always been. Any manufacturer today, for example, who dips into some of the works that have been written will feel a flash of recognition when he comes across some of the complaints his predecessors had to face. In addition an attempt has been made to portray the textile worker through the ages, toiling to produce the cloth. Wool has many virtues, but it does vary a great deal and is not the easiest fibre to handle even with the most modern machinery. The Chairman of Courtaulds, speaking recently to a group of wool textile men, congratulated them on the way they had managed to process such an impossible fibre for so long; but he was perhaps prejudiced, and the fibres that he himself makes have their processing difficulties too. Nevertheless, the remark has point, and if the writer has managed to indicate some of these problems he has achieved what he intended.

The author is concerned – perhaps too much concerned – with the upheaval that the Industrial Revolution made in the lives of the workers. The way in which the processes were carried out was, in a fundamental sense, not greatly changed and it is possible to argue that the only really revolutionary development in the textile trade during this period was the concept of roller spinning invented by Lewis Paul. (It is a pity that some genius did not start the loom on a similar path.) This, however, does not mean that the lives of those workers who left their own cottages and went to the factories did not change. In his introduction to *The Skilled Labourer*, J. L. Hammond has written of the Yorkshire workers:

> Something of the atmosphere of a tragedy, the tragedy that seemed to set science in the lists against happiness, and science and knowledge against freedom, clings to the villages and the grey hills of the West Riding. The bleak and sombre landscape that gives its sad tone to the life and the art of the Brontes seems to speak of the destinies of that world of combers and croppers and spinners and weavers on whom the Industrial Revolution fell like a war or plague. For of all these classes of workers, it is true that they were more their own masters, that they had a wider range of initiative, that their homes and their children were happier in 1760 than they were in 1830. Surely never since the days when populations were sold into slavery, did a fate more sweeping overtake a people than the fate that covered the hills and valleys of Lancashire and the West Riding with the factory towns, that were to introduce a new social type for the world to follow.

To a considerable extent the West Country workers shared the same fate.

It has been fashionable during recent years to argue that the Hammonds overstated the case, but here the author would bring a scrap of personal information as evidence in support of their views, namely, the stories that his grandmother told him of her father, one of the last of the handloom weavers, and of his determination not to go into the factories. This is not much to set against the arguments of the opposition yet there is much truth in what the Hammonds wrote.

The debt to earlier economic historians is very great, above all to those of the older generation who wrote so well, to the Hammonds especially, and more recently to such writers as G. D. Ramsay, E. Sigsworth and S. D. Chapman.

Finally there is a special debt to Miss Julia Mann whose own work on the West Country trade is so keenly awaited. Nothing could have been more delightful than the innumerable discussions the author has had with her about the trade.

For architectural information my debt to Mr K. Rogers is very great.

# PART I

*From the earliest times to the Industrial Revolution*

**Chapter One**                    *Early History*

THE EARLIEST EVIDENCE OF SPINNING
and weaving comes from the Neolithic or New Stone Age cultures of the Mediterranean area, around 5000 BC. These crafts must have developed over many hundreds of years, but certainly by the time of the Neolithic cultures of Crete and pre-dynastic Egypt, spinning and weaving were well established. We can look, therefore, for the first signs of these two crafts in Britain with the arrival of the Neolithic peoples, who reached the South-western coasts of these islands around 2500 BC. They settled on the chalk country and are sometimes known by the name of their most famous encampment, Windmill Hill, in Wiltshire. A little later they built the long barrows, presumably the tombs in which they buried their leaders, and these remarkable monuments are found widely spread over the South-west. Among the finest examples are the West Kennet Long Barrow near Windmill Hill, Stoney Littleton in Somerset, and the picturesquely named Hetty Pegler's Tump, near Uley in Gloucestershire. All lie in the heart of the traditional clothing country of the West of England.

Though archaeologists have found comparatively few remains of either spinning or weaving in these tombs, we know that the allied cultures, from which their builders came, practised both. There can be little doubt, then, that spinning and weaving came to Britain with these skilled Neolithic people.

All the main natural fibres – wool, cotton, silk and flax – have been found among the early archaeological remains that are scattered throughout the world. Each of these fibres was used in different regions and each of the more important early civilisations seemed to have had its preference – the Egyptians for flax, the Sumerians for wool, the Indians for cotton and the Chinese for silk. Generally, though, wool was not as widely used in the Ancient World as flax. It was thought unclean in Egypt and was indeed better suited for a colder climate. When the centre of Western civilisation shifted northward with the collapse of the Roman empire wool was to become its main clothing fibre. The fact that, in recent years, wool has lost a little of its popularity, can be attributed to the fact that we now live so much in a centrally-heated world. The Neolithic inhabitants of Windmill Hill, however, probably processed both wool and flax.

3

Yarn was spun at first without any tools or aids. It is quite possible to spin with the fingers alone although the amount of yarn so produced is small. There were many different ways of hand-spinning and to understand them it will help to divide the process into its three distinct elements.

First there is the drawing out of the fibres to form the yarn. This is now known as 'drafting'. Then the 'twisting' of the fibres, to give the yarn its strength. Finally the 'winding-on' of the fibres, or reeling the thread on to a convenient holder. The hand-spinner drew out the fibres from the prepared bundle and made the thread by rolling them between the palms of the hands, or by twisting them in the fingers of one hand while holding the ends fast in the other. In this manner a thread can be produced slowly but surely. It was not long before a stick was used on which to wind the prepared thread and this in turn led to the idea of the spindle – the first crucial invention in the early history of spinning. It is impossible to over-estimate its importance and it remains in use today in all types of spinning. Originally, the spindle was a thin piece of wood, at first of bone or ivory, but after the end of the Neolithic age, also of metal. Because wood is less likely to survive, it is easy to get the impression that wood was less commonly used than the other materials, though this is not the case.

The next great advance in spinning came when the spindle became something more than a holder for spun yarn. Three changes were made: the spindle was tapered at the top; a notch was made near the tapered end; and a weighted whorl was added to the other end.

The spinner was then able to fasten the spun yarn already wound on the spindle by means of the notch and by revolving the spindle obtain a supply of twist other than that given by her own fingers. Part of this was allowed to slip through the fingers to assist the drafting and the remainder transferred to the yarn when drafting was finished.

The spinning method sketched here was, with certain variations, in use throughout the world. It is unlikely that any of the improvements mentioned originated in Britain. They would doubtless have come over with the many fresh groups of colonisers arriving from the Continent. The simple spindle and distaff method of spinning, still used in many parts of the world, has the advantage that it can be done anywhere, indoors or outside. The spinner can take her work into the fields and at the same time keep an eye on the animals owned by the family, the distaff carried under the left arm or placed in a belt round the waist. Anyone travelling in south-eastern Europe today can still occasionally see the peasant women doing this.

The 'mule' still widely used in woollen spinning, though not in other branches of the trade, reproduces these hand motions mechanically. When showing the famous Sherpa mountaineer, Tensing, over a woollen mill, the writer was delighted to hear him exclaim, after a careful examination of the mule: 'But that is exactly what my mother does in Nepal'.

It is rather more difficult to say how the other main process – weaving – began. Basket work, which many animals do when building their homes, came first, and it is difficult to distinguish between basket work and weaving. For our purpose it is best to define weaving as the process by which one series of threads is interlaced at right-angles with another to produce a fabric.

The earliest method was to tie the lengthwise, or 'warp' threads between trees or posts, or more conveniently, between a tree or post and the weaver's waist, and then to interlace the cross threads or 'weft'. This earliest form of weaving was a kind of needlework, no mechanical aid being used to thread the weft through the warp.

As in so many other crafts, the Egyptians led the way. They were the best weavers of the ancient Mediterranean world and they used two types of loom – the horizontal, and the vertical in which the warp was stretched from a bar by loom-weights.

These looms spread to the more primitive civilisations, such as that in Britain, where, in particular, vertical looms must have been relatively common to judge from the large number of loom-weights to be found in museums.

Later, the Egyptians advanced beyond the simple interlacing form of weaving. They introduced the 'heddle' which gave them control of each individual warp end. This was one of the crucial advances in weaving, and any form of weaving that uses a heddle bears a resemblance to the type of loom used today. The heddle was fixed in a container now called a 'harness'. In the simplest form of plain weaving, the heddles containing ends 1, 3, 5, 7, etc, are fixed to one harness and those containing ends 2, 4, 6, 8, etc, to another. The weaver has then only to lift one harness to form a 'shed' through which he can easily slip the weft 'pick' or length of thread, which before had to be interlaced laboriously, thread by thread. At first the pick was inserted by means of a spool, and many centuries passed before the shuttle was invented for this purpose.

Once the weft 'pick' or thread length had been inserted, the next operation was to beat it up to the 'fell' or the edge of the already woven cloth. This was done by a weaver's 'comb'. Comb-like objects are among the most common textile remains in early Britain, and archaeologists are generally agreed that they are weavers' combs used for 'beating-up'. It is not certain, however, that this was the only use for these combs at this stage. Some of them could have been used also for combing wool to prepare the fibres for spinning – as an alternative method to 'carding' (see Chapter Two).

Originally the 'pick' was a separate length of weft, with the result that the cloth had a frayed edge which easily worked loose. But with the development of the heddle, of shedding, and of the use of a spool holding a greater length of yarn, the weft became continuous and a neat edge, or selvedge was obtained – yet another Egyptian invention.

Pre-Roman Britons, then, made use of both the spinning and the weaving processes. But it is doubtful whether they used the preparatory process of 'carding' or the finishing process of 'fulling' (see Chapter Two). The wool was probably spun much as it came from the sheep's back and the only finishing was perhaps some kind of scouring, though formerly it was thought that both carding and fulling were introduced during the Roman occupation. At one time archaeologists maintained that Chebworth Manor, a beautifully situated Roman Villa near Cirencester, was a Roman fulling establishment, with fulling tubs similar to those shown in the murals at Pompeii, but recent excavations have shown that these tubs were simply Roman baths. In this connection it is difficult to know what significance to give to the weaving establishment at Winchester mentioned in an edict of Diocletian, for there is little evidence to establish that there was any kind of cloth industry on an organised scale. Indeed, Roman Britain was essentially a villa civilisation and any wool produced would have been spun and woven into cloths within each villa. Even if no industry existed, however, the Romanisation of Britain must have improved cloth-making methods.

Probably the most lasting effect of the Roman occupation of Britain was on sheep-breeding. When the Romans came, they found a small native sheep, probably not much different from the Soay still found today on St Kilda (also to be seen at Whipsnade). The Romans introduced new, larger breeds, and some writers have suggested that our present long-woolled sheep may derive in part from these Roman breeds. Here, too, there is insufficient evidence.

We know a great deal about production methods in the main centres of the Roman world, however. Spinning remained unchanged and the Roman loom was no more advanced than that of the Egyptians. Improvements lay in other directions. 'Carding' to separate wool fibres before spinning, was done with the teasel (Latin 'carduus') and the demand for stale urine to provide ammonia for scouring shows that finishing methods must have been more developed. These methods may have spread to outlying provinces such as Roman Britain, but, as we have said, there is little definite evidence.

In Saxon Britain it is unlikely that spinning or weaving were on the level reached under the Romans, or maintained on the Continent.

But nevertheless, excellent embroidery was produced in Britain, of which the Bayeux Tapestry is a typical example, although made after the Norman Conquest. The piece that Brythnoth's widow embroidered to commemorate her husband's death at the Battle of Maldon may have been even finer, while St Cuthbert's stole at Durham is outstanding.

The Norman Conquest gave England closer links with Europe, and led gradually to the development of the urban, medieval wool-cloth textile industries in Britain.

Er omnis femina q̄ incandisam faciat similir q̄ p se sit
· ī manifeste hoc agat.

Ceo est la lei des teliers e des fuluns a Wincestre.

Ceo est savoir ke nul telier ne nul fulun ne peot
drap sechir ne taindre ne a nule marchandise hors de la vile aler· ne il ne poent a nul forain
lur dras vendre· fors as marchanz de la cite. E si ait ave-
noir ke nul des teliers v des fuluns pur la richesce
voulsist hors de la cite aler· pur marchandise faire· bn
leist as prudes humes de la cite prendre tut ceo chatel
e ramener en la cite. e faire de cel chatel cū de chatel for-
fait· p esgard des incurees e des prudes humes de la cite.
E si nul telier v fulun vendist a nul forain sun drap
le forain pt le chatel. e lautre remaint en la merci de la
cite de cink ke il a. ne le telier ne fulun ne poet adtruer
neis ceo ke apent a sun mester· kil ne face le gr̄ al ur
curte chascun an. E nul frac hume ne poet estre atteint
par telier ne par fulun. ne il poent testimoin porter· e si
nul de els enrichoust si kil voille sun mester guerpir· for-
nure le e tuz utilz ostera de sun ostel. e si face tant vers
la cite kil soit en la franchise. E ceste lai unt il de la franchise e de la custume de Lundres. si cū il dient. →

The Law of the Weavers and Fullers of Marlborough
The oldest document relating to the wool textile trade of the West Country, showing that already in the
twelfth century there was an industrial working class in the wool textile trade in this part of the country.

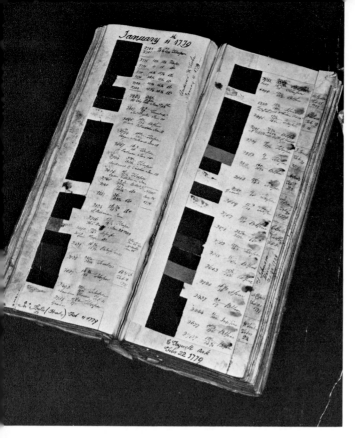

**2  *Salter's (Trowbridge) Pattern Book***
Pattern books of the various clothiers are the best evidence we have of the excellent quality of the cloth produced. The patterns in this case date from 1779 and are of the superfine broadcloths for which the area was famous.

**3  *Letter from Charles I to Prince Rupert***
The full text of this letter, printed in Part III of the book, gives some indication of how trade was affected by the Civil War, see p. 143.

# Chapter Two

# The medieval urban textile industries

BY THE TWELFTH CENTURY IT IS CLEAR that there was a flourishing cloth industry in several English towns. Among them, Lincoln, Northampton, Stamford, York, Beverley and Bristol were outstanding. As far as the West of England was concerned, Bristol was the great centre and we are better informed about cloth-making there than in any other town because, fortunately, in 1346 that sagacious and enterprising recorder, William de Coleford, entered all the guild regulations into a book. They give the best picture of the medieval cloth trade organised under the guild system that we possess.

Then as now, the trade had its two branches: the woollen and the worsted. The term 'worsted' originally came from the East Anglian village of that name in the thirteenth century but the difference was implicit in the way cloth was made even before then. In the medieval period woollens were the more important, but later developments have brought the worsted section of the trade to the fore.

The difference between the two runs almost throughout the production process:

1. Woollens are made from short wool; worsteds from long wool.
2. Wool for spinning into woollen yarns was 'carded'; that for worsteds was 'combed'.
3. Yarn spun from woollen 'sliver' (after the carding) has twist inserted while the yarn is being 'drafted' or drawn out. Yarn spun from worsted 'tops' (after combing) is drafted without twist, or with only a small amount.
4. Woollens are 'fulled' after the cloth has been woven. Worsted cloth is not normally fulled. This difference matters much less today, though in the Middle Ages, when woollen cloths were heavily fulled, it was very important.

Carding and combing apparently date back to pre-history, though their early development has never been clearly differentiated. We do not know which came first, though one might guess that combing was the more logical way of removing entanglements from wool. Carding was done by women and is never mentioned as a guild occupation. Combing, a strenuous and unpleasant job, was done by men, and the combers' guild has an interesting history.

Carding and combing follow the cleaning process and the main object is to separate out the individual fibres in the matted wool, which makes spinning easier.

Carding was done with the short, straight spikes of the teasel. Teasels with hooked spikes are also used to raise the nap on fulled cloth.

The name carding derives from the Latin 'carduus' for a thistle or teasel. In Old English the noun 'taesel' for a teasel and the verb 'taesan' meaning to tease or separate out have a common derivation. The spikes of the teasel are used to open and mix the short wool fibres, a process which produces a mass of fibres lying at all angles, giving a soft thread for spinning. Originally single teasels, picked and dried, were used. Later a number of them were inserted in a wooden frame making what was known as a 'hand card'. By the fourteenth century the teasel had been superseded by the use of nails inserted in pieces of leather fixed to squares of wood. These nails were later replaced by wires. One can get a picture of these by examining the cleaning cards now used for removing fettlings (the dust and waste material left in the card) from a modern carding machine. The medieval worker held a card in each hand and worked the wool between them until she had obtained a bulky lot of wool which the spinner placed on her distaff and from which she drew her fibres for spinning a thread. Card-making remained a common occupation in England for many centuries and Christopher Sly in Shakespeare's *Taming of the Shrew* was 'by birth a pedlar, by education a card maker'.

While the carding process aims at leaving all fibres blended together in the yarn to be spun, combing aims at removing all the short fibres, known as 'noil', which are mixed with other wool for woollen yarn. This removal of the short fibres may not have been a conscious aim in earlier times, when combing was perhaps regarded more as a way of disentangling the fibres from one another. Combing leaves the fibres lying parallel and lengthwise in the thread, producing the flatter, smoother surface of worsteds, which tend to shine after wear. Woollens with the more random arrangement of longer and shorter fibres tend to stretch and bag more easily. As will be seen later, the heavy fulling process to which woollens were subjected in medieval times made this less of a disadvantage.

The advantages of worsted made from combed yarn with its longer fibre were to become more apparent in later centuries as the spinning process developed.

Combing has a very long history. The first known references date from 1500 BC, in the Sumerian civilisation, though nothing is known of the methods used. Nor, surprisingly, are there illustrations from the classical period showing clearly combing as a distinct process. In a painting of the martyrdom of St Blaise, patron saint of the wool combers, the combs with which he is being tortured resemble those in use just before the introduction of machine combing. But the combs which killed St Blaise are not those of the wool combers, nor did he, in fact, have any connection with textiles.

The combing process, unlike that of carding, remained little changed over the centuries; it was indeed the last yarn-making process to be mechanised, continuing to be done by hand until the middle of the nineteenth century. From the point of view of historical record this is fortunate. The versions of how hand-combing operated given by several writers are not entirely accurate, but an excellent pamphlet by H. Ling Roth, curator of the Bankfield Museum at Halifax, based on descriptions and demonstrations given him by an old man who had been a hand-comber in his youth, illustrates the process well.

8

The combs consisted of two or three rows of long tapering steel teeth set in a wooden handle. Before being used they were heated over a fire. This was essential and a stove is always shown in any picture of the process. One comb was secured to a hook on a post, and two pounds of wool, oiled and scoured, were fixed to its teeth. The wool was then worked with a free comb, until all of it had passed on to the second comb. The process was repeated until the opening up of the fibres was completed and the wool taken off as a long sliver, leaving the short 'noils' on the comb.

It is doubtful whether combing, in its early days, removed all the short fibres, something that may have been seen as incidental to the disentangling of the wool. It may well have been that the spinners did not care to lose so much of their wool during its preparation and this could account in part for the predominance, over many centuries, of the carded woollens over the combed worsteds.

Spinning throughout this period, and until the fifteenth century, when the simple spinning wheel was widely introduced in England, continued to be done with a distaff and spindle. The method was little changed from that described in the first chapter. It was slow and tedious with little craftsmanship about it, though great care was needed to produce even or 'level' yarn. The size of the yarn depended on the weight of the carded wool and the amount of stretch given to each draw taken from the carded wool, both of which depended on the hand-spinner's judgement. With continual practice it could be done evenly, but the monotonous repetitive nature of the job led to carelessness. A great deal of uneven yarn must have been produced in those days of hand-spinning.

While the spinning process remained virtually unchanged throughout this period, weaving was continually being improved. Woollens and worsteds were woven on similar types of loom and the loom in use during the thirteenth century was the best piece of apparatus employed by the medieval cloth industry.

The early centuries of the Christian era had seen the development of a loom with pedals to form the 'shed' for plain weaving, by alternately raising and lowering each half of the warp. By the thirteenth century the loom had a take-up beam for winding on the cloth, a let-off beam for releasing the warp, and harnesses with heddles and temples to keep the newly-woven cloth at the correct width. During the thirteenth and fourteenth centuries the size of the loom was increased, particularly in width, so as to make a broadcloth of up to 100 inches wide. For this reason, broad-cloth weaving became an occupation for a man and an assistant, since the passing of the warp was beyond the reach of one worker. This loom made only plain weave, with two interlacings, and differed from the draw loom, which could weave fancy patterns, and was so called because the increased number of 'heals' or 'heddles' needed to raise selected parts of the warp according to the pattern, demanded a series of cords and pulleys by which the selected heddles could be drawn up. It is difficult to say what percentage of the cloth manufactured in the medieval urban textile industry was made on broad looms and what on narrow looms.

After weaving, the cloth was scoured. This was done by the dyers or the fullers, using stale urine, a convenient way of obtaining ammonia, the chief scouring agent. The history of this method of cleaning is long and interesting. It began at the latest with the Roman Empire, where in AD 190 the collectors of urine, the *fulliones*, became so prosperous that Commodius taxed them. Not many years ago people in Yorkshire could remember old fullermen telling how, when they first entered the mills, the urine was collected from the local public houses. It was known under a variety of names, such as old wash, old pot and lant, while in one district the man who collected it was widely called 'piss Harry'.

Of its use in medieval times most of our knowledge comes from Florence, then the world's

9

most important cloth-making centre. Receptacles were placed at the street corners and the inhabitants were expected to contribute to the supply. An observer at that time has reported that the contributions of gentlemen returning home from long evenings at the tavern were not particularly favoured. That most in demand was from the sober citizens and their wives, who enjoyed their evening potions with a substantial meal and then went to bed and brewed their contributions before adding them to the common fund. There is scientific justification for this view, as the liquor with the larger nitrogen content would be the better detergent.

The major difference in the finishing process between woollens and worsteds was that woollens were fulled, and worsteds were not. The fulling process was important at the stage in history under discussion, and was to become crucial in the later Middle Ages. Today, when fulling is rarely as prolonged as it was then, the difference is less clearly defined.

Wool, unlike other fibres, has the property of felting, indeed the fibres can become a fabric under pressure. St Clement, the patron saint of the fullers, before commencing a journey, put soft wool inside his shoes. When he had finished the journey, he found that the wool had been converted into cloth by the action of his feet. His experience summarises the process. Felt-making requires little more than carding and treatment in warm water.

Fulling, originally called 'waulking', meant shrinking the cloth by squeezing it while it was wet. This increased the natural tendency of wool to felt, producing a heavy felted fabric where the individual threads could not be seen. With worsted the intention, on the contrary, became more and more to produce a cloth where the design stood out clearly and sharply. Fulling could also be done by squeezing with the hands or beating with a rod. The east window of Gloucester Cathedral shows St James, with a fuller's club. More frequently, as the name 'waulking' implies, it was done by walking on the cloth, and this was the method used by the medieval fullers of Bristol. It is in fact still done by hand or foot in some parts of the world. To take two different types of fabrics, for example: the woollen shawls of cashmere were fulled by foot, and there have been few finer woollens than these; and in the not far distant past Harris Tweeds were fulled by hand and foot and several 'waulking' songs are known – sung by the workers to help them get through the monotony of the job.

Fulling by foot is the method shown in the vivid mural paintings of the process at Pompeii. The fuller stands in a trough tramping the cloth by foot, and his hands rest on the low side walls. It looks rather as if he is having a hip bath. The baths at the Roman manor at Chedworth in Gloucestershire are so similar to the fulling tubs shown at Pompeii that archaeologists thought they were used for that purpose.

The process was sometimes done by the weavers, and in Langland's famous poem *Piers Plowman*, we learn that Angus Perie of Dunoon at one time fulled his own cloths by foot in the trough, but had given up this method as being too strenuous and too chilly now that he had grown old. In the main cloth-making areas, however, the two occupations of weaving and fulling were separated at an early stage and the fullers lived in their own quarters. In many medieval towns the street they worked in was named after them, showing the importance to the trade of fulling, or tucking, as it was often called.

After fulling, the cloth was 'tentered', that is, dried on racks in the open air, while being stretched to a definite width. This process caused more litigation than any other, and cloth-makers were continually in trouble in the courts for over-stretching their cloths. Some stretching is necessary to get the correct width, as it is never easy to control the exact amount or evenness of shrinking during fulling. This cannot always be done, even with modern machinery, and must have been very difficult with the methods of medieval times. As cloths had to have a definite width, it was necessary, if the shrinking had been excessive, or uneven, to stretch it. This could be done to a remarkable extent without damaging the cloth, but if carried too far would impair its strength. In any case, the cloth would be liable to shrink back to the original width.

After fulling and tentering the cloth was usually dyed and the dyer worked with a small number of dyes using recipes of great complexity involving chemical reactions only understood in recent years. He used a strange variety of processes to produce fermentation and the smell from his dye-house was extremely unpleasant. The most important dyestuff at this period in history was woad and the large quantities used suggest it was the basis not only of blues but also of blacks cross-dyed with weld or madder.

The other vital woollen finishing processes were the raising and shearing. They are related to fulling, because the whole sequence combined to give the traditional woollen broadcloth. The raising of the nap on the face of the cloth was done with teasels with hooked points (those used for 'carding' had straight points). The best woollen cloth was raised and then shorn several times in order to obtain the skin-like finish which later became known as doe-skin and was highly popular. Teasels for raising were fixed in a hand-frame in the Middle Ages and are still used today, though now inserted in a revolving cylinder, to produce the same exclusive type of woollen cloth.

The shearing which followed removed the uneven fibres from the surface so that those which were left gave a nap of even length. This was done with hand shears which over the years developed into a somewhat strange instrument which was yet peculiarly well adapted to its purpose. Early forms were simple, but even those found at Pompeii considerably puzzled the distinguished archaeologist who unearthed them. He thought they might have been used for some sacrificial form of sheep shearing. Later forms can be seen in many museums. Until one realises that the shearman worked over a bench and used the shears with a kind of lever action, it is difficult to understand how they could ever have cut the cloth as evenly as they did.

This processing complex, which made up the manufacture of woollen cloth at this stage in the industry's history, is reflected in the guild regulations of the time – notably of Bristol, the outstanding centre of the West of England town trade. There are no regulations controlling the carding or the spinning, undoubtedly reflecting the fact that they were done by women and completely escaped guild control. But there were many for the weavers, dyers and fullers.

No cloth was to be made unless it was of a definite width. Anyone making cloths of the wrong width was to go before the mayor and be fined. Weft must not be used in place of the warp otherwise the cloth and the loom on which it was woven were to be burnt. Likewise, if the threads were deficient or too far apart ('tosed' as the weavers called it) the cloth and loom were to be burnt. Weavers who worked at night or in upper rooms were to be fined for a first or second offence. A third offence was punishable by exclusion from the trade for a year and a day.

Five shillings and a penny had to be paid for each new loom installed, and further ordinances prohibited any weaver from receiving yarn from outside the family. Bearing in mind the hand-loom weavers' shortage of yarn this is surprising to say the least. No woollen yarn was to be sent outside the town for weaving unless the city authorities had seen it first and no 'thrums' were to be used as weft. Today the word thrums is used to describe the small amount of waste yarn at the end of each warp and it is difficult to see how they could have been used for weft, unless the word has changed its meaning. Finally, each weaver was to have his own mark which had to be put into the cloth so that it could be easily recognised.

Bristol dyers had many ordinances regulating their use of woad, both in preparing it and in the actual dyeing process. Dyeing had to be done on the wool and the type of alum to be used at this stage of the process was also specified.

Especially interesting and important are the ordinances for the fullers, who, in Bristol, seem to have done all the finishing. They are specifically instructed to see that the cloth was properly dressed. Wages are laid down, both for those working at the 'perch', that is dressing the cloth, and those working in the pit or trough. These latter rules are numerous and contain a number of those restrictions to which the medieval spirit was prone. For example, a man must not work in a trough with a woman unless she be his wife. As with the weavers, no work was to be done at night.

Most significantly, Bristol fullers are repeatedly warned to have nothing to do with the rural fulling mills. By the time William de Coleford was recording these regulations (the mid fourteenth century) competition from these rural mills was already beginning, a competition which was to have a tremendous impact on the trade, as we shall see in the next chapter.

Other towns in the south, notably Winchester – where the fair of St Giles was a great selling centre – and Salisbury, had important textile industries. Laws controlling the weaving and the fulling are documented in some detail for both Winchester and Marlborough, about whose cloth trade, however, little seems to be known. Probably both Winchester and Marlborough made mainly burels, a type of cloth then fairly common, but which has since vanished. Documents from both Marlborough and Winchester refer to burellers, who controlled the trade. Chaucer uses both words in the *Prologue* to the *Canterbury Tales*: 'I will run out my burel for to show', where the word clearly means plain clothing, and later 'than the burel folks, although they were kings'.

Salisbury or 'New Sarum' comes into a rather different category. As soon as it was built it naturally became a centre for collecting wool from the Salisbury Plain and a cloth-manufacturing trade began. This development is interesting because Salisbury was perhaps the only major cloth-making town which escaped the general decline dealt with in the next chapter. Being a new town it was prepared to allow the new fulling mills to be used, and, of course, the rivers running through Salisbury were excellent for providing the necessary water power, which proved to be crucial to the next stage of development in the woollen trade in the West of England.

**Chapter Three**

# *The rise of the rural industry*

THE RISE OF THE RURAL WOOL TEXTILE industry of the West of England during the thirteenth, fourteenth and early fifteenth centuries depended on the application of water power to fulling and has rightly been described as an early industrial revolution. The three main wool cloth manufacturing areas of England: the West Riding of Yorkshire, the South-west clothing counties of Wiltshire, Somerset and Gloucestershire and all East Anglia were established by this revolution. It is perhaps the best example we have of the great effect that technical development can have on the history and distribution of an industry.

For the first time one of the main processes of cloth-making – fulling – was no longer carried out by human power. The new invention of mechanical fulling by water-power was adopted by all the main areas engaged in cloth-making, but more fully and with greater effect in the West of England, where it led to that area's great age of Tudor broadcloth. In the West Riding of Yorkshire, the change was of great significance for the future, causing as it did the geographic distribution of the industry throughout the valleys of the West Riding. It may be regarded as the first of many events that led to the establishment of the West Riding as not only the greatest wool textile centre of England but of the whole world. But in this initial period, the shift of the centre of the textile industry from the towns to the countryside had its more immediate and much greater impact in the West of England. In East Anglia during this period, the trade suffered to some extent in comparison with the West of England, because the lower rainfall and the flatter nature of the country meant that the rivers of East Anglia were not so suited to the establishment of fulling mills.

Although this industrial revolution had such a profound effect and although the old urban trade almost completely disappeared, one must not think of it in terms of a short-term revolution. Clothmaking continued for a long time in the old urban areas as is well illustrated by the continual attempts that city authorities made to restrict the development of this new method.

The common method of obtaining power during the early medieval period was by means of the water-wheel – one of the most important inventions of the period known as the Dark Ages, between the fall of the Roman Empire and the rise of the new states in the West. Already by the tenth century the water-wheel was in common use for grinding corn and there are many references to such use in the Domesday Book. The mill at Elcot near Marlborough, mentioned in Domesday Book, was later to become a fulling mill. It must, indeed, have been comparatively easy to adapt the water-wheel used for grinding corn to provide power to drive a fulling mill – though this does not mean one should undervalue the unknown genius who first had the idea. In the fulling mill the water-wheel was attached, by means of a cam, to a shaft which alternately raised and let fall a pair of hammers in imitation of the action of the human foot treading the cloth which was placed in the pit. This type of fulling stock was used until the invention of the rotary machine in the early part of the nineteenth century, by which pressure was exerted between rollers. Even after that fulling stocks were preferred for certain cloths and it was only recently that a well-known West of England firm, specialising in the manufacture of fulled cloths ceased to use them.

There were two types of wheel: under-shot and over-shot. For the first no mill-race or dam was needed, the wheel being turned by the action of the unimpeded current on paddles. This type was suited only to swift-flowing rivers of fairly constant volume. In time of flood or drought, there was the risk of the wheel being swamped or not turning at all. With the over-shot wheel, water stored in the mill-race or pond was delivered near the top of the wheel and caught in buckets or troughs attached to the wheel, which was turned by the water's weight. This method was obviously more satisfactory, but before it could be used the water had to be diverted from the river by a mill-race, stored in a mill-pond and delivered to the wheel by a chute controlled by a sluice. This was the more efficient type of wheel for a fulling mill and the construction of a mill-pond securing an even flow of water must have been important to the clothier. Later written records show the risks the clothiers faced if their mill stood idle because of lack of water.

The cuttings and alterations made to rivers during this period have left outstanding monuments of industrial archaeology throughout the recognised cloth-making counties and in the West of England they are particularly fine. The banks of the Frome divide the counties of Wiltshire and Somerset, the point where the clothing trade was most concentrated and the weirs along this river are of surprising size. The work involved in building, for example, the weir at Stowford, near Farleigh Hungerford, an important cloth-making centre from the Middle Ages to the nineteenth century, must have been enormous for the stones used are massive. The subject of their construction deserves more attention.

The fulling mill became an important feature of the landscape of the Middle Ages, and not only in England. In Cervantes' *Don Quixote*, the noise of six huge fulling mills caused the hero great anxiety. But when Sancho Panza laughed, Quixote replied: 'It might happen that really it is that I have never seen the fulling mill before, though thou, like a base scoundrel as thou art, were born and brought up along with such mean instruments of drudgery.'

Drudgery or not, the fulling mill meant that not only was a greater quantity of cloth processed in this way, thus stimulating production in the industry, but the tendency was to full cloth more and more, and to produce broader, more heavily felted cloth. It is not always realised just how heavy this traditional fulled broadcloth could be. When finished it was anything up to 40 ounces per yard, 58 inches wide – three times the weight of a modern suiting. During these years the heavily fulled broadcloth came to an increasing extent to be the main product of the woollen industry, particularly in the West of England.

Broadcloth originally meant cloth woven on a broad as opposed to a narrow loom (see Chapter

Two). The application of power to mechanised fulling stimulated the increasing use of the broad-loom (more and more cloth could be fulled under the heavy power-driven hammers). Eventually broadcloth became synonymous with heavily fulled and felted cloth and finally the word came to mean the thick, felted fabric which was to remain the chief product of the English wool textile industry for nearly five hundred years. No other cloth has been fashionable for so long. We can still see the excellence of these fabrics by examining the patterns that remain in the clothiers' pattern books, or perhaps even better by examining the fabrics in a costume museum. These broadcloths were so heavily fulled that the tailor had no need to hem his garments. He simply cut the cloth to the shape he wanted, and owing to the heavy fulling there was no risk of fraying.

Broadcloths and the West of England were closely connected, and the full development of this type of cloth led to the great days of the West Country trade. Broadcloths were also made in East Anglia, and were the basis of the so-called old draperies. Between the fourteenth and seventeenth centuries they formed an important part of the wool textile industry of England. Most observers, however, maintain that East Anglian broadcloths, with the possible exception of the cloths of Coggeshall, were never the equal of those from the West. In Yorkshire few broadcloths were manufactured, and apart from some relatively unimportant exceptions, it was not until the coming of the second Industrial Revolution of the wool trade that the great Yorkshire clothier Benjamin Gott began to make broadcloths that really challenged the West. By that time the great days of this trade were passing.

The traditional Yorkshire cloth was the Kersey, a well-milled narrow cloth in which no attempt was made to obtain the completely felted surface which was such a distinguishing feature of the broadcloth. Kerseys were sometimes called Northern Dozens, and were the main production of the new rural trade of the West Riding. They were basically of comparatively coarse cloth made from local wool. The name derives from the East Anglian village of that name, where, presumably, the cloths originated.

The effect of fulling mills on both quantity and quality of production is thus clear. But the most important of all effects of this technological change was to shift the location of the industry, or perhaps, rather, its centre of gravity, from the old towns to villages situated on streams which could produce the necessary water power. This shift was largely responsible for breaking the guild system which had such a tight control on cloth production in the towns. Without the freedom this brought, the trade could never have expanded as it did. The guild system had played a vital part in the growth of the urban textile industry, but, like most economic systems, it became more hidebound as the years passed. If the industry had stayed in the towns under the old guild restrictions then the great expansion which was to take place in the fourteenth and fifteenth centuries would not have come about. This removal from the towns freed not only fulling but other processes from guild control. The records of all the old urban cities are full of attempts to prevent the new method from being adopted. Not only were the towns determined that powered fulling should not take place inside their own boundaries, but they continually passed laws prohibiting cloth woven there from being fulled in what they called the 'upland mills'.

A considerable amount of work has been done on identifying early fulling mills in England. In the West of England a survey made of land belonging to the Templars included a mill at Barton, near Guiting Power in the Cotswolds. A charter granted to the Abbot of Stanley in Wiltshire in 1189 mentions another, but fulling mills were not common, even during the second half of the thirteenth century. At this time there are, for example, only 26 certainly recorded in the South-west clothing counties. Almost all these early fulling mills were the property of the Lords of the Manor. Many were existing corn mills converted to meet the new demands. Others were housed in new buildings. Without doubt the Lords of the Manor found in this invention a welcome new source of income, and they endeavoured to see that all cloth manufactured in the area where their influence extended was brought to their mills to full. The monopoly was so profitable that frequently, when some measure of freedom was granted to the tenants in other matters, the Lords expressly reserved the right to maintain the fulling of all cloths in their own hands. For example, in a West-Riding charter of 1228, granted by the Archbishop of York to Sherburn-in-Elmet, the burgesses 'in this our borough' were 'forbidden on pain of forfeiture to have an oven pan or fulling mill'. Those who made use of the Archbishops' dyepans 'might have in any week a cartload of dead wood in Sherburn'.

But during the fourteenth century fulling mills spread rapidly throughout the valleys of the clothing counties. Increasingly they came under the control of the new clothiers who were leading this industrial expansion.

It is easy to understand the manner in which the decline of the urban and the rise of the rural trade continued, aided and abetted by the restrictions which the city authorities exerted. Their attempt to make the guild system ever tighter as conditions turned against them is typical of what happens in a declining industry. The guild system, which previously had done much for the trade had now become a heavy burden. Not only were the restrictions expensive, but as trade declined other financial burdens increased. The whole urban industry had become completely over-regulated. The system was never intended for an expanding trade, or for a trade which would increasingly look beyond local boundaries for its development. It has always been the fault of those authorities who attempt to control industry to over-do the process. Here at the start of the history of the English cloth industry is a clear example. When a new, and perhaps necessary, regulation was introduced the authorities often forgot to do away with the unnecessary ones of the past.

In the last chapter, the laws of the Bristol trade were taken to represent the best the guild system had to offer. They can equally well be used to show what happened when trade began to decline. For example, in 1409 there is a petition to the master of the craft of weavers complaining of numerous manufacturing changes that do not fall within the guild rules. The ordinances against fulling outside the town are very definite. For example, the ordinances of the fullers in 1406 (in fact, a revision of previous ordinances) began with the usual statement that the laws are not being kept and continued, 'also whereas certain merchants of Bristol have before now been accustomed to full parcels of their cloth in diverse parts of the country round about, the which merchants after the said cloths are so fulled, seeing well that they are not able to be exposed for sale on account of the defaults in them without amendment and labour of the fullers of Bristol, wherefore it is ordained and assented that henceforth no master of the said craft cause any such defective cloth so fulled outside the town to be fulled and amended'.

When one remembers that these upland fulling establishments which were said to do such bad work, represented the future of the wool textile trade, the absurdity of the towns' attitude is apparent. The same position existed elsewhere. When Leland came to Beverley, the great Yorkshire cloth-making centre, he found that though there had been good cloth-making there, it was now much decayed. Bristol suffered more than most towns. Of all the rivers the tidal Avon would have been especially unsuited to fulling mills even if the authorities had allowed them to be built there. Other urban centres of the South-west such as Winchester likewise suffered decline. Bristol held its trading position as a port dealing in cloth as long as Britain kept her Gascon empire, but when that was gone, decline set in. Her cloth trade was gone. The profitable wine trade with Bordeaux was gone. Even later when the Atlantic trade opened out with all its possibilities, Bristol was never quite able to regain the place her position warranted. In London, too, wherever the City's jurisdiction reached the battle against fulling mills went on, legislation being enacted successively in 1298, 1376, 1391 and 1404. After that date the prohibition was alternately lifted and reintroduced. Indeed it was reaffirmed as late as 1483, by which time the rural textile trade had become the source of the most valuable section of England's trade.

This growth of the rural trade had its origin in the changes brought about by the new fulling mills. But it would never have become the most important section of the English textile trade if general economic conditions had not been in its favour. And here the main advantage lay in the difference between duties on wool and cloth. The growth of the urban trade in the twelfth and thirteenth centuries, and the far greater growth of the rural trade in the thirteenth, fourteenth and fifteenth centuries, rested above all on the excellence of English wool. The importance of the medieval English wool trade has long been recognised and well investigated. But rather less attention has been given to the close connection between the wool and the cloth trade. It would be hardly correct to call this a partnership – more often it took the form of half-veiled antagonism, best illustrated by the way the cloth trade during its days of power restricted the export of wool and so kept down its price. The wool grower wanted to sell dear, the cloth manufacturer to buy cheap, and this contradiction has still not disappeared, even today. The interests of both trades, in prosperity or adversity, are intimately linked and the changing nature of the raw-wool supply has had almost as much effect on the manufacturing trade as have technical developments.

It remains something of a mystery why English wool should have been considered the best produced throughout medieval Europe. Spanish wool was eventually to be more highly prized – and at this time the Merino sheep was already established in Spain. So why then, this preference for English wool?

What was the quality which led the merchants of the Low Countries and Italy to come so keenly in search of it? There has always been some doubt as to what the wool was like. It may have been fine or coarse, long or short. Some writers have confused the issue by failing to realise that short wool would be fine and long wool, coarse. The combination of long and fine wool goes against the nature of the animal. The original, primitive sheep had two coats, a short, finer, inner coat and a longer, coarser outer coat. Perhaps the medieval English sheep-breeders supplying this Continental market had successfully bred away the coarse outer coat, leaving the short, finer wool as the main part of the sheep. There is nothing to suggest that the long wool types we know today existed before the improved breeds developed in the eighteenth century by men such as Bakewell. Today a long-wool sheep like the Border Leicester will give eight to ten pounds, while the medieval sheep corresponding closely to the Soay breed (see Chapter One) only carried one-and-a-half to two pounds. This must surely have been short and fine for it to have won the fame it did in the European markets. The fame of the Cotswold area has led to some confusion. Some people think the modern Cotswold breed was the foundation of the fortunes of the medieval woolmen. Yet this is a typically long-woolled breed with a fleece-weight of ten pounds – a relatively modern development deriving from Bakewell's Leicester.

Whatever its qualities, the popularity of English wool in the Middle Ages led the government to tax it more and more heavily, to help finance the dynastic wars with France. By contrast wool cloth was taxed much more lightly. In broad terms, since wool taxation was a complicated business, exported wool carried a tax of $33\frac{1}{3}$ per cent., while exported wool cloth carried a tax of only 5 per cent. It has been suggested that the discrimination was deliberate to ensure wool was used to manufacture cloth in this country. It is more likely however, that the first object was to raise money. It was realised, however, while wool could always be taxed since it could still be used at home, a heavy tax on cloth exports would have led eventually to both sources of income drying up. But whatever the taxation motive, the 'selective' form of taxation gave the dyers and finishers of Europe – and the English clothiers – their chance.

The European dyers and finishers realised that they could circumvent the tax, by purchasing cloth instead of wool. So, from England, and particularly from the West of England, they bought cloth that had been spun, woven and fulled, but not finished, dyed or cloth-worked. At their own centres in the towns of the Low Countries and Italy they converted it into finished cloths for the European market. As a result the weavers of these countries suffered severely, while the wealthy section of the cloth manufacturing industry, the dyers and finishers, prospered.

To meet this market the English clothiers, particularly in the West of England, began to produce white, undyed, broadcloth. Although the West of England led the way, increasingly this trade was adopted by the cloth-making centres of East Anglia. Towards the end of the medieval period, and even more during the early Tudors, we have the outstanding buildings, especially the churches, left by the clothiers, as sure signs of their prosperity. Here East Anglia echoes the West of England. There was a similar movement in the West Riding, though never on the same scale as in the West – no medieval towns, no churches, no country mansions that can compare with those in the South. Houses such as Westwood, Great Chalfield and South Wraxall in the West, or the Paycockes of Coggeshall in the East, or churches such as those of Lavenham and Long Melford do not exist in the north. But what was happening in the West Riding of Yorkshire, poor as compared with the West of England and East Anglia, had the germ of future greatness.

Broadcloth exports from the West were more important than those from East Anglia, where the coloured broadcloth trade did grow considerably, but went mainly to the home market. The export trade apparently required the heavier, more fulled cloths, and the fast-running streams of the South-west made for better fulling mills than the more sluggish East Anglian streams.

Considerable statistical evidence of these exports is available and much can be gathered from customs and aulnage accounts. Inaccurate as these may be they indicate broadly what was happening.

The customs records are the most informative. H. L. Gray, in a pioneer article written in the *English Historical Review* in 1924 was the first person to attempt to use these records. More recently Professor E. M. Carus-Wilson has produced a more complete list covering first the fourteenth century, and now, with Miss Olive Coleman, the whole period. The graphs in this latest volume present fascinating evidence, though this has hardly changed the picture given in Gray's earlier work, for which he deserves great credit. Between 1350 and 1400 the average annual exports of broadcloths increased from 15,000 to over 40,000 cloths – an increase relating to the remarkable development of the rural trade. Some indication can be seen from the figures for London, which in this period was fast succeeding Bristol as the chief port for this trade. In 1366–68 London exports averaged 1,240 cloths by natives, 35 by Hanseatic merchants and 1,678 by aliens. By the end of the century these figures were 4,197, 4,373, 5,353, respectively. Southampton's export figures also show the growth of the trade in the South-west. In the middle of the century Southampton exported 478 cloths made by natives, none by Hanseatics and 62 by aliens, increasing by the end of the century to 4,399, 12 and 5,596 respectively. These figures also draw attention to the closely related Salisbury cloth trade. The figures for East Anglia, at least as far as native manufacturers were concerned show a similar pattern. In 1366–68 Boston was exporting 1,131 cloths by natives, 1,544 by Hanseatics, and 54 by aliens. By the end of the century the figures were 3,379, 326 and 48 respectively. Lynn, not mentioned in the mid-century, presumably because of insufficient importance, was, by the end of the century, exporting 2,336 cloths from natives, 257 from Hanseatics and 9 from aliens. Similar increases are noted in the figures for Yarmouth and Ipswich.

H. L. Gray also attempted to obtain figures from the aulnage accounts to indicate the total production of woollens in the country, though it has been pointed out that these accounts cannot be trusted. Aulnage was an internal tax obtained by sealing each piece of cloth, usually after fulling, before it was sold. This was not done efficiently. The common practice was to farm out the aulnage, and the accounts in many cases were simply the returns that the person who had bought the monopoly cared to put down. But they do probably indicate certain trends, since the authorities would have been aware if the trade was increasing rapidly and even false returns would have to bear some relation to this. So the figures are worth quoting. By the end of the century Suffolk showed an increase of from 312 to 2,797 cloths. Essex, taken together with Hertfordshire for aulnage purposes, showed an increase of from 73 to 2,796. As may be expected, even these important increases were surpassed in the South-west. In the same period, Wiltshire's figures increased from 254 to 7,292, Somerset's from 1,211 to 12,376.

Such an expanding trade as that of the West of England rural cloth industry could only be based on expanding export markets and it is necessary to consider more carefully the structure of this new trade, so obviously dominated by the clothiers. What we cannot deduce from the existing documents we can surmise from the way their names, and more particularly their houses, have come down to us. The word clothier has a rather wide meaning and can, if one wishes, be taken to indicate anyone who is making cloth. Here it is used in a narrower sense as indicating someone who not only makes cloth but organises its manufacture. In this sense it came to have a rather different meaning in the West of England from that accepted in Yorkshire – with East Anglia holding an intermediate position, though perhaps leaning to the West of England interpretation.

The great clothiers of the West of England began to emerge in the rural trade and were essentially capitalists. They bought the wool and gave it out to the hand-spinners and hand-weavers to convert into cloth. Then they carried out the fulling, either at their own mills or at mills still owned by the lord of the manor in their area – finally sending their cloths mainly to Blackwell Hall in London to be exported, undyed and unfinished, to Europe.

A certain number of coloured cloths were made, notably at Stroud, already beginning to emerge as a centre for coloured broadcloths. But generally, the West of England trade, as will be described in more detail in the next chapter, was based on the larger clothier supplying the export market with undyed broadcloth.

In Yorkshire, the word clothier usually meant a working man who had established a small domestic cloth-making industry in his own cottage, helped by his family and perhaps one or two journeymen. His cloths were mainly for the home market and so his marketing methods were somewhat different, giving rise later to the system of cloth halls. Here lies the main difference between the clothiers of Yorkshire and those of the West Country. East Anglian clothiers, such as the Springs of Lavenham, the Cloptons of Long Melford and the Paycocks of Coggeshall were, as suggested, closer to those of the West of England.

Most leading West Country clothiers were to flourish in the Tudor period. Perhaps the outstanding figure of the earlier years of the rural trade was John Tame. He had begun as a woolman living at Fairford on the edge of the Cotswold country. Realising the great days of the wool export trade were over, he turned to cloth-making. He may be reckoned the first of the great West Country clothiers and his prosperity can be measured by the glass he put into the church at Fairford – unrivalled at that time.

**Chapter Four**                              *Tudor broadcloth*

were the great age of the West of England cloth industry. The clothing districts of Wiltshire, Somerset and Gloucestershire represented the chief industrial concentrations in the country. This trade overlapped county boundaries: the important production of Worcester and the varied products of the Kennet Valley in Berkshire can both be considered to belong to the same cloth-making district. The other West Country clothing area, the Somerset–Devon border, was topographically rather distinct; the great days of this serge-making area came in the seventeenth century.

By this period, the thriving and expanding cloth trade had completely replaced the raw wool trade as England's major industry. Sheep still grazed the Downs and the Wolds, probably in similar numbers. But they now supplied directly the English cloth trade, not that of Europe. At the forefront was the expansion of the broadcloth trade, and this expansion was, as one would say today, export-based. During the first half of the sixteenth century exports increased by something like 150 per cent. In 1565, admittedly a good year, cloth made up 78 per cent. of all exports; wool, with 6·3 per cent. came next; all other items together amounted to 15·7 per cent. The trend developing since the 'fulling mill' revolution of the thirteenth and fourteenth centuries (see Chapter Three) and which led to the rise of the rural woollen industry, now reached its climax. The second half of the sixteenth century saw no further expansion.

In the West of England the Tudor period was the 'golden age' of undyed broadcloth. This can be seen from the many records so excellently used by G. D. Ramsay in *The Wiltshire Woollen Industry in the Sixteenth and Seventeenth Centuries* (Clarendon Press) as well as from the assorted gossip of contemporaries, from John Leland's valuable if pedestrian reports to John Aubrey's flashes of genius. There are, in addition, innumerable out-of-door remains which the new study of industrial archaeology has brought to the fore. Using this evidence in its widest sense the overwhelming impact of the trade becomes clear. The published accounts of the successful career of William Stumpe of Malmesbury and that of the Horton family of Bradford-on-Avon are full of interest.

But much more is added by visits to the abbey church which Stumpe used as a loom shed and the family residence of the Hortons at Westwood. The adventures of Peter Blackborough, and later of Anthony Withers (see Chapter Five) are much more amusing if one knows the area where Blackborough operated and can view the bridge at Bradford where the irate clothiers deposited Withers. For towns like Bradford and Painswick it is possible to examine in detail the progress of clothing families and appreciate how they prospered and declined, or, more shrewdly, like Stumpe or Horton, invested in land.

Newbury was an important cloth-making centre, linked with the West Country area, though not concentrating entirely on broadcloths. John Leland described it as being one of the three most important cloth towns in Berkshire, along with Reading and Abingdon. The great days of the Newbury trade came at the time of John Smallwood, better known to history as John of Winchcombe, or in Deloney's fanciful seventeenth-century *Pleasant History* as Jack of Newbury. He lived in about 1520 and Deloney describes his 200 looms and 200 men and 200 pretty boys and 200 maidens all working in harmony together. It is difficult to say just how true this account is. But in Elizabeth's reign there were other wealthy clothiers in Newbury, particularly the Dolman family. Thomas Dolman was a much-envied businessman and he built Shaw House, one of the best Elizabethan buildings in Berkshire, completed by him in 1581. There is also in Newbury a building, now the museum, erected in 1626-27, and sometimes called the cloth hall. Built with money left by John Kendrick it was never a cloth hall in the sense in which the word is used in the Yorkshire trade. Here it was a kind of municipal cloth-weaving workshop intended to give employment to the poor. Originally three wings were intended but only one was built.

Exeter is also of interest, for here originated the important Somerset–Devon border trade in serges, which in the seventeenth century was almost equal in importance to the East Anglian trade. This trade, centred on Exeter, was for many years the mainstay of such places as Crediton, Tiverton and Taunton. Today it survives as a cloth-making industry in a famous mill at Wellington and, until recently, in an industry for producing worsted 'tops' in a few parts of Devon.

By the coming of the Tudors, the West of England trade was already well established and had moved some way towards specialising in the supply of undyed broadcloths to the finishers of Europe. There were exceptions. Stroud, a centre of the undyed broadcloth trade, was also famous for its dyed cloth – the Stroud-water Scarlets. Salisbury, the one town which survived the decline of the urban textile industry described in the previous chapter, continued its individual way, making a variety of cloths, and though in the expansion period it came under the influence of the undyed broadcloth trade, this influence did not last long. When the undyed broadcloth trade itself declined, Salisbury went back to making flannels and other miscellaneous cloths as in the past, although on a much reduced scale.

Almost all these undyed broadcloths went in their unfinished state through the great international port of Antwerp. The importance of this trade (three-quarters of England's overseas commerce) is apparent – as is its vulnerability to political change. It is safe to say that never before or since has the commercial prosperity of the country been linked so closely to the production of the three West Country clothing counties of Wiltshire, Somerset and Gloucestershire.

Such a large export trade calls for a complex organisation – particularly if the produce is handled in a semi-finished state. There must have been some flow of information between the ultimate buyer of the finished cloth in Europe, the finisher and dyer (who may not have been the same person), the London exporter and the clothier in the West Country who was responsible not only for the spinning, weaving and fulling but also for the choice of raw material – perhaps the

4 *Lane Chapel, Cullompton. Interior*
The Lane Chapel at Cullompton is the finest architectural memorial of the Devon/Somerset worsted trade and indeed can even claim to be the best in the West of England.

5 *Lane Chapel, Cullompton. Exterior*
The richly decorated façade shows amply the wealth, even ostentation, of the clothier of the time.

6 *Lane Chapel, Cullompton. Exterior decoration*
This detail shows the clothiers' shears so often used as a trade mark and as a memorial on ecclesiatical monuments.

7 *Lane Chapel, Cullompton. Exterior decoration*
The second detail shows the Lane trade mark and the teasels used for raising the cloth. Together with the shears in fig. 6 they clearly indicate that Lane was a clothier (i.e. a cloth manufacturer) not a wool merchant as is sometimes stated.

6

7

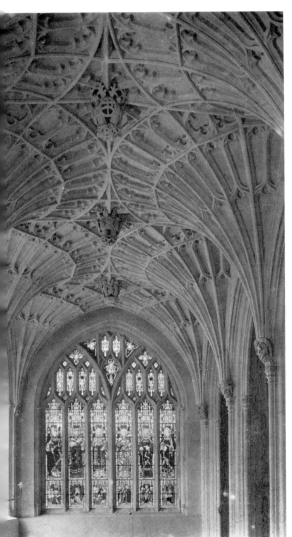

4  5

8 *Lloyds Bank, Trowbridge, c. 1720*
Probably the finest clothier's house in the West of England.

9 *Offices of Winterbotham, Strachan & Playne, Stroud* (above right)
A good example of an eighteenth-century clothier's house, now the offices of the
main West of England group of woollen mills.

10 *Aerial View of Trowbridge* (below right)
The mill in the foreground is Ashton and Court Mill, part of which has recently been demolished.

11 *Westbury House, Bradford-on-Avon*
Another typical clothier's house of special interest. One of the main riots
arising from the introduction of machinery took place outside this house.

most important task of all. Only a manufacturer of cloth can appreciate all this involved and it is strange that we have so little knowledge of how the information passed along such devious and complicated channels.

By this time, too, London had gained a complete hold on the cloth export business. By 1547 London was exporting 90 per cent. and three years later 93 per cent. Bristol had lost its share of the great trade. Here we are concerned mainly with the manufacturing end and unfortunately statistical information is scarce. So far as the writer knows, no reasonable estimate has been made of what percentage of the total trade was in undyed broadcloth. It must have been the major part, though the importance of coloured cloth must not be underestimated. For example, three raw materials (woad, madder and alum) which mainly served the cloth-dyeing and finishing trades, accounted for some 10 per cent. of imports to England. But it is right and proper here to concentrate on the undyed cloth spun, woven and fulled before being sent to London for export. There is no accurate information on the origins of this trade. Customs accounts do not help much because undyed cloths were included in these returns along with all other cloths.

The only special category in customs returns is cloths dyed in the grain, that is with Kermes, an expensive scarlet dye imported from the East. Although it is impossible to draw a close statistical parallel, there is no question that the phenomenal rise of the rural trade in the South-west must always have been closely linked with the undyed broadcloth.

As we have seen in Chapter Two, broadcloth was produced in the plain weave. The broadloom had only two harnesses. It is technically possible to use this for more varied work, drawing two adjacent warp ends on the same harness, or by inserting two weft picks into the same shed, but there is no evidence that broadcloth was ever woven in this way. Consequently these plain-woven broadcloths depended, for their consumer appeal, on the dyeing and finishing. The fulled broadcloth was the background of the final appearance. (Today there is a demand for undyed cloth for piece dyeing to obtain fashion shades quickly. This may well compare with the practice in the period we are discussing.)

In another way, the undyed broadcloth can be regarded as raw material for a separate industry. Its increasing importance coincided with the rise of Antwerp as a great cloth-finishing centre and the dyers and finishers of that city clearly found it the best possible raw material. After all, with the great difference in customs duties, explained in Chapter Three, it was cheaper to buy English unfinished cloth than to make cloth in Flanders from English raw wool.

The difference between the tax on wool and on cloth remained the real basis for the success of the rural woollen industry and the main cause of the clothiers' prosperity.

England's commercial prosperity still rested on the back of the sheep, and the exceptional history of the cloth trade in the sixteenth century, especially in the South-west, can only be understood if it is regarded as a continuation of the older export of raw wool. The most famous and important of Europe's medieval industries, which began with English wool and ended with the cloths of Flanders and Florence, did not disappear: the middle part of the business (spinning, weaving and fulling) simply shifted its location.

But there had been one change which, as yet, has received little notice. In its great days, the raw wool exported from England had been used to make the luxury cloths of Europe, as well as its cheaper cloths. But by the sixteenth century, the best European cloths came to be manufactured from Spanish wool which was now considered to be better in quality than the English wool. English cloth was left to supply the less expensive grades. Miss Eileen Power rightly refers to English wool supplying the luxury cloths of Europe, while Laurence Stone writes of it being

C

used to clothe the North European peasant. By the sixteenth century, the Italian trade, for example, had been almost entirely lost to Britain.

The West of England cloth trade remained a native one. There is nothing to suggest that it was helped by alien immigrations during the sixteenth century, though some have thought otherwise, stressing the community of Flemish weavers that the Protector Somerset brought to Glastonbury. However, this settlement was a fiasco and the only reason so much is known about it is that its many difficulties led to the colony being investigated by a government commission. It is one of the pitfalls of economic history that business generally is never so bad as it tends to suggest because investigations are never made of successful trade but only of failures. The arrival in England of foreign immigrants fleeing from Alva's persecution certainly changed cloth-making in East Anglia, but it is important to stress that in all areas the old broadcloth industry was essentially a native one.

The key position of the West Country clothiers has long been recognised and the trade is best understood if one tries to follow their day-to-day business routine, from the purchase of the raw wool, to the fulling of the cloth, its tentering and dispatch to London. The fulling establishments must have been their business centres, the places where the buying of wool was planned and carried out, and where the hand-spinner and weaver came to collect their wool and yarn. The traditional West Country theme of the cottage weaver making his regular journey to the mill became well established and was to continue until handloom weaving declined in the middle of the nineteenth century. It was the hallmark of the domestic system of the West Country, and an interesting point of difference with the West Riding.

The domestic system was finally established in the West Country during the Tudor period and the term is sometimes used vaguely to mean simply the system under which industry operated between the age of the guilds and that of the factories. But this definition is not quite satisfactory. There were Tudor 'factories' including the famous one of John Winchcombe, or Jack of Newbury as he is known in Deloney's *Pleasant History*, and the less well-known one of William Stumpe of Malmesbury. There had been something approaching this even in Yorkshire in the factory of Hodgkin of Halifax. Generally, though, too much has been made of these 'factories' in view of the final triumph of the factory system in the nineteenth century.

Stumpe in Wiltshire showed that all a factory at that time could do was to gather a number of weavers and finishers together in one building to supervise their work more effectively, regulate working hours more successfully, seek to prevent idleness and generally maintain a more uniform standard of production. However, the one process where uniformity of production was most called for – hand-spinning – was one which very few people ever succeeded in bringing to the factory. Few, indeed, suggested it could be done. It is doubtful whether Stumpe or Jack of Newbury or Hodgkin did this. They could get their weavers inside with their looms but not their spinners. By collecting the workers together under supervision, there may have been some advantage in preventing the petty thieving which must have been common during the domestic system period, and in the saving of a certain amount of waste. However, the advantage was a small one, and when it was found that the Government, for a variety of reasons, was opposed to this development, clothiers in all areas dropped the idea without losing very much. But, to describe the legislation of 1555 as a kind of anti-factory Act, over-states the case.

A great deal has been written in an attempt to define the difference between the domestic systems of Yorkshire and the West of England. In both areas the workers owned the tools or 'machines' they worked with. But in Yorkshire they also owned the material, whereas in the West they did not. The Hortons and the Longs had no real counterpart in the North. No one there built houses like the Longs at Wraxall or the Hortons at Westwood. Nor did anyone in Yorkshire equip factories on the scale that Stumpe did at Malmesbury. No one in the North traded on a big enough scale. But there was one feature common to all – the close alliance between farming and industry – though this connection was much stronger in Yorkshire than in the West. The major West Country clothiers were not farmers. They may have used the money they made in clothing to become landowners, but that was quite another matter.

Doubts have been cast on whether the clothiers controlled the yarn-making as completely as is sometimes thought. Many people were in the habit of buying small parcels of wool in the local market, spinning it and then selling it as yarn. The clothiers objected to this but were quite powerless to stop it. So great was the amount of yarn required that anyone with yarn to sell could find a buyer. The clothiers were also to blame because the wages paid for hand-spinning were so low. It was a part-time job done by the housewife when her other work was finished. Such occupations were always underpaid, and hand-spinning, throughout its long history, can probably claim to be the most sweated of all trades.

Indeed the real wages of all textile workers declined during the period. Money wages remained stationary while there was a considerable increase in general prices. The government made many attempts to regulate wages. The justices were given instructions to fix the rates of pay of any labourers, weavers, spinsters, workmen or workwomen whatsoever, working either by the day, week, month or year, or taking work at any person's hand to be done at home. These assessments were intended to state median wage figures for textile workers. Any clothier who refused to obey the command of the magistrate to pay the wage laid down to his weavers or spinners was to be fined ten shillings for each offence. Where effective these regulations did the workers some good. But the spinners were particularly badly paid, 3d or 4d a day being reckoned normal earnings. Considering the shortage of yarn it remains a mystery that hand-spinning was so badly paid. This encouraged the tendency, among those hand-spinners who had a little money to buy wool, to spin it and sell the yarn on their own account. Low wages paid by the clothiers also resulted in an ever present temptation to improve them by stealing a little wool. Clothiers were continually complaining that they never got back as much yarn as they expected. Even today, using modern machinery, the yield from wool to yarn varies from one lot to another without any very definite reason. This would be even more the case with hand methods, which made any checking by the clothiers almost impossible. The problem was made more complicated because it was necessary, before beginning carding (as with hand-combing) to oil the wool.

Today various oils are used, usually mixed with water. In Tudor times, it was customary to use butter. The weight of the yarn, including oil or butter, should approximately equal the original clean weight of the wool, or in other words, the waste in yarn-making should roughly equal the weight of the oil or fat added. But if a batch yielded, say, only 95 per cent., the clothier would naturally say his workmen had stolen some wool, while the spinner would doubtless reply that the blend had spun badly and made a great deal of waste. One cannot see how such a dispute could easily be settled, although the clothiers could attempt to make the spinner bring back all waste.

The clothiers said – and there is more truth in this argument than many they advanced – that buying yarn in small lots made it impossible to produce level pieces. With a cloth so heavily fulled as the broadcloth it must have been essential to have all the yarn spun from wool of the same quality, otherwise they could hardly produce a cloth conforming to all the regulations. It is difficult to judge wool quality in spun yarn and, in addition, the clothiers would want to have proper control of the amount of twist in the yarn.

The amount of yarn spun by individual yarn-spinners, working outside the clothier's control, increased towards the close of the century, because the growth of large clothiers dominating the whole trade was restricted by Elizabethan legislation. During the last years of the Queen's reign there was an increase in the amount of coloured or medley cloth made, and this trade brought a new group of yarn merchants to the fore. For some years they dominated this trade as the clothier had dominated the earlier undyed cloth trade. The spinner, in the case of this newer trade, did not cease to buy wool and sell the yarn, but worked for a new market. This new trade in coloured cloth made little progress in Wiltshire and Somerset during the sixteenth century, but was important in Gloucestershire.

The chief clothiers, however, must have bought the wool themselves – the nature of their trade and the need to produce a standard article makes any other conclusion untenable. And no problem troubled them more. Wool varies more than any other raw material and has always been bought from an actual sample and not from a type sample or description as is usual with cotton and rayon. At first the West Country clothier took his wool from the sheep on the surrounding downland. In the early growth of the rural trade this meant the downs round the valleys to the west of Wiltshire rather than those near to the Cotswolds. This left Cotswold wool to be pre-eminent in the history of the medieval wool trade, while more local wools were used for the developing rural cloth trade. Later, as the cloth trade expanded, the clothier went further afield for his wool. The woolman, who had previously collected wool for the stapler and the wool export trade, began to cater increasingly for the new cloth-making trade.

From the continual complaints of the clothiers one would think that these woolmen were a new invention, but they were only the descendants of such men as Grevel of Chipping Camden, Midwinter of Northleach and Tame of Fairford. They could claim a longer ancestry than any clothier, and since by this period, government taxation and interference combined with the rising home trade had almost finished the long history of England's medieval wool exports, the woolmen were naturally turning to supply the new home demand for wool. There seems no justifiable reason for the clothiers' antagonism. Probably it was partly fear of competition (some woolmen had turned clothier) and partly a hangover from a long drawn out rivalry between the wool trade and the cloth trade. The woolmen did valuable work in sorting the fleeces and preparing the wool for processing. It is impossible to say why any clothier should have thought it better to go round the farms himself and buy the wool straight from the sheep's back, when the woolman's unrivalled knowledge was available. Today one would think he wanted to swell his expense account. The woolman suffered, and had always suffered, from being thought a middleman – that great abomination of the Middle Ages, and an expression of a hostility that lingered into the Tudor period. But the woolman was no more a middleman than the clothier, and his value to the trade tended to increase, for during the sixteenth century, foreign markets were demanding a finer broadcloth, which made careful sorting of the wool more necessary than ever.

We cannot be certain what the sixteenth century sheep was like. Nor can we be sure how the wool they produced compares with today's product, such have been the changes brought about by Bakewell and the other agricultural improvers in the breeds. In so far as the main object has been to improve or increase the mutton-yielding properties of the sheep, the wool has coarsened. So Tudor wool is likely to have been as fine, if not finer than any wool grown in England today, though not the equal of the modern Merino from Australia. The enclosure movement of the sixteenth century, which began as a means of running more sheep to get more wool, must have started the tendency towards coarser wool. Confining the sheep fattens the animal but coarsens the fleece. Fine-woolled sheep need to be thin and to walk in search of their food. This tendency towards coarseness in the English wool assisted the increasing use of Spanish wool, which by the end of the century, if not before, surpassed the English wool in fineness.

From an early period wool from the Ryeland breed, native of Shropshire and Herefordshire was highly valued and, according to later records, much sought after by West Country clothiers. But by tradition the bulk of England's best wool came from the Cotswold country and the Cotswold sheep, though the nature of this wool during the medieval and Tudor periods is a mystery. Today the Cotswold breed gives coarse, unattractive wool. Certainly such wool would not have been used by the sixteenth-century clothier for his fine woollen broadcloth. One suspects the tradition, then. Perhaps indeed the wool from the local downs was better than the Cotswold for making the heavily fulled broadcloths.

We know little of the state in which the clothier obtained his wool or how he treated it. If it had not been scoured, then he would probably have washed it in the way we know from the eighteenth century – by putting the wool in some kind of container and lowering it into a stream.

As far as the evidence goes, there was very little dyeing of wool or yarn before making up, in the Tudor period. Most cloths were made undyed, the yarn being spun in the white and dyed in the piece.

It was in spinning that the main technical change in the wool production process had taken place. Previously all spinning had been done by hand with a distaff and spindle (see Chapter One). The fineness of work produced under these conditions was amazing: a Hindu spinner could produce 250 miles of yarn out of a pound of cotton with a slender wooden distaff weighted with small pellets. Spinners of woollen and worsted yarn, of course, did not spin as fine as this. Most woollen yarn was much thicker, but it shows what can be done. The first spinning-wheel, which came to Europe from the East, either a Chinese or an Indian invention, reached England by the fifteenth century. By the end of that century it was in wide use, though in districts away from the main cloth-producing areas spinning continued to be done with the simple spindle for many years, particularly where the spinster was producing yarn for her own family use.

The wheel then was introduced in the recognised cloth-making areas where the spinner produced yarn for an established trade. In this period the weavers often had difficulty in getting enough yarn, so rapidly did the broadloom consume it, and the impetus which the wheel gave to yarn production in its turn speeded its own spread in the wool-making process.

This type of wheel, known as the 'old' wheel, or Jersey or 'muckle' wheel, to distinguish from the later and more revolutionary Saxony spinning-wheel, drove a spindle by means of a cord. The spinner still carried her bundle of wool fibres on her distaff. But now she was able to use the spin of the wheel which she turned with her free hand, first to put twist into the thread when 'drafting' or drawing it out from the fibres and secondly, by spinning the wheel faster, to insert further 'twist' into the drafted thread. Next she would change the angle of the spun thread relative to the spindle and wind the yarn on to it, thus converting the spindle into a sort of reel for storing the yarn.

The 'old' spinning-wheel proved more suitable for the spinning of short fibres, which was one reason why its use was more widespread in the areas producing woollens. The later Saxony wheel favoured the spinning of long-fibred wools and was more closely related to the later growth of the worsted trade. Therefore by the end of the Tudor period the spinning-wheel had supplanted the distaff and spindle in the main producing areas.

We cannot be certain whether the 'stock card' (a more elaborate form of 'carding' the wool before spinning, by means of wire 'cards' operated by a system of pulleys) had been introduced at this stage in history. The loom was unaltered. The fulling mills were probably enlarged and improved.

Mechanisation was also applied to the raising process, though there is considerable doubt as to how this was done. This technical development was known as the 'gig mill'. Just what a 'gig mill' was in Tudor times, we cannot be certain. In the early nineteenth century a 'gig mill' in which teasels fitted into a revolving drum were used to raise the nap of the cloth, replaced the older hand-frame fitted with teasels. A fierce legal battle over its introduction was fought between workmen and clothiers. The workmen claimed the gig mill had been introduced and then made illegal by a statute of 1555 in the reign of Queen Mary, and they referred to that statute in their attempt to have the gig mill banned. The clothiers claimed that the gig mill they had introduced was different from that referred to in the Tudor statute – though not so much in the nature of the machine as in its use. They claimed they were using it in the normal and proper way – to raise the cloth after fulling. The Tudor clothiers, they said, used it for raising the cloth before fulling. But, under the Tudors, undyed broadcloth was raised (or more correctly 'dressed') after the cloth left England.

In this case then, the 'gig mill' in Tudor times could not have been used for its normal purpose on undyed cloth. Perhaps it was used in cloth raising or dressing only for Stroud Scarlets and other dyed cloths. Certainly on one occasion the makers of Scarlets argued that the gig mill statute should apply only to the white clothiers and not to themselves. They contended that their cloths had been thoroughly shrunk and dyed before going to the gig mill and so no harm would be done. It was a reasonable plea, but it was not heeded and the gig mills were prohibited.

The question of what use the white clothiers made of gig mills remains. In the parliamentary enquiry in 1806 into the statutes governing the woollen textile trade it was suggested that the gig mill under the Tudors had been used for 'perching' and 'burling' the pieces. Perching means pulling over a 'perch' or bar to examine for faults. Burling means the picking out of the cloth scraps of vegetable matter, knots or anything else which should not be there. Running the cloth over a gig mill would have loosened the bits and in many cases actually removed them, but at the same time the wool fibres would have been damaged and the strength of the cloth impaired. No one wanting to make good cloth would do this. But it does enable fulling to be carried out more quickly and one wonders if this was the Tudor clothiers' object. If so one's respect for their ingenuity increases while one's respect for their honesty decreases. In such circumstances, the Government prohibition was justified, though not its application to the coloured broadcloths.

The prohibition in the Tudor statute specifically referred to gig mills using card wire. Card wire can be used for raising cloth but a different finish is obtained. Teasels give a soft 'doeskin' handle, card wire a blanket-like finish. Certainly the coloured broadcloth superfine which replaced undyed broadcloth as the West of England's main product in the seventeenth century was always dressed on a gig mill using teasels. It was, and remains, the finest example of what the teasel can do. Though the Tudor statute expressly banned card wire, it was interpreted in later years as banning all kinds of raising by mill. The 'red' clothiers argued that they used teasels and that card wire would not give the finish they required. If the undyed cloth, on the other hand, had been run over a gig mill using card wire and not teasels, before fulling, then the damage to the cloth would have been even greater. It is interesting to find that when the nineteenth-century clothiers argued that their gig mills were not prohibited under the Tudor statute, they did not stress this difference between teasels and card wire.

The Tudor clothiers in the West of England, and elsewhere, were, it must be remembered, above all concerned with the production of undyed cloth for export, not with its dyeing and finishing, which was, in this period, mainly done abroad. While it lasted this undyed export trade was a good one and of immense importance to England's economic position. But in the last decades of the Tudor period, the cloth trade was already in a state of transition. The great future of the trade was to be in worsteds not in woollens. And the centre of the trade was eventually to shift away from the West of England.

# Chapter Five

# The seventeenth century: from old to new draperies

THE SEVENTEENTH CENTURY WAS A TIME of transition. It saw the passing of the great days of the Tudor, undyed woollen broadcloth trade, and with it the passing of the great days of the West of England wool textile industry. It paved the way for the new developments in both woollen and worsted trades in Yorkshire in the eighteenth century. But this period should not be looked on as an 'interim' period, lacking in interest. It is above all the period of the New Draperies of East Anglia and the Serges of the Somerset–Devon border. Being for the most part woven with worsted yarns and woollen wefts, the New Draperies came to East Anglia first in the sixteenth century, and by the seventeenth century (between 1600 and 1650) they became perhaps the most important section of the textile trade. Thus geographically the centre of gravity of the industry was shifting, and an important change was taking place in its technical processes, marking a shift in importance from the woollens produced from short-fibred yarn to the worsteds made from long-fibred yarn.

At the centre of this technical change was the introduction into England of the Saxony spinning-wheel, an invention generally considered to have been developed in 1530 by Johann Jurgen, a German wood-carver. It was in the sixteenth century that it made its impact in England and it was to be the most advanced form of hand-wheel until the introduction of powered machinery.

The Saxony wheel included two important innovations. It included the treadle, which enabled the spinner to revolve the wheel faster, while having both hands free. But, perhaps even more important, it introduced the flyer. The 'U'-shaped flyer revolving round the spindle took in the drafted or drawn out thread at the base of the 'U', guided it along the upper arm and thence down on to a bobbin on the spindle. Thus the drafted yarn was twisted and wound on simultaneously, the two operations going on without pause. On the 'old' spinning-wheel, the spinner turned the wheel intermittently with one hand, first drawing out the thread and then, in a second operation, twisting it, finally winding it on to the spindle.

Jurgen put the idea of bobbin and flyer into practice. But the great Renaissance genius Leonardo da Vinci, who died 11 years before the date of Jurgen's wheel, had already sketched a machine with bobbin and flyer. He also worked out a system of adjusting the position of the spun thread so as to build up an even 'cop' or collection of yarn on the bobbin. Jurgen varied the position of the yarn by the rather clumsy device of a number of hooks on the arm of the flyer. The spinner had to move the yarn from one hook to another until the bobbin was filled.

But in Leonardo's drawing the flyer and spindle traversed while the bobbin remained stationary, so that yarn was wound on without interruption, as it was spun. Later, one of Arkwright's workmen improved on da Vinci's idea by making the spindle blade twice as long as the bobbin and allowing the bobbin to traverse. Leonardo's drawings also contain the idea of two spindles and flyers, so that the spinner, theoretically, could spin with both hands and double her output. But it is doubtful whether it was a practical idea. Double wheels were tried later, but never widely adopted because it was almost impossible for the spinner to watch both drafting zones.

Thus Leonardo da Vinci anticipated Jurgen, though it is certain Jurgen did not see his drawings or he would surely have adopted Leonardo's winding-on method. Neither did Jurgen invent the treadle, which probably originated in China, and would have been known before the Saxony wheel was invented. But to Jurgen goes the credit of the practical introduction of the combination of ideas represented by the Saxony wheel.

And the introduction of the Saxony wheel to England led in several areas to the coming of the new draperies, all of which contained some worsted yarn. From the time of its wide adoption worsteds began to challenge the dominant place that woollens had had throughout the medieval period. Given the different methods of spinning between the long-fibred worsteds and the short-fibred woollens, the technical advance represented by the Saxony wheel was more adapted to the former.

Hand-spinning was done in two operations. First the carded or combed wool was reduced to a 'roving' and then the roving was further drafted to a fine thread. To attempt to reduce wool to thread in one operation was not satisfactory. This two-part operation still remains today with woollens, the roving being made on the condenser which is attached to the carding set, while with worsteds the 'top' produced by the comber is drafted by a number of operations until it is small enough to go into the spinning frame.

The short fibres used in woollens meant that these had to be twisted while they were being drawn out, to avoid breakage in the yarn. The old wheel, with its three separate operations of first drafting and twisting, and then, winding on, was more suited to the production of woollens and its introduction in England was followed by the great days of the heavily fulled broadcloth woven from woollen yarn (see Chapters Three and Four). The random arrangement of the fibres in woollens related better to the fulling process than the parallel arrangement of the fibres in worsteds. With the Saxony wheel, where the motion was provided by the feet through the treadle, both hands were free to pull out the thread from the 'top', while the flyer and the bobbin did the twisting and winding on. This method of spinning with the flyer, without twisting, naturally favoured the long-fibred worsted production, the long fibres allowing continuous drafting without the same need to provide guard against breakage.

For the first time it was possible to spin the combed wools, with their long sliver, really fine. There are some remarkable examples of such spinning in clothes in the Costume Court of the Victoria and Albert Museum in London. They permitted the production of a finer, lighter-weight cloth, which fitted well with the trend in fashions of the period.

As the old undyed broadcloth trade declined, the clothiers of the traditional West Country area were able to build a new industry on its ruins. They made a lighter-weight coloured broadcloth, which although never as large a trade as the old undyed broadcloth yet maintained a prosperous industry in much of the area. These cloths may be considered the 'New Draperies' of the West, following the lighter-weight trend developing elsewhere, but not on the same scale. The seventeenth century began to see the shrinking back of the classic West Country areas towards their main centres on the river valleys of Gloucestershire, Wiltshire and Somerset border country. Towns like Newbury, which can be taken as the culmination of the expansion of the old trade along the River Kennet, were never able to play so large a part again. Even in the heart of the area, centres such as Malmesbury, the scene of Stumpe's activities (see Chapter Four) were never again to be clothing towns of fame.

The seventeenth-century success story is that of the Somerset–Devon border country serge trade, and it may perhaps be asked why this is not included in the traditional West Country trade. But it is necessary to stress the complete division between the traditional West Country broadcloth trade and this other new West Country trade of the Somerset–Devon borders. They were quite separate and there was a very powerful topographical reason for this separation. Even today, when travelling from the northern Somerset–Wiltshire border area towards the Somerset–Devon border, the visitor will pass land which becomes heavily waterlogged in winter. It does not need much imagination to realise that this section of Somerset presented a very real hindrance to any communication between the two areas in the period we are discussing.

There were three main manufacturing areas for this second West Country trade: West Somerset around Taunton; the Vale of Exeter with its main centre at Tiverton; and the town of Exeter itself. All cloths came to Exeter for final export and in many cases for the final finishing. There were also two smaller areas, one around Totnes and Ashburton, and the other around Tavistock. The trade had begun earlier, when the Devonshire Kersey, or Devon Dozen, so named because of its length, was the main production. This cloth first appeared about the middle of the sixteenth century. As with other cloths there had first been a switch from undyed to coloured cloth and then slowly the stuff, serge or perpetuanas came to the fore. By 1618 it was already an important export from Exeter. The cloth was made from coarse wool and when supplies began to run short similar wool was brought from Ireland to Devon and Somerset ports. It is from this time that one begins to find demands from the English that Irish wool should be sent to England and that the manufacture of cloth in Ireland should be stopped.

The full development of the New Draperies of East Anglia and the Somerset–Devon border represented the most important section of the history of the English wool textile industry of the seventeenth century. In their introduction into East Anglia, foreign workers undoubtedly played a great part. And there can be little doubt that when the West Country clothiers Brewer and Methuen introduced immigrants into Bradford-on-Avon they were copying a scheme that had been very successful in East Anglia. But these foreign workers did not play anything like the same role in the introduction – or perhaps one should say, the refounding – of the coloured broadcloth trade in the West Country. There had after all been a coloured broadcloth trade in the West Country for many years; Stroud, for example, having established its fame for scarlet cloths.

There is no clear-cut division between the decline of the undyed broadcloth trade and the rise of the coloured cloths, both processes continuing together over many years. During a number of years both were manufactured, mainly however, by different clothiers, and this caused some confusion, and accounts for the mixed reports sent from the district about the state of trade.

The change from the old trade to the new was, as has been said, heavily influenced by changes in the technical processes outlined here. But the decline of the undyed broadcloth trade, pride of England in the Tudor period, the basis of most of the country's exports and source of a good deal of its taxation, was also influenced by a number of important political factors and events.

A great deal has been written about Alderman Sir William Cockayne's project in 1614 to prohibit the export of undyed cloth. The story reads well, and perhaps as a result rather too much has been made of this event. Even if there had been no Cockayne it is difficult to see how the old undyed broadcloth trade could have continued. The peak had indeed been passed earlier in the latter part of Elizabeth's reign. The old trading routes had been disrupted, and not only by the wars with Spain. The driving out of the Hanseatic traders, whose privileges in England were attacked and finally ended towards the close of the century, thus securing the monopoly of foreign trade for the Merchant Adventurers, also had its effect in damaging foreign trade connections.

With the accession of King James I, and his moves to restore relations with Spain, and thus seek to remove some of the disastrous consequences of the Spanish Wars, the trade in undyed broadcloth showed some recovery. Indeed, in 1606 the Merchant Adventurers shipped abroad some 80,000 unfinished broadcloths. But disaster quickly followed.

Sir William Cockayne, and certain others of the Merchant Adventurers, secured King James's agreement to their project to finish all cloth in England before export. In return for a sum of £300,000 a year, the King gave them a patent to this effect. The export of unfinished and undyed cloth was prohibited and the monopoly of the Merchant Adventurers was thus broken in favour of the monopoly of Alderman Cockayne and his friends.

Many reasons were given why broadcloths should be dyed and finished in England before export. The London cloth workers had often attempted to secure this. But the King should have had enough information available to know that they were not able to finish the amount of cloth that would be coming through. Far more important, there would simply be no market for it in the traditional Low Countries centres, which wanted undyed cloth.

Cockayne's project had not long been in operation before complaints began to reach the Government that the normal selling of West Country cloths in Blackwell Hall had come to a standstill, and Privy Council records are full of the efforts that the Council made to keep business moving. The Council did its best, usually by instructions and letters to the Justices of the Peace, urging them to do what they could. They pointed out that good trade was not always to be expected and that when trade was bad everyone should take a part in seeing that the sale of cloths moved forward and workers were kept in employment. This could not be done and the Council soon had numerous reports that many, perhaps most of the woollen workers of the South-west, were unemployed. By the time (1617) the failure of the Cockayne Project became clear, and the old company of Merchant Adventurers had their privileges restored, it was too late to do much about the state of the trade. Some improvement did take place, but this, slight as it was, was soon to be swept away by the beginning of the Thirty Years War and the devastation it brought to Germany, which had been the main ultimate market for the undyed broadcloths after they had passed through the Flanders finishing centres.

Politically, of course, the century was both dominated and divided by the Civil War. In so far as they favoured either side, the clothiers undoubtedly leaned towards Parliament, though probably the majority had no wish to see the King executed. Thomas Ashe, the most notable Parliamentarian clothier, did all he could to help his side to win the war, but he was adamant in refusing to play any part in the trial of the King. Despite this refusal, however, he remained a friend of Cromwell.

Due to continuing bad trade in undyed broadcloths and the production of so many new cloths, complaints of bad inspection by the aulnagers naturally became more common. When trade is difficult the quality of the cloth produced rises, because the manufacturer knows that complaints are to be expected and does everything he can to prevent them. He rarely succeeds, and complaints of bad workmanship are in fact far more a sign of bad trade than anything else. In so far as imperfect cloths are made and sent away from the mill, this is much more likely to happen in times of a boom, not only because the manufacturer knows that there is a good chance that the cloths will be accepted, but also because he may well be short of skilled labour to make the cloths properly.

The Merchant Adventurers – as one answer to the continual complaints arising from the bad trade in the undyed section – suggested that new centres of cloth inspection should be established. The Government thought this scheme too ambitious, but in 1630 sent Anthony Withers and Samuel Lively down to the West to see if anything could be done to improve the standard of cloth production. Lively went back to London quickly, but Withers stayed and had an exciting time. He appears to have been one of those people who was always starting something new, being full of bright ideas but lacking the capacity to carry them through. Formerly a member of the Virginian Company, he had been associated with Cockayne and was once imprisoned in the Fleet.

The rise of the new coloured broadcloth trade had introduced several problems: in particular it had given rise to a new body of merchants, the yarn badgers, who bought wool and organised its spinning in the cottages, and (which may perhaps explain their influence at this time) they arranged for the dyeing of the wool. Possibly the clothiers who were attempting to switch to coloured broadcloths had little knowledge of dyeing and welcomed the opportunity of being able to purchase coloured yarns. We know there was considerable rivalry between the two sections of the coloured broadcloth trade – the one which dyed the fabrics in the wool before spinning, and the other which dyed it afterwards.

However, it is probably fair to see Withers' visit as an attempt made jointly by the Merchant Adventurers and the old white clothiers to do away with both these new rival industries. The recommendations he made certainly suggest this, for he demanded that the same regulations that had for so long applied to the undyed broadcloth trade should apply to the new coloured trade. Withers' capacity for getting into trouble meant that things did not go well: more fatal for the prospects of his assignment he aroused the resentment of the local justices. Inevitably they would have resented the appearance of an inspector from London; moreover, knowing local conditions well it is likely they welcomed the new trade in coloured broadcloth, which was doing at least something to relieve the otherwise almost universal depression. The fact that Sir Edward Baynton at Bromham led the attacks on Withers may be a reflection of the fact that this village had suffered very seriously due to the depression in the older trade. However, Withers was confident that he could introduce a cloth-searching system that would achieve the objects he had in mind; but, never able to keep out of arguments, he became involved in the squabble that was going on between the coloured clothiers and the yarn badgers, and finally he libelled another justice and as a result found himself in prison.

These events reflect the problems of the development of the coloured broadcloth trade in the wake of the decline of the old undyed cloth trade. They also reflect, and perhaps more fundamentally, the fact that the West of England cloth trade as a whole, during the seventeenth century, was sliding down from its former pre-eminent position and making way for the rise of Yorkshire to dominance in the eighteenth and nineteenth centuries.

# Chapter Six

# The eighteenth century: The rise of Yorkshire

THE RISE OF THE YORKSHIRE SECTION OF the industry to a dominant place marks this period of history, for which we have, fortunately, the classic account of Daniel Defoe, a well-informed and keen observer of the woollen trade and, as the records of J. and T. Clark, the old-established West of England firm, show, also a purchaser of cloth.

Though kerseys were still the main branch of the trade in Yorkshire, this century saw the first attempts to manufacture broadcloths, and between 1727 and 1770 output of these better-quality cloths from Yorkshire increased considerably. After 1770 the increase was even more rapid and the 1785 output of broadcloths was six times that of 1727. Thus in almost all fields Yorkshire cloths were rivalling and even supplanting those from the West of England. By 1772, when Britain's total textile exports, including cotton, silk and other types came to £4,500,000, Yorkshire's share of this was £2,500,000 or over half the country's entire textile export trade. At this time Yorkshire was even more important than Lancashire, which was eventually to take first place from her.

Yet, the coming to pre-eminence of Yorkshire textiles must be seen as pre-dating the application of steam power to industry and the general development of factories – the period commonly known as the 'Industrial Revolution'. The vast expansion in Yorkshire took place in what was essentially a domestic system. There were no factories of any importance at all; Professor H. Heaton has said there were hardly twenty factories even by 1800. As late as 1830 half the woollen workers were still said to be outside the factory system and in so far as there were factories towards the end of the eighteenth century, these were the scribbling mills (to be described later in this chapter). The power loom was not to be used for woollen cloths before 1830, indeed the revolutionary inventions of Paul, Hargreaves and Arkwright, associated with the Industrial Revolution, had no effect on Yorkshire's expansion. There can be few such cases in history where a traditional industry has suddenly progressed at such a rate without fertilisation by some new invention.

Yorkshire's worsted trade, on the other hand, followed somewhat different lines, with less emphasis on cloth halls, and with large clothiers and factories playing a larger part – though one should not over-estimate this. Inventions were to play a vital part here – the continuous spinning process for worsted yarn, providing the greater strength needed for the operation of power looms was to have important effects on the relative growths of the two industries. Technical advance, plus the fact that worsteds, not being the traditional trade, might expect a reasonably rapid growth, combined, in the nineteenth century, to put worsteds in first place.

But while the eighteenth century ran its course, the dominant feature was the rise of the Yorkshire woollen manufacture and its competitive pressure on the once greater, now declining West of England trade. It is useful at this point to examine, as far as possible – relating Yorkshire to the West of England – how wool textile manufacturing was carried out: its raw materials, preparatory processes, dyeing, yarn-making, weaving, fulling and cloth working, as well as the types of cloth made.

The purchase of wool had probably changed little over the centuries. Contemporary reports show that the supply of wool of the right kind and its purchase at the right price, remained the major problem. In most cases, it seems, the larger domestic clothiers bought wool themselves. But the smaller ones, the people who were really handloom weavers, would get what they wanted from the local markets. In the West of England a considerable amount of Spanish wool was used, though this was not the case in Yorkshire and it is usually maintained that Yorkshire did not begin to use Spanish wool until Benjamin Gott of Leeds, the famous manufacturer, introduced it at the end of the eighteenth century. Spanish wool at this time, to judge from samples still in existence, was equal to what is now known as a 60/64s Merino quality. It was not as good as the best Australian Merino wool of today, nor as fine as the Saxony wools that began to come from Germany early in the nineteenth century. English wool was probably comparable with that of today. The coarser types would have been used mainly by the Yorkshire clothier for the kerseys, while the finer Down types went into the broadcloths.

There was probably not as much difference between the broadcloths made from the Spanish wool and those made from the best English (Leominster for instance), as is sometimes argued. Those clothiers needing Spanish wool usually bought through factors in London, who were in many cases the same as those who exported their cloth.

## Preparatory processes

Nowhere is the importance of water to the domestic clothier more apparent than in the preparatory processes. The only way then known to scour the wool was to put it into a cage and lower it into a stream.

Dyeing was usually done in the wool, and it was essential in the case of mixtures, the so-called medleys. Many patterns and recipe books are still in existence, so it is possible to find exactly which dyes were in use. Woad had been replaced by indigo for blues and navy, although it was still grown and used as a fermenting agent in the indigo vats. With the coming of the new dyes from America there was a wide range of reds, and cochineal was available for really bright shades. Fustic gave the most reliable yellow, and for browns there were the various woods, such as barwood, brazilwood, and peachwood. Most of these colours were mordanted, and dyeing was a surprisingly complicated operation for the domestic clothier to do himself. In one West of England pattern book, chromium, iron, aluminium and copper mordants have all been found. These natural dyes gave a very good range of colours, and the complaints that had previously been made that English clothiers were behind in this respect were no longer true. The dye recipe books make interesting reading, bringing one very near to the day-to-day life in the mills. The method of recording recipes remained the same as before, and a dyer's recipe book was indeed his livelihood. If he left his job he took it with him, and he usually bequeathed it to his heir.

## Yarn-making

The conversion of wool into yarn, as still done in the worker's own home, had not changed at all, but when the process was moved into the scribbling mill, vast differences emerged of the greatest importance for future developments. The processes in a scribbling mill can be divided into four. First there was the willeying, which had replaced the old method of beating the wool with rods to open it and remove some of the dirt. The willey – really a simple form of carding machine – was essentially a box containing a larger roller covered with teeth, which revolved in such a way that the wool was teased between it and smaller rollers set round its periphery. If necessary, the wool could be passed through the willey several times, and at one stage oil was spread on the material ready for the scribbling proper.

Scribbling is the name given to the first part of the carding operation. The word was introduced to the industry before the machine. W. B. Crump points out that Thoresby has a reference to a Leeds workhouse where poor boys and girls were taught to scribble, a new invention whereby the different colours are delicately mixed. This is one of the earliest uses of the word. The scribbling machine was identical to a carding machine, except that the wire was somewhat coarser. It was designed to disentangle the fibres and deliver the wool in the form of a continuous web. This web passed to the third section of the scribbling mill, the actual carder, which removed any small neps that had passed through the scribbler. Unlike the scribbler, the carder did not deliver a web of material. The last roller on the carder was not completely covered with card wire, but instead had strips across it. As these came in contact with the 'doffing comb', strips of wool, the width of the machine, were separated from the carder.

The fourth and last machine in the scribbling mill was the 'slubbing billy', which was very similar to a 'jenny'. On it the cardings were pieced together and given sufficient twist to enable them to be drafted and wound on to a cop or bobbin. These slubbings were then taken back to the homes of the domestic workers to be spun on the jenny into yarn suitable for weaving.

The spinning 'jenny', invented by James Hargreaves around 1764 (see Chapter Seven) is basically a development of the 'old' spinning-wheel – but here the power provided by the wheel is used to turn not one spindle but several spindles held in a frame. In the hand-loom weaver's house, the jenny was operated either by women or by apprentices, and it was usual to have two jennies working together. These jennies were essentially used in the cottages, and it was only in the very last years of the century that any of them went into factories. Benjamin Gott installed some at Leeds in 1793, although even he did not use power to drive them.

## Weaving

There are many accounts of the hand-loom weavers. The most important development of the loom was John Kay's flying shuttle. Otherwise the hand-looms remained unchanged during the eighteenth century. Before the flying shuttle, the weavers threw the shuttle through the shed. Its introduction meant that, in broadloom weaving, an assistant was no longer necessary. In the case of the narrow loom the job could be done by an assistant much more comfortably. Kerseys had usually been woven narrow, so that the problem of the second weaver had not arisen. It is difficult to say when the flying shuttle was completely accepted in the West of England, but it was certainly not before the end of the century.

## Finishing

Finishing was the great craft, and by the eighteenth century the finishing of broadcloths in particular had been carried to an excellent level of craftsmanship. The finishing routine can be divided into two sections that may be called the wet and the dry, or fulling and cloth-working.

After weaving, and the mending of any faults, the cloth was ready for fulling. The fulling stocks in use were the traditional type that had been common for several centuries. They were used for the two somewhat different processes of cleaning the piece, and then of shrinking and fulling it. There were in fact two rather different kinds of stocks in use – driving stocks and fulling stocks. The heads of the driving stocks came down in a slanting direction. Instead of pounding the cloth, they threw it up and swirled it so that it fell back again as they rose. The heads of the fulling stocks came down almost perpendicularly and pounded the cloth. The driving stocks really performed a scouring or cleaning process which removed the oil added to assist in spinning. It was for this reason that the offensive domestic 'wash' (stale urine) was used, until after the 'twenties, gas-works provided a new cheap supply of ammonia. Lawson of Pudsey described how the hand-loom weavers themselves soaked the pieces before carrying them to the mill, but the fullers also collected and stored their own supply.

Cloth-working was complicated. One of the witnesses of the 1806 Parliamentary Committee which enquired into wool trade statutes, gave a good description of how hand-mossing work was done:

> The cloth dresser first raises the cloth, after that it is cropped wet; it is then taken and mossed and rowed. Mossing is filling up the bottom of the wool after it has been cut with the shears wet, it is done with a handle set with teasels in each hand; after that it is rowed and tentered, after it has been mossed quite wet and rowed down with cards, that is to make the wool lie close; after that it is tentered and dried. If a fine piece it will receive three cuts dry after the tenter; when that is done it is backed, that is, the wool cut off the back side, after that it is burled.

## The Early Factory

Towards the end of the eighteenth century important technical inventions began to have their effect on certain stages of the production process. While roller-spinning developed by Arkwright (see Chapter Seven) was of no use for woollen spinning, Hargreaves' jenny was an excellent machine for all types of woollen yarn. Being small, the early jennies could be used in the cottages and thus fitted well into the domestic system of Yorkshire. Few factories used jennies before the end of the century. Indeed, by the time the spinning factory was fully developed, the jenny had been largely replaced by the 'mule' (see Chapter Seven).

By the end of the century carding and scribbling were largely done by machine. Bourn's circular 'card', in use in Lancashire had passed from thence to Yorkshire. In the West of England, the new scribbling mills were usually combined with fulling mills. But in Yorkshire, perhaps because of the rapid expansion, it seems to have been more common to put up new separate buildings for scribbling and carding – though Yorkshire did have some combined fulling and scribbling mills.

In Yorkshire these factories would be set up on a more or less co-operative basis by a group of

12 *Home Mills, Trowbridge*
The fire of 1862. A local print shows the extent of
this disaster.

13 *Home Mills, Trowbridge*
This photograph represents the building as it was
rebuilt after the sensational 1862 fire. A later fire
in 1931 largely destroyed the mill and it was rebuilt
without the top storey.

14 *Studley Mills, Trowbridge*
Until recently the main mill of Messrs. J. & T. Clark. It was built in 1862 by Gane Brothers, the leading industrial architects in the area.

15 *Bridge House, Trowbridge, c. 1750*
Until recently the offices of J. & T. Clark, and of interest since it shows the workshops which, in the late eighteenth century, were often added to clothiers' houses.

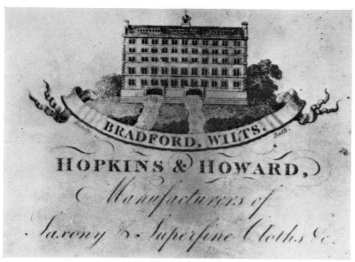

16 *Kingston Mill, Bradford-on-Avon*
The trade mark of one of the owners of Kingston Mill. Note the water flowing through the base of the building to provide power.

17 *Kingston Mill, Bradford-on-Avon*
Built early in the nineteenth century by Thomas Divitt. This was the first mill to go over to the new rubber manufacture that replaced the woollen trade in the area.

domestic clothiers. This important early stage of factory-building came at the end of the eighteenth century, perhaps a little later than the merchants' established finishing shops. It was instituted by the small domestic clothiers for their own benefit, and in consequence it aroused none of the hatred later to be directed towards the new factories.

The position was different in the West of England, where the trade remained essentially traditional, supplying the broadcloths developed in the previous century. The area no longer produced the majority of cloths, but its supremacy in quality was as yet hardly challenged. There were signs of more antagonism between the clothiers and the workers than was the case in the North. Indeed, it is strange that Yorkshire, though expanding so much faster, yet remained a more homogeneous society. Consequently, in the West there can be found interesting examples of the growth of worker's organisations and of the 'combinations' which can be taken as early signs of trade unionism. References to the trade in the Press of the day are more often than not concerned with riots, and there is a considerable pamphlet literature from this period, attacking and defending individual positions.

## Marketing

For information on the markets served by the West Country trade in the latter part of the century, we can turn usefully to Rudder's *History of Gloucestershire*. According to him the home trade was most important, and some manufacturers concentrated on it exclusively. His view is supported by existing records. The West of England offered the home market a wide variety of cloths and there was some export trade, part of it through London, mentioned by Rudder. Another branch of the trade catered for the Army, another for Turkey and yet another for the East India Company.

The coming of the new machinery towards the end of the century did not bring any further significant increase in the particular types of woollen cloths made. As has been pointed out earlier, the new machinery provided manufacturers of worsted cloth with a revolutionary way of producing yarn, it failed to do the same for the woollen trade. Indeed, the whole history of the woollen trade from 1800 onwards can be described in terms of trying to overcome high labour costs, something it never succeeded in doing. Worsteds, by contrast, went ahead.

Thus the West of England traditional cloth trade towards the end of the century was under pressure both from technical developments and the competition from the more rapidly advancing Yorkshire trade. Intelligent observers there soon began to notice the effects of this competition. In 1809 Dr Aiken noted that in Gloucestershire the trade had somewhat declined on account of the rivalry of Yorkshire and other places. At the turn of the century, Gloucestershire was doing relatively better than other areas of the South-west. Aiken's statement that Wiltshire superfine cloths were less affected by the competition from Yorkshire is hardly correct. Wiltshire was feeling equally the pressure from the energetic North, particularly in the production of broadcloths. It was true that a relatively small section of the Wiltshire trade, centred on Trowbridge, to some extent escaped this competition by turning to the manufacture of a finer woollen cloth, the 'cassimere', but by the end of the century, Yorkshire had also entered this field.

Though the West of England trade was not expanding, it retained its reputation for quality and the area remained reasonably prosperous as is shown by the many fine houses the West Country clothiers had built in the main cloth-making towns. Painswick in Gloucestershire and Bradford-on-Avon in Wiltshire can be taken as typical clothing towns, while in Trowbridge, an excellent series of clothiers' houses well indicate the prosperity in the industry. The trade, it is evident, was still profitable, though one might idly speculate that the clothiers would have done better to put more money into their businesses rather than into their homes.

Exeter and Tiverton were the two main centres of the second part of the West of England cloth trade, the worsted trade of the Somerset–Devon borders, whose rise was described in Chapter Five. We are well informed about Tiverton, because Dunsford wrote much about the trade in his book about the town. He is a good authority for he and his family had been serge manufacturers there. By 1700 the trade in both centres was dominated by wealthy, well-established merchant and clothier classes, the former perhaps more entrenched in Exeter and the latter in Tiverton. After 1700, Professor Hoskins notes that fewer new names appear – the trade was obviously settling down to a respectable middle age. At the same time the growth of a distinct working class is noticeable, perhaps even more so in this area than in the West Riding of Yorkshire, which eventually was to take away most of its trade.

The individuality, the push and the commercial success of the small West Riding cloth manu-facturers has been remarked, and it is interesting to note that success in the eighteenth century came to them, the smaller men, rather than the larger, richer merchants of the South-west. The same factors operated to a rather lesser extent in the other West of England area farther north.

Although a number of serges were made in Exeter, the town really had more importance as a marketing and exporting centre, and the fame of its serge market has been well chronicled both by Daniel Defoe and by Celia Fiennes (1662–1741). Tiverton, on the other hand, was essentially a manufacturing centre, and a large proportion of the cloths made there went through Exeter, although in many cases the selling was controlled by Tiverton merchants and not by those in Exeter.

It is worth trying to place the Somerset–Devon worsted trade around 1700 in its correct context in the British wool textile trade. We have seen how the old broadcloth trades of the West of Eng-land (i.e. the northern section) and of East Anglia had lost their markets, and how they had been replaced in the West of England by a lighter broadcloth, and in East Anglia by the New Draperies. The serges were in some respects a branch of the New Draperies, although it is not easy to see the exact routes by which the trade settled there. However, by the last decades of the seventeenth century some of the serges made in England were from East Anglia. Although serges from the Somerset–Devon area were of worsted warp and woollen weft, they were quite heavily fulled. Miss Fiennes drew attention to the importance of the fulling process in Exeter. On the other hand, the cloths made in Sudbury, Suffolk, were not fulled and were really bays. It is best to distinguish these fabrics one from the other.

According to Professor Hoskins, from 1688 to 1715 the serge manufacture of the Somerset–Devon borders was the most important section of the British wool textile trade. Out of a total export averaging about three million pounds, it accounted for £850,000.

The Exeter and Tiverton trades differed in several ways. In Tiverton a few really wealthy clothiers – Oliver Peard was a notable example – obtained control, and then an interesting situation arose as Exeter merchants, among them Charles Baring, one of the early members of the great banking family, tried to move in. For the Exeter merchants, although powerful, were kept rather in the background in their own city. One notices this tendency in ecclesiastical centres, for a somewhat similar development can be seen in Salisbury. There were other differences: for example, whereas the spinners, as in the other cloth-making areas, worked at home, the Exeter weavers almost without exception seem to have worked on the clothiers' premises. They no longer owned their looms, and even though they worked in the owners' workshops they seemed to have been expected to pay a rent for the use of the looms. This was clearly an unsatisfactory system, and may have had some effect upon the decline that followed. The finishing was carried out in workshops much as in the other parts of the West of England, but the methods by which the smaller domestic clothier had kept control over his destiny – so noticeable a theme in the West Riding of Yorkshire at the time – did not exist in the Somerset–Devon area.

Although many of the cloths made went to London for export, this section of the cloth industry of Britain was one of the few where the out-ports, in this case mainly Exeter, had been successful in keeping some of the local business.

After about 1715 the trade began to decline, particularly in serge exports to Holland, which fell from 425,000 cloths in 1710 to 147,000 in 1721. Exeter lost about two-thirds; the Spanish trade was hard hit by war and never fully recovered; moreover, Exeter fabrics were failing to hold their own against the stuffs that were being made in Norwich, the full force of that competition becoming apparent by the 1720s. The decline was evidently rapid because in Tiverton, according to Dunsford, 1720 was almost a peak year. Abroad, fashions changed in favour of worsteds, as had been the case with serges in the 1670s, though this change was caused partially by the better techniques used at Norwich which gave a better appearance to the fabric at a lower cost of production. Professor Hoskins thinks that labour costs were considerably lower in East Anglia than in South-western England, with a difference of something like 40 per cent. in weavers' wages in the 1760s. The expansion of the Norwich trade immediately after the Treaty of Utrecht in 1713 is particularly noticeable.

Tiverton endeavoured to copy Norwich cloths and to reduce costs by importing Irish yarn. The combers resisted this and, helped by the weavers, their fight with the masters led to a stormy chapter in the town's history. The attempt to rival Norwich failed, while competition from the north, especially from Halifax, increased.

By the early 'forties it was a common saying in Exeter market that there was a trade but no profit. In 1750 things improved a little, but serges never regained their previous position and the outbreak of the war of American Independence again hit business. In so far as the Exeter trade continued afterwards, it was on a different basis and of comparatively little importance in the wool-textile trade of the country as a whole.

# PART TWO

*The Industrial Revolution: Machines*

PART TWO

**Chapter Seven**

# *Inventions: Spinning and Carding*

century the West of England wool trade had lost its former position at the head of Britain's textile industry. Enveloping this change, however, was an even larger one. Wool was by this time no longer the major textile fibre, its place being taken by cotton. This change coincided with the great textile inventions which formed a crucial part of the Industrial Revolution, one of the results of which was to bring the Lancashire cotton industry to the position where it dominated the British industrial scene for nearly a century. For the great textile inventions came almost entirely within the cotton trade, spreading later to the wool branch of the industry.

In the next two chapters we shall examine the nature and background of these main inventions and their application to the two main textile processes: spinning (including the 'carding' or preparing the wool for spinning) and weaving.

It has often been said that the spinning industry was transformed because the adoption of the flying shuttle in weaving brought about a shortage of yarn. But this point has been overstressed. Yarn had been in short supply for many centuries as is shown by the number of spinning schools which had been set up in many European countries. These are sometimes regarded as early factories, but in fact they were simply attempts to collect a number of hand-spinners together. The few factories, if one may use the word, that did appear before the eighteenth century were quite the exception and too much has been made of them. The lines of Thomas Deloney which are so often quoted are a case in point. The sixteenth-century mill at Newbury, which he praised, had few successors.

As noted in earlier chapters, wool was prepared for drafting and spinning by two main methods, 'carding' in which teasels were first used and later replaced by nails or wires fixed in leather, and 'combing' in which a comb with metal teeth was used. Carding was the general practice with the short-fibred woollens and combing with the long-fibred worsteds. Combing was the last yarn-making process to be mechanised and it continued to be done by hand until the middle of the nineteenth century.

The mechanisation of carding began with the patent that Lewis Paul took out in 1748 – a variation of the stock card (see Chapters Two and Four). Paul covered a flat, rectangular board three feet by two feet with 'card clothing' nailed in parallel strips and made it so that it could be turned by means of treadles.

Before carding started, the card-covered table was fixed by means of a treadle so that the points of the card wire were pointing away from the operator. The material was carefully spread over the table and the upper card which was completely covered with card clothing was brought into contact with it and worked to and fro. As the points of the card clothing on the upper card were pointing towards the operator a carding or working action resulted. When the material had been opened the table was turned through an angle of 180 degrees, consequently when the top card was again brought into contact with the wool on the table a stripping or doffing action resulted and the wool was transferred to the other card. The process could, if necessary, be repeated on the same or a different card. Paul included in his specification an ingenious idea for removing the carded material by means of a thin stick covered with card wire and then placing it on a ribbon. It is clear that this was not very far removed in principle from the method of doffing later employed with a single ring doffer, but it took a long time to make this change. Strips taken off by Paul's system resulted in discontinuous pieces from the carding set and these had to be joined together, whereas with the ring doffer the strips came off continuously. Many years passed before the connection occurred to anyone.

This patent of Paul's raises several interesting points. It has never been made clear whether it was used in practice or whether the needle stick was already in general use with the larger stock cards – it is likely that it was, and it could therefore be questioned whether Paul had any right to claim it as a patent. A little later in the same year (Patent 636) Paul introduced a circular card. He included it in the same specification as the one detailed above, but the important point is that he had been anticipated by Daniel Bourn whose Patent No. 628 came earlier in the same year.

Bourn's circular card was the first revolving card to appear on the patent list and was one of the crucial inventions in textile development. Bourn changed what had been an intermittent process to a continuous one by the simple method of giving rotary action to a movement which previously had never been conceived in these terms. His card had four rollers and he included a traversing device. The patent does not give any clear idea of the way it worked, and although no one can doubt its importance, it is a little difficult to see how the two distinctive actions of working and stripping were actually obtained. Doffing was presumably done with a needle stick. Probably this machine did not have very great practical application as it stood, but the greatest credit possible is due to the inventor for his revolutionary conception of cylinder or circular carding. He suggested that the card could be driven either by hand or by wind or water power.

Paul's circular card was different. He had only one cylinder which was covered with parallel strips of card wire, whilst underneath was a concave card completely covered on the inside which was in contact with the roller. The cylinder was driven by hand. The setting of the concave card could be adjusted and also lowered sufficiently to be turned at right angles. Doffing was obtained by a needle stick.

As it stood, this card was as impracticable as Bourn's, but like Bourn's it had in it the germ of a very important development. Paul began the present system of carding used in the cotton trade in which the fibre is carded between wire placed on a roller and wire placed on a stationary flat.

The actual inventors of the many improvements which followed those of Bourn and Paul are not known, but there is no doubt that as in the case of drawing and spinning it was the great practical genius of Arkwright which co-ordinated all these ideas into a machine which worked and which employed most of the principles we now know as carding. By the time Arkwright took out a patent in 1775 the carding engine already included an automatic feed consisting of a continuous revolving apron on which the cotton was spread evenly and carried to the cylinders. This invention has been credited to several people; John Lees was probably the originator and Arkwright improved it by rolling up the material into lap form and feeding it to the cylinder by means of a feed sheet and a pair of feed rollers. He has always been given the credit, even by his enemies, for making an improvement here, although it is difficult to see its exact nature.

The main cylinders of Arkwright's card were covered with strips of card clothing with gaps between them, as was the case with Paul's machine, and the working action took place between these and the stationary flats which he put over the top of the machine. His card was fitted with a doffing comb, and he probably invented this ingenious contrivance although it has been claimed for Hargreaves. Ure, usually well informed, said:

> This is the crank and comb contrivance so unjustly claimed for Hargreaves in the law-suit against Sir Richard Arkwright. This elegant instrument takes off the material in a fine transparent fleece like the aerial web or woven wind of Aurungzebe's daughter.

By this means a web fibre was produced and this was drawn through a funnel and a pair of rollers so that it emerged as a thick sliver of carded cotton which was then coiled into a can. Later, in 1839, Ure illustrated a machine which was the same as Arkwright's, and one needs only to look at a modern cotton card to see how directly it derives from the great inventor. The woollen trade has preferred to use all rollers rather than flats.

It has been thought best to give a brief account of the early development of mechanical carding because the inventions of Paul and Bourn have a claim to be in a very real sense the starting-point of mechanised spinning, but before Arkwright perfected their ideas the really crucial spinning inventions had taken place. These early inventions of Paul or Bourn were not made in Lancashire or Yorkshire; both men worked in the Midlands, but the improvements that made their brilliant ideas workable were made in the North.

Already the North, particularly Lancashire, had been quick to seize on John Kay's invention of the flying shuttle, and although its influence has been over-estimated it did stimulate the search for a method of producing yarn more quickly.

The mechanisation of spinning developed on two quite different lines, and the interesting point is that in many ways they coincided with the two types of hand-wheel, the Saxony wheel which gave continuous spinning and was ideally adapted for long material, and the simple wheel which gave discontinuous spinning and was best for short material. The mechanisation of the first, however, was based on an entirely new idea, roller spinning, in which the drawing out of the sliver was done by having a series of rollers revolving at different surface speeds. The second approach was an attempt to copy the action of spindle drafting on the simple wheel in something approaching a mechanised form. It was not in any way as revolutionary an approach as roller drafting.

The writer would maintain that the idea of roller draft was the most sensational development ever introduced into the textile trade, and it has proved the basis of most modern spinning systems. In addition it was adopted for the processes between carding and spinning, and today drawing out from the large sliver coming from the card to the final fine thread is entirely done by rollers in the worsted section of the wool textile trade, but not, it should be stressed, in the woollen section. It was an entirely new concept, and was patented by Wyatt and Paul in 1735, but it did not really become a practical proposition until Arkwright brought together the many ideas that were being discussed in Lancashire and embodied them in his patent of 1759.

There has been a great deal of discussion as to who was really responsible for the first original idea, but it has now been firmly established that Lewis Paul, whose carding inventions have already been mentioned, was the brain behind it. He stands out as one of the most original minds in the textile trade. The second method, which imitated spindle spinning by the use of a moving carriage and reproduced the essential movements of the old hand-wheel, was the invention of James Hargreaves, and his spinning jenny dates from around the year 1764. Owing to the fact that he had made a few spinning jennies before he attempted to obtain a patent, he was not successful in maintaining any patent rights.

Both these methods of spinning were introduced into the cotton trade and spread to other trades. It is interesting to note that they fitted exactly into the two branches of the wool trade. Roller spinning was excellent for worsteds and spindle spinning for woollens. The fact that there were these two quite distinct inventions consolidated the definite division already existing between the two types of cloth made from wool. The cotton trade used both methods.

Stress has been laid on the important differences between continuous and intermittent spinning which the two contemporary inventions confirmed and further defined. Roller spinning was continuous; there was no need to deliver a length of slubbing, then stop and draw it and twist it and wind it on to a container. Given two pairs of rollers working at slightly different surface speeds, and suitable material, the drawing out took place continuously and as the yarn left the second pair of rollers the twist was put in and the winding-on accomplished at the same time by means of the ingenious apparatus invented by Jurgen.

Spinning on the jenny was intermittent; a length of slubbing was delivered then drawn out and finally wound on to a spindle, exactly as is still done with the mule system of spinning woollen yarn.

Although at first the jenny was the more widely used, the development of roller spinning was so important for the future that it deserves to be treated first. The original patent of 1738 was taken out in the name of Lewis Paul, Wyatt appearing only as a witness. Considering this it is surprising that so many people in the past have tried to claim Wyatt as the original inventor. The original specification is not very clear, but it is certain that several pairs of rollers were used and that each pair revolved faster than the pair before it. In this lay the genius of Paul's invention. The actual patent read:

> The said machine engine or invention will spin wool or cotton into thread, yarn or worsted which before it is placed therein must first be prepared in the manner following: All those sorts of wool or cotton which it is necessary to card must have each card full, bat or roller joined together so as to make the mass become a kind of rope or thread of raw wool. In that sort of wool which it is necessary to comb, commonly called jersey, a strict regard must be had to make the slivers of an equal thickness from end to end. The wool or cotton being then thus prepared one end of the mass, rope or thread or sliver is put betwixt a pair of rollers, cylinders or cones or some such movements which being turned round by their own motion draws in the raw mass of wool or cotton to be spun in proportion to the velocity given to such rollers, cylinders or cones. As the prepared mass passes regularly through or betwixt these cylinders or cones a succession of other rollers, cylinders or cones moving proportionately faster than the first draws the rope or sliver into any degree of fineness which may be required. Sometimes the successive rollers, cylinders or cones (but not the first) have another rotation

besides that which diminishes the thread, yarn or worsted (viz): they give it a small degree of twist betwixt each pair by means of the thread itself passing through the axis and centre of each rotation. In some other cases only the first pair of rollers, cylinders or cones are used, and then the bobbin, spool or quill upon which the thread, yarn or worsted is spun is so contrived as to draw faster than the first rollers, cylinders or cones give, and in such proportion as the first mass, rope or sliver is proposed to be diminished.

There were no drawings attached.

Three points stand out: first of all, and most important, the really brilliant and original idea is contained in the first part; secondly, the inventor only complicated this idea by suggesting that the second pair should 'sometimes' give twist as well (any attempt to introduce twist in this way will make roller drafting impossible, and Paul's failure to produce a practical machine probably came from his failure to see this); finally, the last part of his patent has nothing to do with the first, and is really only a form of spindle drafting which Paul complicated by presumably attempting to wind the yarn simultaneously. This is clearly impossible, for one cannot use the spindle for drafting and winding at the same time; drafting and twisting or twisting and winding with the help of the flyer are possible, but not drafting and winding.

The idea was by no means widely adopted; the inventor had obviously not properly developed his original conception. Indeed Paul, in a specification for another patent twenty years later, virtually abandoned the roller and returned to the alternative method of drafting between the spindle point and a pair of rollers. There is in fact little doubt that Paul had given up hope of making a successful practical machine based on his original idea. Many people tried to improve it and make it work but none of them achieved a great deal. When Arkwright finally brought it to a successful conclusion many people in Lancashire had already decided that it would never be done.

Paul and Wyatt were a strangely contrasted pair. Paul was, or liked to claim that he was, of French extraction and he was sometimes called Monsieur Paul by his friends. Little is known about his early life but he has been credited with the invention of a pinking machine before he met Wyatt in 1732; it was used for making the edges of shrouds and it is said that, unlike his other machines, he made some money out of it. It is not known when he began working on the idea of a spinning machine, nor when roller drafting occurred to him. Clearly work must have been going on for some time before the patent was applied for. Paul had a streak of real genius in his make-up, obviously, but it was mixed with much else that made him both an impracticable and difficult man to live or work with. On the few occasions when he had any money, he spent it, and when he had none, as was more often the case, he would live as best he could on his friends. All this can be seen in his relationship with Wyatt, to whom however great credit is due for recognising the genius of his difficult friend who expected to be kept when things were not going well and yet at the same time would write to Wyatt with the air of a scholar and a man of education addressing one whom he thought his inferior.

An interesting sidelight on the life of Lewis Paul is his friendship with the great Samuel Johnson. It has been said that the great writer had been a lover of the dissolute wife of the inventor but there is no foundation at all for this. Paul was an entertaining companion and a convincing conversationalist, and it was this that appealed to Johnson. He even managed to obtain some money from Johnson in order to further his grandiose schemes.

Wyatt was a different man, without the genius of Paul but much more honest, hardworking and perservering. There is no doubt that he had a great deal to put up with when working with his occasionally brilliant but very erratic associate. Wyatt himself never claimed to have invented roller drafting; from the start he said that this idea had come from Paul, but he added, and there is little doubt that this was the truth, that he had made a number of practical suggestions which he thought made the machine a better proposition. The claim that Wyatt was responsible for the basic idea originated with his son and was not made until many years later. The son said that Wyatt had thought of the method in 1730 and had spun thread by means of it at Sutton Coldfield in 1738. There is no truth at all in this, but Wyatt deserved credit for what he did do. He was without doubt a better practical mechanic than Paul, who was inclined to regard himself as above such details, which was probably one of the reasons why the idea never came to fruition. Truly great inventors combine the theoretical and the practical. Paul regarded himself as the presiding genius who did not need to worry about practical details. Wyatt rather added to this by himself appearing somewhat as the skilled assistant working with a chief. He was a very sober, conscientious man, a little inclined to be taken up with his own importance, and he wrote a number of bad verses. His prose was better and his letters are well put together, yet his whole attitude towards Paul appears that of a slow-thinking honest man confronted with a much more lively and unstable one. He was certainly strictly honourable and rather at the mercy of those who were not. He must ultimately have come to regard his association with Paul as unsatisfactory because once it started he was never out of debt, and whereas this certainly never worried Paul, he himself hated the condition. He always hoped that the spinning machine would repay his efforts and as it never did he was always letting good money follow bad. One can only regret that he never had the satisfaction of knowing that he would be remembered as playing a part in bringing to life one of the greatest of all textile inventions.

If one can trust the interesting references in John Dyer's poem 'The Fleece' (1757) it seems that the card was used, also a spinning machine based on the second patent:

> But patient art,
> That on experience works from hour to hour,
> Sagacious has a spiral engine formed
> Which, on an hundred spoles, an hundred threads
> With one huge wheel, by lapse of water twines
> Few hands requiring; easy-tended work
> That copiously supplies the greedy loom.

Dyer's footnote reads, 'Paul's engine for cotton and fine wool'. Later he continues,

> We next are shown:
> A circular machine of new design
> In conic shape: it draws and spins a thread
> Without the tedious toil of needless hands.
> A wheel, invisible, beneath the floor,
> To every member of the harmonious frame
> Gives necessary motion. One, intent,
> O'er looks the work: the carded wool, he says,
> Is smoothly lapped around those cylinders
> Which gently turning, yield it to yon cirque
> Of upright spindles which, with rapid whirl,
> Spin out in long extent an even twine.

Dyer's footnote here reads: 'A most curious machine, invented by Mr Paul. It is at present contrived to spin cotton, but it may be made to spin fine carded wool.'

Wyatt and Paul made several attempts to produce a practical version of their machine but they were never able to test it in a factory of their own and, after many failures, by 1744 had obviously given up hope; after 1746, with one exception, they bothered no more with the idea, Wyatt devoting himself to other inventions and Lewis Paul disappearing from the scene. During the years between 1738 and 1744, however, they did manage to convince their friends that their ideas had great possibilities, and they obtained a considerable amount of money with which to develop them. There was no doubt that the invention was basically sound; what one might call the prototype machine seemed exciting, and demonstrations that the inventors put on were enough to secure cooperation. One feels that the trouble lay with Paul, who instead of working away at producing a good machine lost himself in grandiose schemes for making thousands of pounds, and as a result his backers were led to expect far too much too soon. It was at this point that Johnson and his Birmingham acquaintances, Thomas Warren, Robert James and Cave, became involved. They all put money into the project and Paul led them to think that they were going to make huge fortunes. Cave gave a large sum and was given a licence to set up a frame with 250 spindles. When one considers that even a small practical machine had not yet been worked over a period, one gets some idea of the whirlwind of words by which Paul must have inveigled his backers. When the scheme crashed, Johnson did his best to act as an intermediary and there are letters of his in January 1741 to Paul in which he tries to get some satisfaction.

We know little of what happened next, only that slowly the knowledge of what had been done reached the North, particularly the greatly expanding Lancashire cotton trade, and several people there attempted to perfect roller spinning.

Information probably came partly through the mill that Daniel Bourn, the inventor of the rotary carding machine, set up at Leominster. This mill is first mentioned in the same year as he took out his patent for a carding machine, and it has been suggested that it may have been this that influenced Paul in applying for a patent for his own. In any case the mill at Leominster was partly owned by men from Lancashire, so that the North soon learned of the latest technical developments. Bourn's mill was burnt down in 1754 and was not rebuilt. After that date, experiments continued to be made in Lancashire where the carding machine was certainly used to a considerable extent, a slightly different variation of it known as the scribbling machine becoming equally popular in the wool textile trade.

Although originally intended for wool spinning, such machines as were tried out were never used for anything but cotton, and it was for the cotton trade that Arkwright finally devised a machine that was successful. Later, of course, it became the recognised machine for spinning worsteds.

Before Arkwright revolutionised spinning, the raw material in the cotton trade after the usual opening and cleaning was still usually carded by hand so as to obtain a well-opened batch, and the slubbing was drawn out of this and slightly twisted on the spinning-wheel so making a roving. This roving was then spun again on the wheel. Arkwright's work swept all this away and established the spinning factory as we know it. All the cruelty of these early mills with the horrors of child labour should not blind us to the importance of what was done.

E. Baines, in his *History of Cotton Manufacture* published in 1835, referred to Arkwright's unrivalled sagacity in estimating at their true value the mechanical contrivances of others, and this opinion has been quoted and requoted by industrial historians with the result that Arkwright's own genius has been greatly underestimated. It is only necessary to read Paul's specification and to try to visualise the machine the inventor had in mind, and then to go and look at Arkwright's water frame in order to appreciate just how unfair writers have been to Arkwright. His machine is much nearer to the modern spinning frame than it is to the contrivance Paul so completely failed to explain in his patent or to make work in the mill.

In his 1769 specification, Arkwright said that he had, by great study and long application, invented a new piece of machinery never before found out, practised or used for the making of wefts or yarns for cotton, flax and wool, which would

> be of great utility to a great many manufacturers as well as to his majesty's subjects in general by employing a great number of poor people in working the said machinery and by making the said weft or yarn much superior in quality to any heretofore manufactured or made.

In his original model there were four pairs of rollers, and a total draft of 6·25 was obtained. The machine was of wood, and the winding of the yarn that was spun was carried out on the same basis as that of the flyer of the Saxony wheel. Here at first Arkwright was rather unimaginative. He still used the device of placing pins on the flyer so that the spinner could guide the thread on to the bobbin evenly. This meant that the winding was still to some extent intermittent, which certainly went badly with the continuous process he had succeeded in bringing to the drafting. In his specification Arkwright said that the machine was to be driven by a horse, but water-power was soon preferred and became the usual means, consequently the machine was given the name of water frame. Other Lancashire inventors continued to work on the frame and several improvements were made, the most important being the patent of 1772 by Coniah Wood, a workman of Arkwright's, who introduced a movable rail in place of the pins used to guide the yarn during winding, which made the whole spinning process continuous.

Arkwright's specification, unlike Wyatt's and Paul's, was accompanied by an excellent sketch, and anybody wishing to see what it was like can examine the excellent model in the Science Museum.

It has been well and truly said that Arkwright was the chief architect of Britain's cotton industry. The more one studies him the more he seems to epitomise, in both his greatness and his narrowness, the famous trade he foreshadowed. There is the same determination to work hard and long that made the cotton trade of the nineteenth century one of the main foundations of Britain's industrial power; but this was combined, one must admit, with a certain amount of prejudice and lack of spiritual insight which was the whole period's greatest fault.

Nevertheless, the story of Arkwright's life invigorates one in a way that is different from that of any of the other textile inventors. One can still feel his presence in the industrial world he founded both in Lancashire and in Yorkshire, where the worsted section of the wool trade is based almost entirely on his ideas, but even more strongly in Derbyshire whence he moved, frightened by the possibility that the workers would destroy his machines. Whereas the growth of the cotton trade in Lancashire has tended to obliterate the monuments of the early Industrial Revolution, it is otherwise when one moves south and comes to the Derwent Valley, for there it did not expand much from its early stages. The houses that were built in the days when Arkwright moved there remain today. It was there that, when success had come so fully to him, when he was High Sheriff of the county and when he had been knighted by George III, that he began to build Willersby Castle, a castellated mansion and now a Methodist guest house, beautifully situated with the river running below. He hoped to spend his last days there, but he died before it was finished. His life is the perfect example of the self-made man. First of all there were the early years of poverty, when he was the youngest in the family of thirteen in Preston. Next came the years when he was a barber and advertised a clean shave for half a penny at Bolton. He had purchased the hair of girls going into service, dyed it, and developed a trade in wigs. He was over 30 years old before he started on the mechanical inventions that were to bring him fame and fortune. Success followed success rapidly. He left his native county and moved to Derbyshire, and at Cromford the two mills he built remain, the first a prison-like range of buildings without any windows on the ground floor, the other a brick building much more open and confident looking. Together with Willersby Castle and Thomas Wright's portrait they give us a picture of a most remarkable man.

One must turn now to the vexed yet ever interesting question of how much credit should be given to Richard Arkwright for what he said he invented. Many have been the attacks made against him, perhaps the strongest being in R. Guest's early book of 1823 entitled *A Compendious History of the Cotton Manufacture*. The author was determined to claim that Arkwright invented few, if any, of the machines he patented. This book is essential reading for all who are studying the early history of the cotton trade but it is certainly very biased.

'The machinery employed in the cotton manufacture is little known except to the manufacturers themselves, and the history of its progressive improvements perhaps scarcely to them. For the greatest improvements we are indebted to a man in humble life, whose poverty and want of patronage prevented him from either reaping the pecuniary reward or establishing his claims to that fame which his ingenuity entitled him. By following his ingenious inventions, the late Sir Richard Arkwright lived to acquire a princely fortune and died with a reputation of being one of the most eminent of those individuals who have enlarged the resources of their native country, and made her manufacture and her machinery the wonder of surrounding nations; while the man to whose painful labours and ingenious contrivances Sir Richard was indebted for these honours lived in obscurity and died in indigence.

Sir Richard Arkwright was a rare instance of one who from a very inferior situation in life, by dint of indefatigable perseverance, unity of object and able management of the men he had to deal with, amassed a large fortune and raised himself to great eminence. With no original invention to boast of in the department of mechanics to which he devoted himself he possessed unweary zeal and patience in obtaining discoveries of others and great skill in combining them and turning them to his own purposes.

He had the same appalling obstacles to surmount which Highs himself had, nothing could be done by either without capital. The modest spirit of Highs shrunk from the humiliation of soliciting partnerships or patronage; but the sphere of Arkwright was in the world and amongst men.

In 1761 Arkwright married Margaret Biggins and his marriage brought him acquainted with Highs and his inventions. His knowledge of them, however, was not obtained from Highs himself; he went to work in a more crafty and circuitous manner. Having learnt that Kay, who then resided in Warrington, had been Highs' workman he introduced himself to Kay in the summer of 1767 by employing him to make some brass wheels, and when he had called two or three times on Kay he took him to a public house and treated him with wine telling him that he was endeavouring to discover perpetual motion and that the turning brass was for a machine of that principle. Kay dissuaded him from the attempt and advised him to turn his attention to making a machine for spinning cotton. Ah, said Arkwright, that will never be brought to bear; several gentlemen have almost ruined themselves by it. Kay replied that he could bring it to bear. This was exactly what Arkwright wanted and the following morning early he went to Kay's bedside, reminded him of their last night's conversation, and eventually succeeded in procuring from him a model of Highs' machine, the water frame or throstle. In this model, Arkwright found the perpetual motion he wanted as well as the philosopher's stone.

Sir Richard Arkwright died at Cromford and his life and labour are a worthy subject of contemplation. Highs continued to make reeds. While gold was flowing in copious streams into the coffers of Sir Richard, Highs was struggling for the pittance of a day labourer.'

It is a good story, but the present writer does not think that it contains very much truth, although one would like to know more about the somewhat mysterious Thomas Highs and what, if anything, he did invent. Perhaps the most one can say is that the roller spinning scheme as an idea was well known in Lancashire around 1766, and certainly no one then had the right to claim it as their own, for that honour belongs to Lewis Paul. The widespread interest in the idea comes out very clearly in the evidence the clockmaker Kay gave when the question of the validity of Arkwright's patents came before the courts in 1785. It is certainly true that Kay was in Warrington in 1767 and while there met Arkwright, but whether he was in any way an intermediary passing on knowledge obtained from Highs to Arkwright is extremely doubtful.

However ignorant Highs may have been, if indeed he had invented what Arkwright's enemies said he had, he certainly acted in a peculiar way and did nothing to protect the work he had done. He did not even continue making roller spinning frames, but for five years occupied himself in quite a different manner, and during these years he appears to have met Arkwright on several occasions without showing any feelings that he had been robbed of the credit for his successful machine.

Re-reading the evidence of the trial one feels that the other cotton manufacturers were determined to break Arkwright's patent and seized on Kay and Highs; not being sure which to make their leading inventor they came very near to making a mess of their case. That they did manage to break Arkwright's patent was probably nothing to do with anything Kay or Highs had done, but was due to the fact that everybody recognised that the idea went back to Paul and had been common knowledge in Lancashire for many years. Arkwright in fact had no right to claim that the idea of spinning by rollers was his, and the writer is not aware that he actually did. What he was certainly justified in saying was that he had made the first machine that really performed the operation of roller spinning successfully.

Earlier in this chapter it was stated that there have always been two distinct methods of spinning, known by various names but best described as (1) continuous and (2) intermittent spinning. The first method is epitomised in roller spinning as brought to perfection by Arkwright and it has come to be the generally accepted system for fibres above a certain minimum length.

Looking back it is clear that, even with the original hand-spinning before the wheel came in, something approaching continuous drafting was done, but at that time twisting and winding were done separately and later. When the spinning-wheel came into being, its effect was to introduce spindle spinning to the trade, and the simple big wheel itself remained entirely a spindle-spinning machine; with the development of the Saxony wheel and flyer, spinning became continuous except for the stops caused by moving the yarn on the notches of the frame. Arkwright's water frame perfected continuous spinning and at the same time as he was working on this James Hargreaves, who often crossed his path, introduced the spinning jenny which was to develop into the mechanised version of the spindle-spinning method. James Hargreaves was a weaver living near Black-

18 *Avon Mills, Malmesbury*
Architecturally speaking perhaps the most charming of the early nineteenth-century woollen mills.
It is now an antique shop.

19 *The Weir at Bradford-on-Avon*
The River Avon flowing through Wiltshire and then Bath and Bristol has many weirs,
most of them built in the late Middle Ages to provide power for mills.

burn and is generally thought to have invented the jenny in 1764, but he did not patent it until 1769 after Arkwright's patent of the water frame. There was no question in this case that Hargreaves had sold jennies of his own manufacture before the date of his patent, and consequently when his case came to the courts there was no doubt that his patent was invalid. His first machine had eight spindles and was driven by hand, and although one rightly gives the jenny an important place in the history of the mechanisation of spinning, it should be made clear that from the beginning to the end of its career the spinning jenny was usually hand driven. It was a clever contrivance which employed the principle of spindle draft and partly mechanised the process in the sense that it increased the number of spindles that one person could work. The small early jennies were comparatively easy to make and were widely taken up in the cotton and woollen trades, being extensively used in the cottages by the home hand spinners. Later water power was sometimes used to drive them and as many as 120 spindles were used, but by this time the jenny had been largely replaced by the mule.

Arkwright's water frame was excellent for producing strong yarn for the warp, but it was not as good as the jenny for spinning the soft weft desired. The two inventions were therefore in a very real sense complementary. Arkwright and Hargreaves knew each other well, and both experimented in improving the carding process; on one occasion Arkwright said that Hargreaves had stolen his idea of the doffing comb for removing the cotton from the card. It is possible that the truth was the other way round. Hargreaves' patent for the spinning jenny was:

> For a method of making a wheel or engine of an entire new construction, and never before made use of in order for spinning, drawing and twisting cotton and to be managed by one person only and that the wheel or engine will spin, draw and twist sixteen or more threads at one time by the turn or motion of one hand and a draw of the other.

The inventor further described the process:

> One person with his or her right hand turns the wheel and with the left hand takes hold of the clasps and therewith draws out the cotton from the slubbing box, and being twisted by the turn of the wheel in the drawing out then a piece of wood is lifted by the toe which lets down a pressure wire so as to press the threads so drawn out and twisted in order to put the same regularly upon bobbins which are placed on the spindles.

Although this description refers to a slubbing-box, the rovings were later placed on bobbins in a fixed creel in the lower part of the machine. The spindles, which were slightly tilted in towards the creel, were mounted on a fixed frame at the end of the machine and were turned by belts from a tin roller which itself was driven by a belt from a wheel which the spinner operated with his right hand. The rovings were led up from the creel to a carriage which traversed the length of the machine. On the carriage there was a clamp consisting of two large pieces of wood which opened and closed rather in the manner of a parallel ruler. Each roving passed through this clamp, then round a peg, back through the clamp and thence to the spindle. Thus the spindles were fixed and it was in effect the let-off motion which moved.

Hargreaves remains the least known of the three famous textile inventors and he may well have been the most likeable of them all. From what we know of him, one imagines him to have been a man greatly interested in the trade and one who had thoroughly studied spinning; the idea of the jenny is said to have come to him when his spinning wheel fell over and worked for a moment on

E

its side. The spinning jenny was in many ways the most attractive of all the textile inventions, but it lacked the scientific precision of the roller spinning frame.

In the cotton trade the frame produced the warp yarn and the jenny produced the weft. The third great invention, the mule, could spin either. In the wool trade the frame was used for worsted yarn, the jenny for woollen, and when the latter was replaced by the mule it was in fact a different machine from that which Samuel Crompton the inventor had in mind. He was a shy man, extremely fond of music, who never wanted his machine to be generally used. His intention had been to make a mule for himself and thereupon spin the yarn which his family would weave, and any surplus he would sell. This surplus yarn was so good that people living round him adopted almost any method they could to see how Crompton was able to spin so fine. There are many stories about this. Arkwright himself is said to have visited Crompton's house in an effort to discover what his machine was like. Most of these stories are inaccurate, but it is true that Crompton never patented his machine. He had begun his experiments in 1776 and the machine was working five years later. In its original form it combined the roller spinning principle of the water frame with the moving carriage of the jenny, the spindles being placed on the carriage and the rollers on the frame, exactly opposite to the position used by Hargreaves. The spinner pulled the carriage out and the back rollers gave out the sliver, and drafting took place between the rollers and also between the last roller and the spindles. With the most common mule in use today there is only one pair of rollers and spindle draft alone is used. This type of modern mule is essentially a spindle drafting machine, and is therefore nearer to Hargreaves' jenny. Crompton's 'mule' is still used in the cotton waste trade but otherwise it has developed as indicated above and is now confined mainly to the woollen trade or for roller drafting alone in the cotton trade, the so-called carriage gain being used solely for stretching the thread, and the jacking motion for smoothing out soft places. The general·motion of the machine is well summarised in the contemporary phrase 'let the spindles move out to twist and in to wind'.

Crompton called his invention the 'mule' because he considered it to be crossbred, like the animal. His mule was a cross between Hargreaves' jenny and Arkwright's frame. This is a fair description. In terms of originality it does not rank with either the frame or the jenny, but it had important effects on the development of the cotton industry as it proved for many years a much better practical machine than its rival.

Crompton's mule was also called the muslin wheel as it was the first machine that could spin cotton fine enough to compare with the Indian hand-spun yarn which had hitherto been used for the manufacture of muslin. It is for this reason that the mule was so important in the Lancashire cotton trade, and it would be true to say that the first part of that trade's expansion was due largely to its invention.

Crompton's life has been more fully described than that of any other textile inventor. Like Hargreaves, he was originally a weaver, and he did not wish his machine to be used outside the family. He took this course because of the great dislike his fellow workers had of any labour-saving device. Crompton seems to have regarded himself as one of them; and he certainly did not wish to fall out with any of them. He was a man of very mild temperament who dreaded being placed in any awkward position. It may also have been partly for this reason that he took no steps to cover his invention by patent. Unfortunately for Crompton, the mule was such a good machine that all his efforts to keep it hidden failed, as did his efforts to avoid being brought into the limelight himself. When the mule became widely used in Lancashire many people recognised that Crompton had obtained nothing for what was bringing great wealth to others, and attempts were made to collect for him and to petition parliament that something should be done on his behalf. The account of Crompton wandering around London trying to solicit Members of Parliament is a sad story.

Spinning reached a remarkable degree of efficiency during the days of Crompton's hand-mule. The spinner could use either kind of draft, roller or spindle, according to which was most suited to the material. This, incidentally, is what the old hand-spinners could do and the hand-mule was the only machine with which it was possible. All the main motions – delivery at the first rollers, the carriage movement, the spindle speed – could be controlled to a very fine degree. Crompton's genius was to have kept this all under such careful control in a machine that was fully mechanical in the sense that one source of power drove everything. His mule carried out all the motions we now associate with the self-acting mule except the control of winding-on of the spun yarn and the resetting at the end of the cycle ready for the next draw.

Compared with the jenny the hand-mule had two advantages: optional roller drafting and mechanisation of the control of the draft scroll, which led to the drafting being more uniform.

Crompton made himself a mule with 52 spindles and later other builders increased the number and introduced additional improvements. Machines with a hundred spindles were in use by 1790, by which time water power was in use enabling large numbers of spindles to be used. Until water power was applied to the mule, Arkwright's frame was the only power-driven spinning machine, and this, combined with the advantage of continuous spinning, led to its wide adoption, but it was found that the yarn produced was uneven. The reason for this was the lack of control of short fibres between the rollers. Roller spinning was a wonderful idea, basically simple, but the operator could not do much to remove any unevenness whereas the spinner on the jenny or mule could adjust numerous controls so as to get the best yarn possible. Today, with the improved control recently introduced, roller spinning approaches perfection, but it is easy to see why at the time of the great inventions the yarn from the mule was definitely the best, and there was the additional advantage that the yarn wound on the mule cop could be used for weaving without rewinding.

The life of Samuel Crompton illustrates better than any other the problems and difficulties facing the inventor of the period. He had worked seven years in his so-called conjuring room at Hall in the Wood before he succeeded in producing the yarn he sought which was both strong and light and suitable for both warp and weft. We do not know why he did not patent his machine; in addition to the reasons already given it has been suggested that the wide terms of Arkwright's specification ruled it out, but one can hardly credit this. It was after 1790 that Crompton's mule really began to mould the cotton trade. Watt's steam engine was used to obtain power, although for some time water power was preferred as it caused less vibration.

The coming together of the two great names of Crompton and Watt leads one to reflect upon an interesting fact. The inventors in the textile trade were mostly men who had no recognised schooling, and although many were certainly geniuses, they were in the main practical rather than theoretical men. On the other hand, those who made the great discoveries in engineering were naturally skilled engineers, but they also had real knowledge of the theoretical background based on good technical education. There seems to have been something strangely accidental about the development of mechanisation in the textile trade. Paul hit upon a great idea but he did not know how to use it, Arkwright was a business man of great genius, Hargreaves and Crompton were practical men of the highest possible quality, but why they all came together is unaccountable.

When one turns to later developments in spinning, the most notable name is that of Richard Roberts, who perfected the self-acting mule in 1825. He made many ingenious additions to the mule as left by Crompton, including the quadrant winding motion for controlling spindle speed and the shaper for controlling the faller wires which thereby controlled the making of the cop. The only advance during the 130 years since Roberts has been to make the winding-on motion, which used to be hand operated, fully automatic. The mule cop itself is certainly a most remarkable package and has been described as the most beautiful and the most scientifically constructed package in the whole of the textile trade. This seems rather extravagant praise and anyone well acquainted with the mule will set against this statement the numerous bad cops he will have seen which were neither beautiful nor scientific.

There were other figures besides Roberts, but taken as a whole the second period of development lacks the excitement of the first. Although the machines of 1790 were still crude they contained all the essentials, and nothing of what was to come equalled in interest or importance the great work of Paul, Arkwright, Hargreaves and Crompton.

Almost all early textile machines were made of wood and in most cases the manufacturers built them themselves. It was during the first years of the nineteenth century that iron began to be used and the textile machinery-making industry emerged as a trade in its own right.

Arkwright, always attempting new ideas, had used steam, but the power produced had been obtained on the Newcomen principle and could not have been really satisfactory. A steam engine made by Boulton and Watt was used in the cotton trade in Nottinghamshire in 1785, and after 1800 the use of steam-power increased considerably, so that mills became concentrated in the towns rather than being spread over the countryside in search of water-power.

When the mule became a factory machine its outstanding ability to spin all types of yarn led to a relative decline in the use of Arkwright's water frame. When after the Napoleonic Wars power-looms became more common the increased demand for stronger yarn in the cotton and worsted trade led to a return of the water frame in its larger and more economic form, known as the throstle. In this the spindles, instead of being grouped four or six to a head with each head separately driven, were grouped in two long lines driven from one driving belt. A coping rail was introduced and the whole process was greatly improved. An alternative system was developed by Danworth; here there were flyers, and the spindles were stationary and covered by a conical cap which revolved at a high speed. This was a simple machine and produced yarn softer and more fleecy than that spun on the throstle, but it also made more waste so the throstle remained more popular with cotton. The cap spinning system was preferred for making worsted yarns for the hosiery trade and has remained in use.

Ring spinning, which was the ultimate answer, was invented in America in 1828 and was soon tried in England, but it did not really establish itself until the second half of the century.

# Chapter Eight

# Inventions: Weaving

THE HISTORY OF THE MECHANISATION OF
weaving is a much less dramatic story than that of spinning. There was no Lewis Paul to set the
process on entirely new principles and no Hargreaves or Crompton to adapt new ideas to an
expanding industry, and certainly no Arkwright to put new machines into practical operation.

The only new ideas involved in the long sequence of events that led to the final successful mechanisation of the loom came early, and were in some ways not a mechanisation at all. Perhaps it is
here that one can sense a difference between the development of spinning and the development of
weaving, for the idea of roller drafting was brilliantly suited to machine development, and has up to
the middle of the twentieth century pointed the way to full automation.

There are two memorable names in the history of weaving, John Kay (inventor of the flying
shuttle) and Edmund Cartwright. They were very different types of men. Kay was born and brought
up in textiles and obviously thought in terms of the trade. He is without doubt the leading figure.
Cartwright was a clergyman who knew nothing about weaving, a man of great if rather indecisive
ability, who was led to attempt the invention of a power-driven loom because he knew how successfully power had been applied to spinning. It remains a mystery why no one inside the cotton or
the worsted trade did the job himself.

Kay's flying shuttle was one of the crucial inventions of textile machinery and of those who
turned their attention to the loom, John Kay was the most outstanding figure. There had been great
inventions previously – that of the heddle which enabled the alternate warp strands to be raised at
once, forming the 'shed' through which the weft could pass, comes to mind – but this came at a
very early stage. The Egyptians are credited with this invention, though the name of the genius
responsible remains unknown. But, before Kay's invention there had been no outstanding developments in weaving, either in the broad, the narrow or the fancy drawloom. During the first half of
the eighteenth century, weavers were making their cloths on looms that differed little from those
used four hundred years before. The same differences still existed between plain and fancy weaving,
though there had been a tendency in plain weaving to increase the number of harnesses from two

to four, thereby making it possible to weave a slightly wider range of fabrics than before, but not on a scale comparable to what could be produced on the drawloom.

A partial exception to all this – lying outside the mainstream of textile weaving – is the Dutch or swivel loom, used for weaving ribbons. Ribbons were originally woven on a narrow loom, one at a time, but the Dutch loom enabled up to forty to be woven together. The shedding of the warp, the throwing of the shuttle and the beating up of the weft were all accomplished by an ingenious system of cranks and tappets.

Power was applied to the Dutch loom many years before any other loom. It was introduced into England from either Germany or the Netherlands, and may have been separately invented in both centres, but the date of its introduction is uncertain.

Apart from this the loom remained little altered for several centuries before 1738, when John Kay, a native of Bury in Lancashire, invented the flying shuttle. It was not his first textile invention: five years previously he had considerably improved 'reeds' (a comb-like structure which carries out the 'beating up' process on the loom) by using brass wire for the 'dents' or teeth. Previously the reed had been made of split cane. Kay's idea of changing to metal was a good one and most success-ful; the reed now used by the weaving industry derives from it.

But as far as weaving is concerned, Kay's chief claim to fame remains the flying shuttle. It came before the introduction of machine spinning and writers have often held the view that his inven-tions, by enabling the weaver to weave more quickly, thus increasing the demand for yarn, pre-cipitated the mechanisation of spinning.

It is very doubtful whether there is much validity in this point of view and it is better to consider the phenomenal success of the spinning inventions of the second half of the eighteenth century as being due to the accidental fact that several mechanical geniuses, all working in the cotton industry, happened to be alive at that time. The great attention given to spinning inventions in Lancashire at this period derived from several factors, all more important than the coming of the flying shuttle; the chief factor was probably the general prosperity of the cotton trade, due largely to the fact that for the first time there were large supplies of the raw material coming into the country, and the arrival of the printed calicoes from India had created a new fashion. Partly because of this increased activity, there were many men in the trade who felt that if only they could get Lewis Paul's idea of roller-drafting to work, they could really ride the tide of this boom and stimulate trade even more. All these factors led to the intense interest in spinning, and the increased demand for yarn played only a part. Weavers had always been short of yarn during the days of hand-spinning, and although the coming of the flying shuttle aggravated this shortage, it did not do more than that. If the shortage of yarn had been capable of bringing about the mechanisation of spinning, there appears to be no reason why it should not have happened years before. In any case, it is extremely doubtful whether an increased demand from one branch of the trade for certain products necessarily leads to an invention in another so as to bring supply and demand into equilibrium.

Before Kay's invention, the weaver threw the shuttle from one side of the loom to the other, which meant that if he was weaving on a narrow loom, the work could be done by himself, although it meant he must continually bend over the loom. On the other hand, if he was weaving on a broadloom, then it was necessary for the weaver to stand at one side and have an assistant to catch the shuttle at the other and return it to him. The eighteenth-century poet, John Dyer, whose poem 'The Fleece' has already been quoted with reference to the spinning inventions, tells how pleasantly the two loom workers passed the day in conversation, but one doubts whether broad-loom weaving was quite as enjoyable an occupation as the poet paints it. Kay's invention did away with the necessity of an assistant when weaving on a broadloom, and consequently it should have been there that the effect was most pronounced. The West of England woollen trade, which made many more broadcloths than any other area, was, however, notably slow in making use of the invention and this of all areas would appear to have been the one which could most have profited by it.

On the narrow loom, however, the flying shuttle was also a considerable improvement, in that it meant that weaving could be done more rapidly, more comfortably and with greater evenness, and it was more widely adopted by the cotton weavers of the North using narrow looms than by the broadloom weavers of the woollen trade.

Kay added about a foot on either side, to the width of the lay sword – that part of the loom which carries the shuttle while it traverses the warp and then moves forward to beat the pick-up to the fell of the cloth. In this additional space he provided a container into which the shuttle could pass as it emerged from the side of the cloth. The shuttle remained in this receptacle while the lay sword was used for the purpose of beating up the weft. Then the shuttle was knocked back to the other side of the loom where the other receptacle was waiting for it. The introduction of these containers on each side of the loom was the first part of Kay's invention; the other – and this was the reason for the name flying shuttle – was more novel and here for the first time one meets the picker, which has since so dominated weaving. The picker was simply a piece of leather, or some similar material, which by means of a handle held in the weaver's hand could be used to knock the shuttle through the shed formed by dividing the warp threads. Previously it had been thrown by the weaver. Kay's chief difficulty here had been to obtain sufficient momentum to drive the comparatively heavy shuttle across the whole width of the cloth at one stroke. It may have been this problem that accounted for the invention's comparatively slow adoption by broadloom weavers. Kay was probably the first man to place wheels on the bottom of the shuttle in order to achieve this momentum.

It is easy to appreciate the beneficial effects of Kay's ingenious invention. Once the weaver had become used to manipulating it so that he made each stroke with uniform power, it was possible to insert the weft much more smoothly and regularly than before. It is worth while recalling that previously most woollen cloths had been heavily fulled, and to some extent this must have been necessary because of the unevenness of the wefting. From the general adoption of Kay's device, it became common to weave woollen cloths that showed a design, whereas previously they had usually been plain. In the worsted trade, evenness of yarn was extremely important as there was no fulling process to follow.

More generally, Kay's invention made possible the power-driven loom that eventually followed. It would obviously have been quite impossible for Cartwright, or anybody else, to think of a method of driving the loom by power whilst the weaver still threw the shuttle across by hand. More immediately there were, of course, the advantages of the saving of labour on the broadloom already mentioned, and the speeding up of weaving generally. In addition, the weaver was now able to sit in an upright position and propel the shuttle by means of a flick of the wrist instead of, as with the narrow loom, having to spend most of his time bending double over the loom. Kay certainly made weaving a more comfortable job. This method of hitting the shuttle remains the one in general use today. When the power-loom was introduced, the hitting motion previously conveyed from the hand was replaced by a cam working through a picking stick which can be regarded as the equivalent of the weaver's arm, and the picker in exactly the form that Kay invented it was adapted to this. Many inventors have endeavoured to find a better way of weaving, but without success except for the recently developed Sulzer loom. Looking back, one could almost feel that Kay's invention was virtually too good. It was so neat and such a great improvement that for years nobody tried to alter it; indeed, it came to dominate the whole conception of weaving with what one feels were rather unfortunate results.

Kay took his invention to Lancashire and introduced it there. At the time a large part of that county still made woollens, although the cotton trade was beginning its great advance. The invention was not widely used there, however, until twenty to thirty years later. Kay made a muddle of his plan to patent the shuttle and landed himself in a great deal of trouble. Those weavers who realised it was a good idea were determined to use it but were equally determined not to pay the inventor for so doing. They formed what were called shuttle groups to provide funds to support any of their member weavers against whom Kay might proceed in the courts in an attempt to assert his rights. In those days the patent laws were very different from what they are today, and it is difficult to realise the antagonism that was felt by people against the idea that inventors should be allowed to profit by their inventions. There seemed almost to be a feeling that any invention should be common property. To some extent this was due to the fact that during the early days of the patent laws people had attempted to take out patents for what were in no way new inventions. There is a typical case of this in the West of England trade which had, about this time, changed to a large extent from making fabrics in plain weave to those in twill. One leading clothier, Mr Yerbury of Bradford-on-Avon, took out a patent which contained a great deal about angles and so forth and was, in fact, an attempt to patent the weaving of twill cloth. Twill cloths, although not previously produced in the West of England, had of course been made elsewhere since prehistoric times.

John Kay himself, feeling unfairly treated, went to France, giving as the reason his inability to maintain the rights that had been granted him under his patent. This seems to have been the real reason, and there is little evidence to support the often-quoted view that he left because of riots occasioned by his labour-saving device. No one who has studied the history of the introduction of textile machinery and the consequent coming of the factory system will doubt the great tragedy of the riots, but they are sometimes made responsible for things which had quite different causes.

In France, Kay made many other inventions, including a machine for twisting silk, a warping mill, a new type of spindle, an improved carding machine, improved jennies and, in a different field, a machine for making hat brims. They all show a mechanical ability of a very high order, but there does seem to have been something about John Kay that always prevented him from getting the reward he deserved; it is almost as though it was a defect in his character. Not only was he, like so many other inventors, without business ability, but in addition he was both obstinate and suspicious. His earlier experiences in England may have been responsible for this but hardly justify it. In France he was well treated, and this is proved by the fact that he either did not return to England, or if so only for a short time. For many years John Kay was a rather shadowy individual and writers have often confused his inventions with those of his son. Fortunately, however, Miss Julia Mann has clarified the account of his career and set his work in the right perspective.

In 1760, around the time the Lancashire cotton trade was adopting the flying shuttle more widely, John Kay's son Robert invented the drop box. This invention, although not as crucial to the future development of weaving as his father's, was nevertheless an important step forward. It fitted in well with his father's work. Instead of having one receptacle (known in the trade as the shuttle box) on each side of the loom, Robert Kay had two, three or four and introduced a contrivance by which the weaver, by means of the hand he was using to pull the lay sword backwards and forwards, could bring whichever shuttle box he needed to the level of the lay sword. It is obvious that when he then pulled his picker it would be that shuttle that was in the shuttle box level with the lay sword that would be hit across the loom. The advantage is clear, and it became possible to use different colours in the weft without any time-wasting changes. Previously when one had wanted to use different colours each shuttle had to be taken out and placed on a box or possibly on the already woven cloth, and whichever method was adopted the weaving would have been held up. The disadvantages of the hand change would have been much more evident once the flying shuttle came into use, and perhaps it was this that partly led to the new invention. Just as the father's invention has remained with us, so has the son's, and the rising and falling shuttle box remains the most common method of introducing a variety of wefts by woven cloths today. It was taken over from the hand-loom into the power-loom, and in the fancy trade it was usual to have four boxes on each side of the loom. Mechanisms were easily arranged to raise and lower these boxes, and in the so-called dobby loom the movement was worked in conjunction with that for raising and lowering the harnesses. In the early power-looms the boxes were mechanically raised but were allowed to drop by their own weight, as had been the case with the hand loom. This caused some trouble as it made moving from box one to box three difficult, if not impossible. Some time passed before the dropping motion was also made positive, but once this was done the system became traditional and is part of the wefting mechanism of the power-loom which is now tending to become out-dated. Incidentally, it has never proved possible to have multiple shuttle boxes on both sides of the loom when automatic shuttle changing is used, and this has played a larger part in preventing the general adoption of so-called automatic weaving than any other single factor.

This group of inventions was responsible for important changes in the types of cloth being made. Instead of the old traditional plain-weave solid-colour fabric, and the very different type of cloth woven on the draw loom, increased quantities now began to appear of an intermediate group of fabrics which, without involving the complications of the draw loom, yet moved considerably away from the old plain cloth. All that we know today as Gun Clubs, Glen Check, Pick and Picks, Hairlines, etc., owe much of their development to the inventions of John and Robert Kay.

Once spinning had been mechanised, people wondered whether it would be possible to do the same for weaving, but very little was accomplished during the eighteenth century. The problem consisted simply of finding a way of applying power to the many jobs performed by the weaver. These included the working of the harnesses, propelling of the shuttle, and beating-up of the newly inserted weft against the fell of the cloth. There were other processes, such as the letting-off of the warp and the taking-up of the cloth, but most early attempts left these alone and concentrated on the three first mentioned. By far the most difficult of these was the propelling of the shuttle. Once that had been accomplished it was clear to anyone with a reasonable knowledge of mechanics that the other weaving processes could be power driven. The first necessity was to discover a means of allowing the power from whatever source, whether water or steam or any other mode, to be trans-ferred to the picker. Looking back, it does seem that everybody thought it a much more difficult problem than in fact it was.

Be that as it may, those in the industry, as is sometimes the case, said firmly that it could not be done, and it was left to a man from outside to show that it could. This difference between spinning and weaving inventions is interesting. The whole sequence of inventions that revolutionised spinning was made by men who were in the trade, and one is amazed by the amount of experimen-tal work that was done on this subject. Few people outside the trade tried their hand at it. With weaving it was quite different. The trade gave up the problem without really trying to solve it. Edmund Cartwright made his first attempt in 1784, and the story has often been told. He had been with a number of friends who were in the industry or well acquainted with it, and had heard them say that great though the advantage of driving a loom by power would be, it was unlikely ever to be accomplished.

Cartwright was a man of many gifts, a good writer of English prose and an equally poor one of verse. His own account of the power loom which he wrote for the first edition of the *Encyclopaedia Britannica* is excellent:

Happening to be in Matlock in the summer of 1784, I fell in company with some gentlemen of Manchester when the conversation turned to Arkwright's spinning machinery. One of the company observed that as soon as Arkwright's patent expired so many mills would be erected and so much cotton spun that hands never could be found to weave it. To this observation I replied that Arkwright must set his wits to work then to invent a weaving mill. This brought on a conversation in which the Manchester gentlemen unanimously agreed that this thing was impracticable; and in defence of their opinion they adduced arguments which I certainly was incompetent to answer or even to comprehend, being totally ignorant of the subject, having never at that time seen a person weave. I contraverted however the impracticability of the thing by remarking that there had lately been exhibited in London an automaton figure which played chess. Now you will not assert gentlemen, said I, that it is more difficult to construct a machine that shall weave than one that shall make all the varieties of moves that are required in that complicated game. Some little time afterwards, a particular circumstance recalling this conversation to my mind, it struck me that, as in plain weaving according to the conception that I then had of the business there could only be three movements which were to follow each other in succession, there would be little difficulty in producing and repeating these. Full of these ideas I immediately employed a carpenter and smith to carry them into effect. As soon as the machine was finished, I got a weaver to put in the warp which was of such a material as sackcloth is usually made of. To my great delight a piece of cloth, such as it was, was the product. As I have never before turned my thoughts to anything mechanical, either in theory or in practice, nor had ever seen a loom at work, or knew anything of its construction, you will readily suppose that my first loom must have been a rude piece of machinery. The warp was placed perpendicularly, the reed fell with at least the weight of half a hundredweight, and the spring which threw the shuttle was strong enough to throw a Congrieve rocket. In short, it required the strength of two powerful men to work the machine at a slow rate, and only for a short time. Conceiving in my simplicity that I had accomplished all that was required, I then secured what I thought was a valuable property by a patent on the 14th of April, 1785. This then done, I condescended to see how other people wove, and you will guess my astonishment when I compared their easy methods of operating with mine. Availing myself of what I had seen, I made a loom in its general principles nearly as they are now made.

Cartwright's second loom was indeed a different proposition from the first. His study of the loom had shown him that weaving, although consisting of three motions, had other auxiliary functions which a loom must perform. For example, the point at which the beat-up touches the cloth changes with every pick; this can be controlled by the hand-weaver, but the beat-up mechanically driven will always come to the same point. The edge of the cloth must therefore always be at this same point, which implies an automatic relation between the beating-up, letting-off and taking-up motions. Again, with hand-weaving when a weft thread breaks it is at once seen and attended to; but the mechanically driven shuttle flies at the same rate all the time driven by the same force, whether carrying the weft pick or not. Dr Cartwright was quick in seeing these facts, and reconstructed a loom with additional motions to cope with these needs. His new loom stopped without the interference of the attendant on the breakage of either the weft or the warp threads; it sized the warp on its way to the healds; it regulated the supply of warp and the winding-up of the woven fabric on to the piece beam; and it adjusted the temples. Cartwright, from attempting too little, went to the other extreme and tried to make his loom do too much. Sizing, although a necessary part of the weaver's duty, should be done before the warp goes into the loom, thus the addition of a sizing apparatus was unnecessary and seriously hindered the operation of the loom. The weft stop motion was essential but the warp stop was too ambitious and failed to attain the object aimed at while adding to the complexity of the mechanism. Nevertheless, the ideas that Cartwright introduced in his machine were comprehensive and, although imperfect in many details, showed the way to weave cloth by a power-driven loom.

This new machine, however, in spite of proving itself capable of weaving cloth, found little acceptance with the manufacturers. Determined to show what could be done, Cartwright, unluckily for himself, built a power-loom factory at Doncaster where he set about weaving all kinds of fabrics. At first in 1787, the whole of the machinery both for spinning and for weaving was driven by horse-power; but in 1787 a small steam engine was introduced into the factory. Shortly afterwards, however, the whole enterprise was abandoned after having caused the inventor a loss of several thousands of pounds. Perhaps one of the cases of the collapse of the Doncaster factory was the decline of Cartwright's interest in his invention. His quick fancy had been caught by other projects. Instead of stubbornly sticking to the power-loom until he had perfected it, he turned his attention to wool combing which was then still entirely a hand process. He took out three patents for a machine and then abandoned it for attempts to improve the steam engine. Next, this busy man of ideas invented a dough mixer, a reaping machine, a three-furrow plough, a wheat-planting drill and various other contrivances. Everything he tried showed strength of intellect and a good understanding of mechanical principles, but he lacked the perseverance to make any of his contrivances thoroughly practical and therefore profitable.

In 1801 Cartwright undertook the management of the Duke of Bedford's model farm at Woburn and while there met Robert Fulton, the celebrated American engineer and famous as the first to make steam navigation practical. Fulton seems to have found the inventive clergyman a congenial companion and confided in him his project for the steam propulsion of boats. Cartwright seized on the idea and constructed a small steam boat which was floated on the pond in the grounds of Woburn. He does not seem to have carried the idea further.

Towards the close of his life Cartwright realised that he had greatly impoverished himself by his desultory inventive pursuits. In 1806 therefore he petitioned Parliament for monetary reward for his inventive services to industry and the nation. Though he claimed to have spent £30,000 on the power-loom alone, Parliament could not be brought to grant a sum so great for any individual achievement, but he was given £10,000 in recognition of the great service he had rendered to the public by his invention of power-loom weaving.

With part of the money Cartwright purchased the farm of Hollenden at Sevenoaks, and there spent the remainder of his long life in leisurely pursuits, inventing, writing and experimenting till the last. At the age of eighty he was hail and vigorous, writing thus of himself:

> I cleave to earth to earth-born cares confined,
> A worm of science of the humblest kind,
> With mind unwearied still will I engage,

In spite of failing vigour and of age,
Nor quit the conflict till I quit the stage.

During his stay at Woburn, Cartwright received from his university the degree of Doctor of Divinity, and was made a Fellow of the Royal Society. He enjoyed the reputation of being a poet on the strength of a legendary poem known as Arminia and Elvina, which was favourably received by contemporary critics but is never read now. He was said to possess a fine wit, and the poet Crabbe, a good judge of people, commented of a meeting with him at Tunbridge Wells: 'Few persons could tell a story so well, no man could make more of a trite one. I can just remember him, a portly, dignified old gentleman of the last generation, grave and polite but full of honour and spirit.'

Such was the man who was mainly responsible for the introduction of power-loom weaving, and anyone today who has devoted time and study to the loom will feel that there is something appropriate in the connection between this amateur genius and the equally ingenious contraption which has resulted from his labours.

Cartwright, by his ability to produce a loom that worked, had shown that a power-driven loom was a possibility, and other people quickly followed in his footsteps, notably Robert Millar of Glasgow, who patented a loom in 1790 which was not directly derived from Cartwright's and has hardly received the credit it deserves. He used eccentric wheels or wipers to drive the shuttles through the shed, and his loom was used to some extent in Scotland in the early years of the nineteenth century.

With cotton weaving, the sizing of the yarn was important. Cartwright had attempted to do this combined with weaving but it was not successful and it was left for Thomas Johnston to solve the problem. He saw that the correct place to do the sizing was not at the loom but while the yarn was on the warping mill, and the process has continued to be done in this way ever since.

# PART III

*The Industrial Revolution: Men*

# Chapter Nine

# The revolt of the shearmen

THE TECHNOLOGICAL AND ECONOMIC pressures on the wool textile trade, as has been noted, were shifting its centre of gravity from the West of England to Yorkshire; they were reducing the importance of woollens and elevating that of worsteds; and they were having an impact on the traditional way of life of the workers in the trade, which, as the nineteenth century dawned, was to result in violence.

The vigour, and sometimes desperation, with which the wool workers attacked the introduction of the new machines may have been heightened because an old, traditional craft trade resented having to adopt ideas from the cotton industry – seen as its rival.

Though there had been earlier outbreaks, the main troubles developed in 1802–3, and at the start there was a united movement of opposition by the workers in the West of England and Yorkshire. At first the former played an equal part, though understandably they were later to show less staying power.

Riots were largely organised by the cloth workers or finishers and can only be understood in the context of the history and development of finishing machinery which had been made specially for the trade. There had been few riots due to the coming of either the new spinning machinery or the flying shuttle. But the question of whether the weavers had been apprenticed played a part in these disputes.

It was, indeed, the introduction of machinery specially introduced for the trade which sparked off the main outbreaks of violence. The finishing of woollen and worsted cloths presented special problems and the answers to these were found within the trade. There were two important inventions: the shearing frame which ultimately replaced the old hand-shears and the circular milling machine which replaced the fulling stocks. This latter was invented by John Dyer of Trowbridge and patented in 1833 (there was a controversy with Yorkshire as to who did invent it) and closely resembled the machine now in use. The only difference is that Dyer used three top rollers and a short spout.

The milling machine, however, did not affect the disturbances in the West of England trade, which are the subject of the following chapters. The invention of the rotary cutting machine and the consequent departure of the old hand shears is a subject of more interest for several reasons. There is the effect on the riots and, in addition, the invention had a considerable importance beyond the field of its original intention. The potential of the circular cutting machine was recognised by a Stroud engineer, Mr Budding, and from it he produced the modern circular lawn mower.

When the problem of replacing the old hand shears was first faced, the original idea was to place a number of shears into a frame and work them together. This idea had occurred to Leonardo da Vinci but as with his other textile ideas, nothing came of his sketch which was not known to the trade and it was only in 1784 that James Harmer, a clergyman of Sheffield, placed several pairs of shears into a frame and operated them by means of a crank. These machines were used to some extent in France, but never widely in England, partly, one suspects, because of the great opposition that the machine-shears evoked from the workers, partly because they were technically not very successful. It was the invention of the rotary machine that was important. The first version was made by an American, Samuel Dore, and patented in England in 1794, though, for some reason, no more was heard of it here. In America, however, machines based on it were produced. The machine arrived in France in 1812 and 1818, John Collier, who already had a number of woollen patents to his credit, produced the circular machine. This machine, too, was not very successful and without doubt the first really effective rotary cutting machine in Britain derived from a patent by J. Lewis of Brimscombe, near Stroud, in 1815. This is usually regarded as his own independent invention, but this is somewhat doubtful, since drawings of the American model had been brought to England in 1811 and Lewis may well have seen them.

These earlier versions are basically the same, though they may differ in detail. The one important change was that while in the earlier machines the cutting blades worked from list to list, as the circular machine developed, the blade was made the same width as the cloth and the cloth passed through the machine lengthwise. Once the circular machine was perfected, the days of hand-shearing were over, and this came by 1830.

The riots which followed the first ideas, and the legal arguments which followed in Parliament are some of the most interesting of all the aspects of the West of England wool textile trade. The letters passing between the local magistrates and ministers of the Government in London, give the impression that England in 1802 was on the verge of civil war. Certainly the ministers spoke and acted as if they expected civil war to break out at any moment, while down in Wiltshire, the local magistrates appear to have thought the same. Both groups, determined to maintain their power, did not hesitate to use unfair means to do so. In some cases, ministers and magistrates were not unsympathetic to the workers but they were determined to stamp out any disobedience. On the other hand, the workers were equally determined to fight for what they felt were long-established rights. Most of them regarded themselves as their own masters, not as the employees of the cloth-iers. To work in a factory meant the end of a way of life and they were prepared to use any and every means to avoid it. On one thing both those who wanted change, and those who opposed it, agreed: a struggle was taking place that was, for them, more important than the war in Europe.

In a sense it is incorrect to speak of those in power as being for the 'established order' because in many ways theirs was a revolutionary position, while the workers were fighting to maintain a traditional way of life. These men in the woollen industry of the West, the oldest established in

20  *Abbey Mills, Bradford-on-Avon*
The last woollen mill to be built in the West of England, *c. 1875*, by the Gane Brothers.

21 *Mill at Shawford, c. 1800*
A delightful small mill, typical of many in the area. It is now a theatre.

22 *Clothier's Mill in the Stroud Valley, c. 1750*
Whereas most Wiltshire mills are in the towns, many Gloucestershire mills were built in the river valleys.

England, had been craftsmen for centuries, working usually in their own homes, in small groups and retaining a considerable degree of independence. Therefore their opposition to the new machines was complete and very bitter.

During the eighteenth century, as already indicated, the supremacy of the West of England had been rudely shaken, not only by the rapidly expanding cotton trade, but within its own field by the rapid expansion of the two sections of the Yorkshire industry – woollen and worsted. The West of England clothiers still thought they made the best cloth – and there was some truth in this, though not as much as they reckoned; but the days of their dominance were already passing, if not passed.

Already in the cotton trade of the North, operatives confined in large factories were working long hours. Those who tried to remain outside were finding themselves poorer all the time. As yet, however, the woollen trade had withstood this threat and the workers in the clothing towns of the West of England, as well as Yorkshire, remained independent men.

The shearmen were the aristocrats of the woollen workers. They usually worked in shops which belonged to the manufacturer or clothier, but maintained a large measure of independence. Only men of considerable strength could use the huge shears which cut the nap of the cloth so close that the resultant fabric was as fine as a skin. The new factory system appeared to them as a form of slavery, and they were determined to stop its growth by whatever means lay within their power.

Everything combined to encourage the sense of close companionship; above all the great secrecy in which the affairs of the union were shrouded. Before anyone could join there was the oath swearing the members to complete secrecy, and anyone who disobeyed this knew that their fellow workers would ostracize them. But it was not fear that kept them secret and faithful to their oath, it was rather the deep sense of fellowship with their workmates which combined to give them a pride and sense of community in their work.

The struggle was a bitter one, with strikes and riots and mill-burnings on the one hand and combinations, some wise some not, on the other; attempts to co-operate with the masters, attempts to frighten them, and finally a grand appeal to Parliament. All were tried. On their side the local magistrates and the Government in London had the power, including the army, and they did not hesitate to use spies and informers. Even the courts, which should have been independent, and indeed sometimes were, usually fulfilled their wishes.

The shearmen met regularly as the threat to livelihoods increased, and discussed the possible ways in which they could meet it. Some advocated direct action, such as setting fire to mills that had introduced machinery, while others thought that the laws which had been on the statute book for years protected them and that they should appeal to Parliament – in particular to the statute that prohibited the use of the gig mills used for nap-raising which the clothiers were introducing even faster than the new shearing frames. The shearmen knew that the power-driven gig mills were an improvement, whereas the shearing frames being made at that time were no great advantage. Another law laid down that every worker in the woollen trade had to serve seven years' apprenticeship, and the members of the shearers' union were determined that this apprenticeship rule – which had been relaxed in many branches of the trade, notably weaving – should be maintained. In addition, there was another old statute which said that no clothier should own more than two looms.

On the gig mill the teasels were placed in a cylinder, supported between two posts, which revolved rapidly, and the cloth passed from a cylinder below to one above. It took a man working nearly a hundred hours to raise the nap on a piece of cloth by hand, but with this machine a man (without using anything like the strength of the hand-worker), helped only by a boy, could do it in

F

12 hours. It was these cloths that came from the raising, either from the hand-worker or alternatively from the machine, that the shearmen worked on. The nap or face of these cloths was long and shaggy and the shearer cut it down with heavy shears. Already a few clothiers had introduced shearing frames (in which several shears were fixed in a frame) and some of the shearers must have seen them working. The finished pieces were said to be uneven and rough, but it was likely that some day a better method would be developed – and there were no laws on the statute book prohibiting machine shearing. It was for this reason that many of the workers realised that if there were to be a fight, either legal or otherwise, it should be now and the issue should be the gig mills.

The problem was, however, that gig mills had been in use in Gloucestershire for very many years, and despite great discontent, the clothiers had succeeded in keeping them. The workers there had several times attempted to stop their use, but the clothiers maintained that they were not the same machines as those prohibited by law (see Chapter Four). As a matter of fact, nobody knew whether they were or not, as there were no records of what the old machines were like.

The clothiers retaliated against the workers' struggles in many ways, and on one occasion they suggested to the Government that those shearmen who were unwilling to shear cloths raised on the gig mills should be press-ganged into the army, pointing out that between three and four thousand extra soldiers could be found in this way.

There were close connections between Yorkshire and the West of England. Shearman several times brought joint actions against the users of the gig mills, arguing that they were prohibited by the old law from Tudor times, but always the clothiers maintained that these mills were different and therefore not covered by the old Act. Nevertheless, no grand jury had been found willing to say that they were in fact the same and so allow the Act to apply. The shearmen thought that in the end they would win their case. For some reason the Wiltshire clothiers had never used gig mills, but they were now saying that they would have to do so to maintain their trade because the cloths finished on them were better and consequently they were losing trade to their Gloucestershire competitors. This attempt to introduce the gig mill in an area where it had not so far been used was the main reason why the West Country shearmen played so large a part in the forthcoming struggles.

Some of the shearmen thought the question of apprenticeship more important. They considered that everybody ought to go through the same training, but in fact in this they were misled by their own position because, taken as a whole, most textile workers had never been apprenticed and consequently this was not an issue upon which the workers were ever likely to join together. The shearmen were one of the few groups of workers where apprenticeship was regular and recognised. It was certainly not common amongst the weavers.

The other Act which the woollen workers thought protected them was more difficult to understand, and many of the members of the shearers' union did not know what it was about. Many years before, an Act had been passed which prohibited the clothiers from owning more than two looms. It had never been an important issue, because the clothiers had never been particularly keen on having their weavers all in one building and were quite prepared for the weavers to continue to weave on their own looms and in their own homes. Recently, however, a few had endeavoured to organise weaving shops, and this had led to considerable ill-feeling; in Yorkshire, unlike the West of England, there were a number of small clothiers, who were willing to combine with the workers against their larger rivals. Although as yet power-looms were not used in the woollen trade, both sides knew that they were being tried out in the cotton trade, and the workers feared, and the clothiers hoped, that one day they would be suitable for woollen cloth. Incidentally, both sides to the dispute appear not to have known that a special addition to the original Act exempted the Western clothing counties from the prohibition.

At the back of the minds of all the workers was the fear that they would be driven into the factories. This had already happened in the spinning section of the trade, but the people involved there were, to a great extent, either women or children. The use of child labour in the spinning factories of the textile trade was one of the cruellest aspects of the growth of the industry, but it must be admitted that it was not against this outstanding evil that the weavers and shearmen were prepared to unite. What was happening to their children, although it must have been present in their minds, did not have the effect on them that their own fears about their own future had.

One of the leading clothiers in the West of England was John Jones of Staverton. He was regarded as the great enemy of the shearers, perhaps a little unjustly. The new mill he had built at Staverton was looked upon by the workers as a symbol of all that they feared most. His fellow clothiers, although sometimes following his lead, were perhaps rather jealous of his apparent success. He appears from his letters as a man of considerable power, not only because he was the most important manufacturer in the area but also because he was a magistrate. Most clothiers, however, had not followed Mr Jones, feeling perhaps the organised hatred of those amongst whom they lived.

The great campaign of the workers of the West against the introduction of gig mills came to a climax when these mills were introduced into the clothing towns of Wiltshire. The first attacks took the form of minor riots, and were more spontaneous than organised. The early outbreaks were at Warminster and Bradford, but they soon shifted to Trowbridge, the main centre of the trade and the meeting place of the shearmen's union. The workers at this early stage were supported in their slightly theatrical gestures by the feeling that there was a great deal of public sympathy for their cause. Several people in authority trying to prevent these actions complained that they could not get the support they would have expected and wished for from those people not engaged in cloth making. Jones himself, in a report he sent to London, complained of the difficulty he was finding, in his capacity as a Justice of the Peace, in obtaining the additional special constables he thought were necessary. At this time in Trowbridge, there was another dispute about wages, and early in July 1802 the shearmen came out on strike. But it was the threat of the gig mills, suggesting in turn the threat of the factories, that was the driving force behind all these events and accounted for the support the men gave to their leaders. The shearmen met regularly at their headquarters at Trowbridge, and communicated regularly with their friends in other parts of the West Country and in Yorkshire. All members of the union had a ticket without which it was impossible to get work as a shearman in any part of the country; written across it were the words: 'May industry and freedom unite us in friendship.'

The local justices and clothiers were greatly concerned about these clubs, as the unions were called, and following a meeting decided to appeal to London for further help. As a result, Mr James Read, a London magistrate, was sent down to enquire into details about them, and to help in dealing with the riots that had taken place.

Mr Read was a rather dogmatic Londoner and inclined to underestimate the intelligence of both the workers and the clothiers; he knew nothing about cloth-making and he did not think that the clubs were of such long standing as had been generally thought; he also considered that the guiding power was in Yorkshire. He started intercepting letters and thereby obtained a certain amount of information, but it was not long before the shearmen discovered this and began sending their vital messages by carrier. The main leader in Yorkshire, himself a friend of many of the

Trowbridge shearmen, was George Palmer; he had been to the West earlier and there appears to have been complete trust between the two groups. One of Mr Read's early achievements was to bribe a member of the shearman's union to give him a great deal of information about the Trowbridge meetings and about the shearmen's plans, but here again the shearmen soon learnt what was happening and turned the culprit out of the union. All this, however, comes rather later in our story, and during the events leading up to the attacks on the Trowbridge and district mills, and throughout the whole of the period of the strike for higher wages, the clothiers made no attempt to break the shearmen's union by the underhand methods that were to be introduced by Mr Read from London.

Some of those in authority said that among the leaders of the shearmen were men who had been discharged from the army, but there was no truth in this. The chief members had been shearmen for many years, and the cause for which they were fighting was their own. They were certainly not the revolutionary men that some of their enemies thought they were. One of the clothiers, carried away by the fear that his own mills might be the next to suffer, was heard to say that this was no assembly of a common mob but an organised body of armed men who had received their training in the army.

However, there were a few woollen workers returning from the armed forces who found it difficult to get employment. One of them, an inhabitant of Bradford, wrote a letter to Mr Benjamin Hobhouse, M.P. for Hindon and a man whom the workers thought sympathetic to their cause. The writer appealed to Mr Hobhouse for those who, he said, had served for many years in His Majesty's Service in defence of their country and now that peace had come had been sent home to starve. Surely, he contended, the masters did not mean to do this? He went on to deal with the problem of those who were losing their work because of the coming of the factories and said: 'We know that it has been mentioned to our great men and ministers in Parliament by them that have factories, how many poor they employ, forgetting at the same time how many more they would employ were they to have it done by hand as they used to do.' As a result the workhouses were full of people who would otherwise have been employed and consequently the poor rates were not collected. Unless things were altered there would certainly be a revolution, 'and the Lord will sooner or later punish those that want to abate the hireling of his wages. The burning of factories or setting fire to the property of people we know is not right, but starvation forces nature to do that which he would not had he sufficient employ. We have tried every effort to live by pawning our clothes, and chattels, so we are now on the brink of the last struggle. Do with us and for us as you would wish to be done unto, that we, before we give up the ghost, clasp our hands and say Hobhouse forever.'

The writer signed the letter dramatically: 'From a soldier returned to his wife and weeping orphans.'

**Chapter Ten**                    *The mill burners*

IN TROWBRIDGE DURING THE EARLY
summer of 1802 the men were meeting regularly, debating their course of action. It would appear
there was some disagreement between those who thought that any mill which introduced new
machinery should be attacked and those who believed that strike action was better. The real
difference perhaps lay between those who were most afraid of the new machinery and those who
were more concerned to safeguard the existing wages.

Finally, however, the shearmen's union organised a number of attacks on the clothiers who were
either using or intending to use gig mills. Their first act was more a gesture than anything else.
They cut down a number of trees that one of the clothiers had recently planted in the drive leading to his house.

The shearmen also sent a number of letters to those clothiers whom they knew were, or thought
might be, going to introduce either gig mills or shearing frames, saying that if this took place they
would do everything in their power to destroy them. As far as could be seen these preliminary
moves had no effect on anyone.

Then towards the end of April 1802, the shearmen planned their first attack. It was set in
Warminster. A small but expanding clothier, Mr Warren, had introduced gig mills into his factory.
He thought there might be trouble and his mill was well guarded at night. The local shearmen had
hoped that the guard would quit when they appeared for the first attack; when it did not they were
not prepared for violent action and withdrew, and after talking amongst themselves set fire to a
hayrick belonging to a clothier who had never thought of introducing any gig mills himself. It was
not a well-organised attack and the fire was discovered before the rick was well alight and was
promptly put out. The Warminster shearmen were determined to try again and they succeeded in
setting fire to a dog kennel and another rick, both of which, this time, were completely burnt.

A few days later a small group of shearmen from Warminster came across the Downs following
a Mr Bailey of Calston Mills, near Devizes, and whilst he was on the Downs near Imber, his cart
loaded with cloths, they caught up with him and six of them with blackened faces took the cloths

out of the cart and cut them into pieces. The damage was reckoned at two hundred pounds and Mr Bailey was certainly unfortunate as the rumours that he was about to introduce gig mills were apparently untrue. He said this to the attackers, but it did not help him and the Warminster shearmen appeared pleased with their efforts.

The Warminster group then organised an attack on 23 June, when during the night, one of their members fired a gun into the window of the house of a worker employed by Messrs Bleeck and Strode, clothiers in the town. This man had agreed to shear cloths that had been raised on the gig mill. The next night another attack was made on a rick belonging to a Mr Dunn, but this fire was put out. Another group attacked a rick owned by Mr Tugwell, a manufacturer of Bradford, and this was successful. Mr Tugwell was intending to install gig mills and apparently a letter sent to him warning him of the consequences of this had been ignored.

Encouraged by these successes, a group including workers from Trowbridge and Westbury met some shearmen from Warminster late in the evening of 29 June near Arn Down, and, shortly after midnight, they went to the house of the chief clothier in Warminster, Mr Henry Wansey, and fired a gun into his bedroom. Mr Wansey's family had been clothiers in Warminster for many years and it was not at all certain that he had intended to introduce gig mills. Reports merely said that he was considering it.

A few days later shots were fired into the house of Mr John Jones of Staverton, and in Warminster into the house of Thomas Baker, a worker employed by Mr Wansey. Baker had said that he would work on cloths even if they had been raised on the machines. This type of renegade worker was regarded as even more obnoxious than the clothiers who brought in the machines. Meanwhile in Trowbridge similar action was carried out against Mr Stancomb, another clothier; he had a narrow escape as this shot, fired when he was sitting in his room one evening, flattened against the wall above his head.

Feeling perhaps that these attacks were having some success, the men then decided to burn the barn, stables and other property of Mr Warren, the Warminster manufacturer whose property they had previously attacked and with whom they were particularly angry. The attack was completely successful and the buildings were totally destroyed. At the same time, a letter was sent to the other chief Warminster clothier, Mr Wansey, warning him that the same thing would happen if he proceeded with the suggested idea of bringing in the machines.

On 4 July the biggest attack so far was organised against Mr Jones' mill at Staverton. The shearmen from Bradford and Trowbridge met at 11 o'clock at night outside the town and came across the fields to the high ground above Staverton Mill. There were about a hundred shearmen, and when they reached the mill they fired a number of shots at it, breaking a few windows, but at this point a counter-attack was launched by men whom Mr Jones had brought in to act as guards; these guards did not fire over the men's heads as on several previous occasions, and some shots came very close to the shearmen, who thereupon withdrew having made what they hoped was a worthwhile gesture.

The shearmen of Warminster, two nights after the Trowbridge and Bradford workers' attack on Staverton, organised what may be regarded as their most successful attempt yet. They went to Clifford Mills at Beckington, the property of Mr Newton, and started a fire which consumed the entire mill. The damage was estimated by the owner at £15,000 and, even more important, many of the inhabitants of the village turned out and prevented those who wished to stop the fire from doing so.

Back at Trowbridge Mr Naish, a clothier with several workshops in the town, had installed the hated machinery, while at the same time a Mr Heath, who rented a mill at Littleton from Mr Naish, had done the same. It was against this mill that an attack which was to have fateful consequences was now planned.

Meanwhile Mr Jones was endeavouring to enlist help for the Government. In his position as magistrate, he had had occasion to send reports to London and as the riots increased these became more regular and brought him into direct contact with the Home Secretary, Lord Pelham, who appears to have had a considerable respect for his judgment.

A few days after the attack on his own mill, he sent Lord Pelham a description of what happened. He explained that the attacks had considerably increased during the month of June with the result that the neighbourhood was greatly threatened and disturbed. It would have been more true to say that the clothiers were threatened and disturbed, because most of the inhabitants of the area, whether working in the cloth trade or not, were sympathetic with the cloth workers. Mr Jones went on to describe how, at about 2 o'clock in the morning, a considerable number of armed men had attacked his mill without any provocation and, according to him, effected much mischief by firing at it for more than half an hour with ball slugs and small shot. He admitted that no lives were lost, but added that children living in the house of his resident overlooker had been in great danger and only saved themselves by creeping under their beds. The attacks had been quite unexpected and there had been no time to escape out of the house. Mr Jones himself, as soon as he had been informed, had ridden down from his own house at Berryfield and had taken with him a detachment of the Queens Dragoon Guards under the command of a Captain Quantock who, he took the opportunity of saying, was always willing to afford him every assistance. Before they arrived at the mill, however, the rioters had gone away, and Mr Jones assumed that they had heard of his approach.

He went on to tell the Home Secretary that the meetings of the workers were so well concealed that he had not been able to obtain any definite information as to who was responsible, though he assumed that the same group had burnt an unoccupied dwelling house and mill about five miles away belonging to a Mr Newton. It was clear Mr Jones thought that the area should be placed on a more regularly guarded basis, and he arranged with Captain Quantock that nightly patrols should be carried out so as to secure the peace of the country and to afford all possible protection to the lives and property of the inhabitants. He arranged for the commanding officer at Bristol to quarter a troop of Dragoons at Trowbridge and another at Bradford, for he felt that with their support he would be able to prevent any further mischief. If the riots still continued, with these forces at his disposal he felt sure that he would quickly be able to restore peace. He went on to point out that the riots made it quite impossible for him and the other manufacturers to continue their normal business, and they were all very greatly alarmed for the future of their trade. He was also concerned as to how these rioters had obtained their arms. It had been reported that many of them were members of the associated corps, who, having originally purchased their muskets, now retained them as their private property. He would, he said, endeavour to find out if this were the case when the late commanding officer, who was away at present, returned home. In conclusion, Mr Jones said that he was enclosing a copy of a letter which he had received that morning from a group of manufacturers in Trowbridge. Unfortunately the acting magistrate there was ill and incapable of organising the necessary measures. As a result the clothiers there wanted the Government to take action to protect them from the turbulent temper and conduct of the shearmen. They considered that the Government should call a meeting of the manufacturers and allow them to join together with those in the neighbouring towns to make a stand against the fate that was threatening them. Mr Jones enquired whether he, with the help of the other Bradford magistrates, should organise this.

It is clear that the position in July was tense and complicated. The two issues, the strike of the shearmen at Trowbridge and the workers' attempts by threat, riot and legal action to stop the spread of machinery, were naturally mixed, in most people's minds, into one large issue. The strike had gone on for some weeks, but before any settlement was reached the main attack on Littleton Mill was made. Incidentally, it is rather puzzling that Mr Heath's mill, rented from Mr Naish, was attacked rather than Mr Naish's own mill in Trowbridge. Perhaps a country mill was easier to get at than one in the town.

Ralph Heath, aware of the recent outrages and burnings, and knowing that Mr Naish was very unpopular with the workmen, had been afraid his rented mill might be attacked and had therefore employed several people to keep watch with him at night. On this night (as he was later to report) he was sitting in his house next door to the mill with his wife and John Pearce, Stephen Richardson and Daniel Goodship. At about 1 a.m. Daniel Goodship, thinking that he heard noises, looked out and saw four men, all armed with muskets, pistols and bayonets, their faces blackened; and it was clear that there were more in the background. The leader brushed Daniel Goodship aside and rushed into the room shouting, 'Stand up, you!' The other three followed, pointing their weapons at Mr Heath and his servants who had had no time to collect their own arms. They were told to stand up and not move. A man about five feet six inches tall with his face blackened was particularly excited and rushed round with a fixed bayonet shouting: 'Blast your eyes, are there any other soldiers or guards here?' The leader attempted to calm him down, but failed and ordered him outside. Then, leaving another shearman on guard, he went outside himself.

A young shearman was left on guard. He was tall, and like all the rest his face was blackened, but this could not disguise his protruding front teeth. Mr Heath looked at him closely and then said, 'I know you.' The shearman made no reply, but silently kept his watch, his pistol pointing towards Mr Heath and his three servants. Once, Mr Heath moved, and then the shearman spoke for the only time, swearing that if everyone did not keep still, he would blow all their brains out. No one spoke or moved again and very shortly the other man, the impetuous one, came in and shouted: 'Blast your eyes, we came to set fire to your mill and we have damn well done it.' No sooner had he spoken than the leader entered, told him to get out, and addressing Heath said: 'Your mill is on fire because you are going to introduce shearing frames.' Heath attempted to argue but was told to keep quiet and the shearman continued: 'We remain on guard, and if you come out and attempt to put out the fire, we shall shoot you.' With that he left.

Outside he joined his companions, about 30 or 40 in number, all of whom had done their job well, and they watched the fire with satisfaction.

Inside the house Mr Heath could see the light from the fire, and after a few minutes he went to the door and opened it. The tall man, the one he thought he knew, was still there with his pistol which he immediately pointed at Heath telling him to go inside and stay there, otherwise he would shoot him. Heath realised that he could do nothing and went back into his house and stayed there for some time. When he went out again the mill was completely in flames and there seemed no chance of saving anything. All the shearmen had gone home. He went round to the back of the mill by the canal and, helped by his servants, began to throw buckets of water on to the burning buildings. They partly saved one end, and when it was light Mr Heath climbed in through a window and rescued several cloths.

The attack on Littleton Mill was over. But the drama, whose chief actor was to be the young shearman Mr Heath thought he recognised, had only begun.

**Chapter Eleven**                    *The counter-attack*

IN TROWBRIDGE THE NEXT MORNING everybody knew about the burning of Littleton Mill. It was certainly the most sensational success yet achieved in any of these organised attacks and the weekly newspaper put the point of view of the clothiers very clearly when it stated that the workmen were proceeding in their outrages in defiance of all the laws of the country and were thereby attempting to dictate to their masters how their businesses should be run. This attempt at intimidation by violence should, it continued, be stopped, not only in the interest of the clothiers themselves but also in that of all who believed in law and order. If this were not done the very foundations on which civilised society rested would crumble.

Even before the attack on Littleton Mill it was clear that events were moving to a climax. Only a few days previously Mr John Jones, acting in his joint capacity as a magistrate and leader of the manufacturers, had at last been able to obtain the names of the committee of the shearmen's union. He suggested in a letter to the Home Secretary that he should arrest all thirteen and endeavour to seize the papers and books of the union. He went on to report that the workers were now attempting to collect money throughout the whole country in order to support those who were on strike and that many people had helped them in this way by giving donations.

Mr Jones had also discovered that the committee issued pass tickets to their members and that these were valid throughout the country. Indeed, without one of them it was impossible for a shearman to be accepted by his fellow workers in other areas.

Mr Jones went on to say that he considered the power of the union was increasing daily and that at his mills workers who had continued to come were now being forced to stay away and follow the instructions of the union. Unless something was done he felt certain that he would have to shut the whole factory.

This last statement makes clear the dilemma Mr Jones was facing. Like many other people who find themselves in the same position, he was not quite honest in his reports. Mr Jones above all wanted his business to prosper. He was not opposed to the workers' union as such. This becomes clear when one follows his actions upon hearing of the news of the burning of Littleton Mill. Instead of rushing to arrest someone his first thoughts were how to stop the strike of the shearmen which was still going on and which he saw as both a threat to the industry as a whole and as the basic cause for these attacks. Accordingly, now that he knew the names of the committee, and despite his previous letter to the Home Secretary in which he had suggested that he should arrest the whole lot, he now decided to approach the shearmen's union in order to see whether he could negotiate and reach an agreement to call off the strike. His action in doing this was later to be criticised by the authorities, but it probably had the support of his fellow clothiers.

As a result of these moves a deputation of seven shearmen went on 26 July to Mr Jones' house near Bradford. It was quite a formal meeting and amongst those present was Mr Hobhouse, M.P. for Hindon, the man to whom the unemployed Bradford-on-Avon cloth worker had written (see Chapter Nine). He was regarded as one of the most liberal of M.P.s and the fact that Mr Jones had invited him to be present could be taken by the workers as a gesture of his sincerity. At this meeting Mr Jones made an offer that he would give work to anybody at present unemployed in Bradford and that he would always give preference to the employment of men of that parish rather than use the frames for cutting or shearing the cloth. A rather involved argument arose out of this and there was a considerable difference of opinion as to the number of people actually employed in Bradford. The deputation endeavoured to make him agree to throw out the machines he had installed, but this he firmly refused to do and because of this the deputation finally rejected his offer.

A report of this meeting was forwarded to the Home Office, and with it the names of the shearmen. They were Samuel Jones, John and James Mead, Henry King, Benjamin Pitman, William Sheppard and Thomas Tuck. It is worth noting that James May, whom we know from other sources was the leader of the shearmen's union in Trowbridge, was not present. The report stated that Mr Jones had offered to employ all the men belonging to the parish of Bradford who were out of work and who, according to him, numbered 30. He would give preference to the employment of such people rather than use the frames and would continue to do this while any such people were out of work. In addition, he offered to do no gigging or shearing for any other clothier. This offer, the report stated, the workers had rejected, acting, as they said, on behalf of the body of shearmen who had deputed them to attend the meeting. They went on to declare that it was the resolution of the shearmen throughout England, Scotland and Ireland, not to work after machinery, that is on cloth prepared by machine. Samuel Jones had loudly declared that for himself he would rather be hanged than recommend that the shearmen should accept Mr John Jones' offer or ever agree in any way to work on cloths that had been partly treated on machines.

At this time Mr Jones, the magistrate, must have been a very worried man. His business was not as successful as was generally thought, and although he was regarded by many as being the enemy of the workers this was an exaggeration. He was fast becoming the leader of the clothiers, and at the many meetings they were to have, he was to restate the position he had maintained at this meeting with the workers. As he saw it, the clothiers must maintain the right to be able to introduce any new machinery they felt was necessary for the continuation of their business, and this machinery must be protected against any attacks. On the other hand, the manufacturers should promise to find work for all persons in their factories. This might, of course, involve a change of occupation, but ample and sufficient wages should be paid to anyone whose job had been made unnecessary by the introduction of machinery. The final, perhaps unnecessary, proviso was that this would only apply as long as people behaved properly.

The connection between this considered opinion and what had happened at the meeting held at his house immediately following the attack is clear. Mr Jones had in fact given some thought to his problems, both as a manufacturer and as a magistrate. He considered that the conclusions he had come to and the suggestions he had made were both fair and generous. He did not, however, give sufficient weight to the feelings of the workers and he certainly did not see that these negotiations which he had initiated were doomed because of the existence of the Combination Acts of 1799–1800. Nor did he realise that in the interpretation of the Combination Acts there was considerable difference of opinion as to whether the Combinations which were made illegal included those of employers as well as those of workers.

From the workers' point of view there were certainly some who saw the problem clearly, and perhaps credit can be given to James May, the secretary, who does emerge slightly from the shadows as a distinctive figure. May, and those like him, knew that the one strong point the union possessed was the Act on the statute book that declared gig mills to be illegal. They felt that riots and demonstrations were perhaps a mistake and that if they could get the authorities to put the various Acts into force then their battle had been won.

The news of the meeting at Mr Jones' house led the authorities to send a letter back to Mr Jones almost immediately. It was brief and to the point. The Home Office had, they said, consulted the law officers of the Crown and these gentlemen were of the opinion that the conduct of the individuals who came to Mr Jones' house would support an indictment for a conspiracy and they would recommend that such an indictment should be prepared and sent down to the assizes shortly due in Wiltshire. This indictment would charge the seven men with such a conspiracy and Mr Hobhouse, together with the other people present with Mr Jones, should attend at the assizes when the grand jury considered the matter. This communication was signed by two ministers, Spencer Percival and Thomas Manners Sutton, and illustrates exactly the problem facing the workers. If they attempted to negotiate then they came under this risk; if they attempted to use more violent action then the risks they ran were equally obvious.

In the meantime Mr Jones had written another long letter to the Home Secretary. In it he stated that these recent outrages which had been committed in the clothing districts of Wiltshire and Somerset were a complete disgrace to any civilised country. He again stressed the great secrecy that these unions managed to maintain and despite all his efforts he had been quite unable to get any information as to who led these nightly raids. He lamented the general state of intimidation which had attained such a hold over the area that nobody appeared willing to come forward with information. Actually it was not so much intimidation that prevented people coming forward but the general sympathy that many had with the workers in their fight. Mr Jones reverted to his previous suggestion that strong measures were necessary if any discovery was to be made, and he reiterated his suggestion that the committee should be seized. In addition, he introduced for the first time the idea that letters passing between the workers in various parts of the country should be opened. He then proceeded to make the point that as he was not going to be able to attend the forthcoming assizes at Salisbury, and as he did not have the honour of knowing the judges there, he suggested that the Home Office should stress to the judges the dreadful destruction that had taken place; also that they should bring to their notice the great dangers occasioned by this combination of workers which were in fact threatening complete destruction of the long-established woollen trade. Warming to his task at this point, which so closely touched himself, he ended by repeating that he and his fellow clothiers were surrounded by a most wicked attempt to ruin their businesses and their livelihoods. Unless something was done to change the position, he foresaw the complete annihilation of the woollen trade in the area.

In this letter Mr Jones rather allowed his feelings to run away with him, and he concluded that unless the Government was prepared to support and protect the factories the clothiers would suffer the demolition of establishments that had taken many years to build. He had, he said, no hesitation in saying that this had become a question of national importance, one to which the Government should give its full attention. The effect of these combinations of the workers to force the clothiers to do as they wished was even more to be dreaded than the riots that were taking place.

It was this letter that led the Government to send the London magistrate Mr James Read of Bow Street to the West. This was not exactly the result that Mr Jones had hoped for, and it would appear that he was later to regret the arrival of Mr Read and to wish that he had not, on this occasion, allowed his feelings to express themselves quite so strongly in his letter to London. It was, however, a few days before Mr Read arrived and in the meantime, crossing his own letter, Mr Jones received a communication from the Under-Secretary at the Home Office stating the opinion given by the Crown officers that steps should be taken against the committee, and repeating that proceedings should be started against the deputation that came to Mr Jones' house. Lord Pelham, the Home Secretary, had no doubt that the conduct of these individuals was sufficient to support an indictment for conspiracy.

Mr Jones did not like this letter. More than any other clothier in the area he wished to stop the attacks on the mills, particularly on his own. This was natural enough, for his own livelihood was at stake: the financial sources available to his firm were smaller than was generally thought, and at the present time he and his associates were losing money. Nevertheless, he could not approve of this method of proceeding as he had given his word, and he immediately replied direct to Lord Pelham acquainting him with the fact that the seven men who had come to his house had been given his assurance that no advantage whatsoever would be taken of their attendance upon that occasion. Many of the clothiers had considered this meeting advisable, and the gentlemen who had acted as intermediaries had made this very definite promise which Mr Jones had accepted. He agreed that it was most necessary to make examples of those workers who were in these combinations, but he must for his part stress that he himself would become most strongly reprobated for his apparent deception if proceedings were started against these men who had every right to consider themselves secure from all proceedings. Not only the workers but many of the clothiers would consider a movement against them as entirely unjustified. He therefore requested Lord Pelham to order the suspension of the proposed prosecution for without hesitation he considered that it was unjustified in such a case.

Meanwhile in Trowbridge events moved fast. The shearmen who had been out on strike decided to go back to work. According to information later sent to London by James Read the Bow Street magistrate, this strike had thrown 600 people out of work. But Mr Read is not entirely to be trusted as a witness; for example, he said that at the meeting at Mr Jones' house the clothiers had given way all along the line to the shearmen. However, a combination of factors, partly the feeling that with the firing of Littleton Mill they had gone too far, partly the feeling perhaps that the negotiations at Mr Jones' house might lead to something, did lead to work being resumed.

Certainly at this time it would seem that many of the shearmen came to feel that they were winning their battle, and there was a reversal of opinion against the riots and burnings and a belief that they would do better to concentrate on their legal rights. Acting upon this belief, on 31 July they sent one of their members, a man named Howell, to the Salisbury Assizes where they presented a paper to the grand jury in which they complained of the introduction of the gig mills and shearing frames and alleged that a number of workers were being thrown out of work because of their use.

There were differences of opinion on the other side. So far as the clothiers were concerned, business was reasonably good, and as is natural under such circumstances, many clothiers felt that the best policy was to accede to the shearers' claims and get work started again. Others felt that things had come to such a pass that order must be restored at any price. Matthew Davies of Warminster was one of these, and feeling that his fellow manufacturers were taking too lenient a line, he himself wrote to the Home Office saying that there was, in his opinion, no doubt that these daring outrages had been committed by the workmen employed in cloth manufacturing. These men had, for many weeks, refused to work because some clothiers had introduced machines that were necessary for their business. They were endeavouring to destroy these and prevent their introduction throughout the kingdom. It was clear that these men had no visible means of support, and there was, Mr Davies said, every reason to think that they were supported and encouraged by the help which they received from innkeepers and other inhabitants of the area who should have known better. He felt that the Government must make some very strong declaration stressing the illegality of all that was going on. This should be circulated and brought to the notice of the neighbouring magistrates who had in the past been too sympathetic with these men who were on strike.

The clothiers, like the workers, were more and more trying to get the Government to decide between them, but as so often happens in such cases they confused the issue by sending contradictory opinions as to what should be done. Thus another clothier gave it as his view that the offer made by Mr Jones on behalf of the clothiers, that they would not use shearing frames when there were any shearmen available to do the work and in addition would always find employment for anybody without work, was reasonable to all concerned. The promise, he considered, should have satisfied the workers, and a definite public engagement by the manufacturers who would introduce machinery to find such employment for all on this basis would have deprived the workers of any general prejudice against the clothiers and the machines. If this engagement had indeed been made public, it might well have satisfied the workers, but there was never any clear understanding that this would be done. In any case, by this time there was such a general feeling of distrust between the two groups that it was perhaps almost too late for any agreement to be reached. The strike and the riots had left such a feeling of enmity that anybody who now tried to bring the parties together faced very grave obstacles. In addition, certain other groups, lying as it were between the large clothiers on the one side and the workers organised in unions on the other, were making matters more difficult. Thus the so-called master shearmen, men who in several cases owned shearing shops, were not keen to see a settlement reached. They foresaw that if the large clothiers, such as Mr Jones, installed shearing frames in their own factories, then their days of owning shearing shops would be past. A somewhat similar position was taken up by the many small clothiers, men who owned a few looms worked in many cases by members of their family. They feared the growth of the big manufacturer, and although not themselves members of the union, they certainly regarded any attempt to destroy the position of such people as Mr Jones with favour. The smaller manufacturers and the master shearmen had much in common, and provided a considerable backing for the workers' attacks on the clothiers.

In addition, there was a certain amount of unemployment caused by the disbanding of the army and navy, and this would have led to a surplus of workers even if machinery had not been introduced. Naturally, however, the workers did not see it in this light and they blamed all unemployment on the machines. So in the days that followed the attack on the Littleton Mill, there must have been many meetings of clothiers and of workers in Trowbridge. It was felt that the position had reached a climax and something must be done on both sides, as is usually the case when two groups stand opposed to each other. Amongst the manufacturers were those who felt that the intentions and the ideas of the workers must be squashed completely once and for all. Then there were those who did not agree with this. They had themselves, in many cases, started as small clothiers and they knew intimately or were friends of the leaders of the other side, and the last thing they wished to do was to push matters to a serious clash involving possible bloodshed. They sympathised with much their opponents stood for, and felt in a very real sense that they were all members of one trade.

In between there were men like Mr Jones, leaning perhaps a little more towards the right but nevertheless hoping that terms could be arranged. They knew that they could never run their businesses successfully if all their workers were opposed to everything for which they stood. This was a view that James Read of London was never able to understand.

The division on the workers' side was similar. There were those, the rash spirits, who believed that by burning down the mills and firing guns into the houses and surrounding the new factories they would bring back the old days. They were both violent and conservative and there is nothing more dangerous. The others, and they were the majority, were those who believed that there were many clothiers who wished to come to terms with the workers, though they were rather vague as to how this should be done. But even this group had not yet come to see the inevitability of machinery, and it was their failure to appreciate this that was to lead finally to their downfall. Nevertheless, they tried very hard to reach a settlement. Inside this centre and moderate group it is possible to feel that the secretary, James May, stood out. There were obviously others like him, but he must have been a leader. He appears to have been an intelligent man who had come to understand clearly that the Acts on the statute book, if they were put into operation, would give them all the protection they sought. This was a correct assumption; the Acts on the statute book, if they were in fact implemented, could give them all the protection they were seeking, but James May suffered from the same illusions as his friends. He did not recognise that machinery had come to stay or that in the last resort the Government, whatever its wishes and whatever its view of the legal position, would not use these old Acts to stop the coming of the machines. This was the tragedy of the shearmen's case.

Meanwhile, both sides continued their communications with their friends in Yorkshire and this, particularly the letters that passed between the workers in the two areas, caused great anxiety to the authorities. Earl Fitzwilliam, the Lord Lieutenant of Yorkshire, advised the Home Secretary that he was entirely in agreement with the wishes of the Home Office in arranging for a meeting in London of the merchants and manufacturers of Yorkshire with those of the West of England. He pointed out that he had given the reasons for this meeting to Mr Cookson, the Mayor of Leeds, who had declared himself confident that the Yorkshire manufacturers would accept the arrangement provided it appeared that they had been summoned to the meeting by the Government. If the impression were given that the idea of this meeting originated with the manufacturers they would run the risk of appearing to form a combination, which was of course illegal. Lord Fitzwilliam felt certain that the Home Secretary would be willing to fall in with the manufacturers' wishes in this case, particularly as there most certainly existed sufficient cause for the Government to call together such a meeting. There had certainly been illegal gatherings of the workers in both the West of England and Yorkshire, and it was most important that some enquiry should be made.

If the Government called the meeting he felt certain that no one would dare to attack the propriety of, or occasion any other form of vengeance against, those who were attending. It was, he concluded, a subject of infinite moment and at the same time of the greatest delicacy.

Earl Fitzwilliam enclosed with his own communication to the Home Secretary a letter he had received from Mr Cookson, in which the importance of Government action was stressed. Without it, Mr Cookson was very doubtful whether many clothiers would attend.

It is a little difficult to see how this attempt at negotiation would have worked out if the local body had been left alone, but it is possible that they might have come together and reached a form of agreement. James May and John Jones, if they had ever reached the stage of having discussions free of political overtones, were both capable of reaching an agreement advantageous to both sides of the industry. Whether this point could have been reached, however, is doubtful. In Wiltshire the authorities began to put more pressure on the workers. The driving force behind this was without doubt Mr Read, the London magistrate; he had no knowledge of the trade and not unnaturally regarded the whole question as one of the maintenance of law and order. In some ways it is strange that this different emphasis became apparent at this time, for the workers had clearly decided to desist from riots and burnings. However, Read pushed the local authorities into positive action and on one occasion he reported to London that he had arranged for the local justices to meet daily, adding that he had found the Combination Acts an excellent pretext for having the shearmen brought before the magistrates and examined under oath at considerable length. He did, in fact, have a considerable number of the shearmen examined in this way, including James May and the other members of the committee. They were very closely questioned and cross-questioned but were surprisingly successful in keeping their heads and withholding any information. James Read was inclined to feel that this failure to obtain the information he hoped for was due to the fact that the local justices were not prepared to go as far as he was in the way of threats, arrests and similar drastic measures. In this respect Read had run into a number of difficulties. The clothiers as a whole were honest men and when, like John Jones, they were also magistrates, they felt uncomfortable in their position. In fact the clothiers who were magistrates should certainly have refused to sit on any case that concerned their workmen, but none were prepared to take this stand. In some ways this did not matter as much as it might have done, for the majority of the local magistrates were not clothiers, and in some cases they were not without sympathy for the workmen. They did not, of course, approve of the riots, but being landowners they were not sorry to see the mill-owners in difficulties. In Wiltshire in particular there had long been considerable rivalry between the clothiers and the well-to-do country gentlemen who normally filled the ranks of the justices of the peace; this was less than it had been in the past, but was still an important factor in local events and probably accounted for some of the comparative mildness with which the workmen were treated. It is noticeable that when later there were agricultural riots the justices were considerably less sympathetic; in this case, however, it was only with considerable difficulty that James Read was able to persuade them to make any arrests at all.

Throughout these anxious days the journeys and the messages between the West of England and Yorkshire continued. Here James Read was much more thorough than John Jones in organising searches for letters passing backwards and forwards. He attempted to interview or have brought before him anybody who was suspected of having come from the North, but he never managed to obtain any valuable information in this way. In fact the best he could report to London was that he had seen Richards, the agent of the important Yorkshire firm of Wormall and Gott. As Richards had come to Trowbridge quite openly to attempt to get workers for Benjamin Gott, it was no great achievement for James Read to have interviewed him. However, he reported that he had learnt that the shortage of workers in Leeds arose because the shearmen would no longer work for those manufacturers who had taken on apprentices at the age of 14 and had indentured them for a shorter period of time than was stipulated in the statute dated in the reign of Queen Elizabeth. As the Home Secretary had received a number of letters from Yorkshire telling him just this, he must have felt that James Read was rather wasting his time in the West.

The failure of attempts to induce shearmen to leave the West of England and go North does show the strong solidarity of this group of men. Mr Gott, who sent Richards to the West, was himself the largest clothier in the whole country. In Trowbridge the local shearmen read with interest the notice that Richards had posted on the front of the chief local inn: 'Wanted immediately at Leeds in Yorkshire a number of journeymen shearmen, sober, steady, good workmen, will meet with constant employment, good wages by applying to Messrs Wormall, Gott and Wormall, at their manufactory near Leeds. Further particulars may be known by applying to Jacob Richards at The George Inn, Trowbridge, or to Mr Henry Richards near the Market Place, Frome.'

In Yorkshire Mr Gott himself visited the Lord Lieutenant, who reported the meeting to Lord Pelham. He had, he explained, been in conversation with two other friends when Mr Gott, whom he described as a most extensive manufacturer and considerable merchant, had presented himself in order to describe the events that had taken place at his mill that very morning. He had regarded it as very serious. All 80 of the shearmen had given Mr Gott notice that they would leave his employ as soon as they had finished cutting the pieces on which they were then engaged. Henceforth, they said, no shearer in Yorkshire would cut a piece for Mr Gott. Earl Fitzwilliam went on to say that the menace did not stop there, for the shearmen gave Mr Gott to understand that their places would not be filled by any other shearmen either from Yorkshire or from any other part of the kingdom. They would not, they said, allow anyone else to do the work for him. In other words, they were determined that Mr Gott should have no means of escaping from the threat their withdrawal of labour indicated. If he attempted to get his pieces cut at another factory they would see that the shearmen there refused to handle the work. Mr Gott pointed out that this action did not arise from the resentment of any harsh treatment he had given his workers, nor was it a scheme to obtain higher wages. The one cause was that he had ordered indentures to be prepared on two boy apprentices, neither of whom had reached the age of fifteen. The shearmen regarded this as a breach of the regulations and their action was taken to try to uphold these regulations.

One would have thought that even the Lord Lieutenant would have felt that there was some error in writing to the Home Secretary to suggest that Mr Gott was under the ban of the shearmen for breaking their regulations when in fact what he had actually broken was the law of the country. This law might be a bad one, but for the time being it remained the law.

In Trowbridge James Read continued his endeavours to find someone prepared to betray the union and his friends and reveal the truth of what was going on. At last he thought he had found such a person, a shearman named Beaumont of Bradford-on-Avon. He had worked at Mr Jones' factory at Staverton and had apparently left because some of his friends had done so, but he had been heard to say that his reason for leaving was because the other workers had forced him to do so. James Read arranged for him to be questioned, and it was clear that Beaumont was suffering from a sense of grievance, but it was impossible to get anything really logical or sensible out of him. James Read concluded, probably rightly, that he was afraid of what would happen to him if he mentioned any names or gave any definite details. Nevertheless Mr Read remained convinced that he had found in Beaumont a possible source of valuable information, and he proceeded

23 *Dunkirk Mill, Freshford (Token).*

24 *Dunkirk Mill, Freshford*
This quite magnificent ivy covered mill ruin was once the centre of activities for Joyce, a leading clothier of 1802–3.

25 *Mill and Clothier's House at Chalford*
Another typical Gloucestershire, or Cotswold, mill grouping.

26 *Mill at Staverton*
The Staverton cloth mill, largest mill in the area for most of the first half of the nineteenth century. Since this photograph was taken the upper storeys have been removed.

27 *Heathcoat's Lace Works, Tiverton*

John Heathcoat, famous in the lace industry, moved to Tiverton early in the eighteenth century and occupied an empty woollen mill, here illustrated. It was burnt down some years ago and has been replaced by a modern factory. The early eighteenth-century school built by Heathcoat can be clearly seen on the right.

TIVERTON. Lace Works

28 *Ebley Mills, c. 1840*
This contemporary print shows one of the finest mills in Stroud. It still operates as a carding and spinning mill.

to commit him into custody for refusing to give evidence. After being in prison for three weeks Beaumont changed his mind and gave Mr Read a certain amount of information. He then went back to work at Mr Jones' factory, but the other shearmen who were on strike talked to him and he left his work again. Mr Jones said, quite rightly, that the only reason for his doing this was because he feared for his own life if he continued to work at Staverton. This was what Beaumont told Mr Jones when they met. He said that, for himself, he was happy to go on working, but he was afraid to go against the warning he had received. Mr Jones offered to provide him with all the protection that was necessary while he was in the factory and also arrange for his house to be guarded, but Beaumont was not willing to take the risk. Mr Jones further offered to guarantee him constant work and said that he would pay him 21s a week instead of the 14s which he had been earning before, and at this point Beaumont said he would accept Mr Jones' earlier offer and would be back at work the next day. But he did not keep his promise. Instead he completely disappeared from the district. Mr Jones arranged for a close watch to be kept on his house and on his wife at Bradford-on-Avon, so that if Beaumont returned home, he could arrange to receive him again.

It was by such means as these that the shearmen held their organisation together. The majority were wholeheartedly in support, and those who wavered, like Beaumont, were in a minority. James Read thought that Beaumont had probably gone to Yorkshire and the authorities there were asked to try to find him and further examine him. The justices thought that they might now learn something of Beaumont from the letters that were passing between the West of England and Yorkshire and which they were opening.

In September the manufacturers began a series of meetings, ignoring the Combination Acts which made such gatherings illegal. The Acts were only enforced against the workers. At these meetings the manufacturers agreed to make a determined effort to stop the riots, and, what was more important for the future, decided to try to persuade the Government to change those laws on the statute book which, as they now realised, made their own position illegal. They appointed a number of their members to go to London and submit their case to the Government. The shearmen likewise, under the influence of James May, turned increasingly to the legal aspect of their case. In so doing they found themselves in sympathy with the weavers of the Stroud district and, even more important, the workers of the West Riding who felt that this was the correct course to take. Before September the shearmen had learned that the manufacturers were intending to persuade the Government to repeal the Acts regulating the woollen trade. They had realised for some time that this might happen, which is why they had decided to concentrate on their legal rights whilst such rights existed, rather than fritter away their efforts on strikes and riots which would end by bringing them nothing. They therefore decided on another attempt to force the Government to apply the existing statutes at once.

This decision was probably made at about the same time as the burning of Littleton Mill and it was the conjunction of these two events that was to leave Thomas Helliker, a certain young shearman, exposed to the fury of the authorities.

**Chapter Twelve** *A scapegoat*

AT THIS TIME A NEW DIVISION BEGAN
to appear in the shearmen's ranks. James Read thought this was because the shearmen's wives were becoming impatient with the loss of earnings their husbands were suffering due to the strikes. During the early days of the strikes, many of the inhabitants of the West Wiltshire towns had sympathised with the men, and shopkeepers had been generous with credit and even in contributing to what one might call a strike fund. But as the strike went on with no signs of an agreement, and as the riots began to turn public opinion against the workers, this generosity wore rather thin. Some workers and their families began to suffer real hardship. James Read recognised this and in a letter to his superiors in London he recommended them to allow the manufacturers their main point but then to impress on them that they should be willing to take back their original workers and try to guarantee them regular employment. There must, he said, on no account be any attempt by the manufacturers to penalise the workers.

But still there were many shearmen who felt the only hope of maintaining their position was to continue their attacks on those mills that were introducing machinery. As there were signs that the strike was beginning to collapse, those who held this view were inclined to organise these attacks without delay. Certainly this group still had considerable authority with many of their fellow members. As always, it is a little difficult to estimate their real strength, but it was probably less than it appeared for they, the violent ones, were those who talked the most. As a group they regarded another attack on Mr Jones' factory at Staverton as the essential next step. An attack was planned, but it was badly organised and the workers who went found there were many sentinels on guard. One or two of the more daring spirits fired off a few muskets, but when the sentinels returned the fire, the shearmen became nervous, and when, in addition, they heard sounds of a further patrol approaching, they decided to withdraw.

Much more important was the attack organised in Trowbridge which was the biggest yet. This mill belonged to Mr Naish, who also owned the mill at Littleton rented by Mr Heath, which had been destroyed. Mr Naish had introduced the hated machinery into his mill at Trowbridge and this one, too, was destroyed in a well-conducted attack. Mr Naish had been warned that this was going to happen and had tried to persuade a number of his workmen to protect the factory, but they had refused and he realised there was nothing he could do. He decided that his best policy would be to leave Trowbridge for the time being, which he did, so that when the rioters arrived at the unprotected mill in The Conigre they were easily able to set fire to it, having first destroyed the hated machinery.

Amid these events the assizes were held at Sarum, and the constables of the district around Trowbridge and Bradford reported on all the riots. This brought forth the expected response of what might be described as the 'Establishment', and in their own words 'it was unanimously resolved that all responsible people must get together to put an effectual stop to such behaviour and prevent such riotous and tumultous events in the future'. The justices stressed that they would make every effort, both as private persons and as justices of the peace, to see that this was done; they would punish all those guilty of these improper proceedings. They advised that in the riot areas there should be frequent meetings of the magistrates, together with other responsible local people, to put this resolution to effect.

At Trowbridge such a meeting was called, and most of the local celebrities were there. These gentlemen were at pains to express their horror at the outrages that were taking place throughout the district, and in an official statement which they issued they referred to the noisy assemblages that were taking place which they said were made so much worse because some of the persons appeared disguised. They went on to stress that the deplorable burning of properties and destruction of mills, combined with the threats upon the lives of innocent people, must stop immediately. They further declared, that as the best means of bringing this about, and in order that the offenders should be brought to immediate justice, they would hold daily meetings at 12 noon in the main centres affected. Thus Thursdays and Saturdays would find them assembled at Trowbridge, Tuesdays at Warminster, Fridays at Melksham and Mondays and Wednesdays at Bradford. At these times they would be ready to receive any information that might be brought to them that would assist in keeping the peace. They called upon all constables and other officials in these areas to be diligent and painstaking in their duty, and to report at these times as stated with the latest information, in order that this deplorable state of affairs might be brought to an end. It was further stated that anyone who appeared in the area disguised, with his face blackened, or in any other way appearing as a suspicious character wandering about at unreasonable hours and not being able to give a completely satisfactory account of himself, should be reported to them. They concluded by saying that they knew that all well-disposed inhabitants were more than willing to exert themselves to the very utmost of their power to restore law and order, and that they had arranged for any law-abiding citizens to have the full support of the army if necessary.

Meanwhile, the manufacturers continued to organise their case, and despite the Combination Acts held regular meetings at Bath, at the White Hart Inn. Bath, which had once been a woollen centre, was now much more a place of fashion and the manufacturers felt it was better to meet there rather than in one of the clothing towns. One of the first decisions they made was to offer a considerable reward to anyone who could assist in identifying those responsible for the actual burnings. For this purpose a subscription was started amongst them, and a statement to this effect was issued, duly signed by John Jones, whom they had appointed their chairman. A considerable sum was subscribed. At a slightly later meeting they issued another statement giving a list of all the attacks that had taken place on the property of the clothiers. There was a certain air of the defensive about these early statements, which were clearly designed as tentative attempts to influence public opinion in their favour.

Thus, in introducing the list of mills that had been burnt, they stated that they had themselves requested the authorities to prevent these alarming outrages, which had been committed by people who had unlawfully assembled, bearing arms and disguised with blackened faces. They were at pains to inform the public further, that in order to make easier the apprehension of these people, the King had agreed to bestow his most gracious pardon upon anyone who was willing to come forward and give evidence. Anybody who had actually set fire to premises, or had written particularly threatening letters, was excepted from this offer.

But with these exceptions anyone who should come forward to assist the authorities in tracing the leaders of these attacks and their accomplices could feel that any ill-doings they might have committed would be pardoned. Lord Pelham, the Home Secretary, signed this promise himself, and as it incorporated an offer of a reward of £500 to be paid upon the conviction of the offender the manufacturers felt that it should certainly tempt someone to come forward and give the necessary information. In addition, they issued notices offering special rewards for the apprehension of those responsible for particular burnings, among them being the attack on Littleton Mill. The public notices explained that this attack had taken place on the night of 21 July, and that it had been made by a group of armed men with blackened faces who had set the premises on fire, as a result of which the mill had been totally destroyed. In particular the authorities were seeking a person answering the following description, who had been actually concerned in the attack: he was a man of ample size, with black eyes, thin of face with large teeth in front and wide apart. His nose was short, and he had black hair which during the attack had been tied behind. Finally he had been dressed in a blue jacket. If anybody could give this person's name, or any information leading to his capture, he would receive a reward of £500.

Another notice offered a smaller reward of five guineas. This notice explained that many scandalous and false reports were being circulated by the shearmen and other people working in the woollen trade, to the effect that in consequence of the introduction of machinery these people were threatened with unemployment. This led many benevolent but unwary people, who did not understand trade, to sympathise with the workmen and in some cases to go even as far as bestowing relief upon them. The manufacturers felt they must, in justice to themselves, take this opportunity of issuing a caution to the inhabitants of this area that they should be on guard against such impositions, as for their part they would wish to assure all good people that there was no danger of the cloth workers becoming unemployed because of the machinery it was necessary to introduce. They hoped that this warning would be sufficient, but if in spite of it people persisted in offering their help to these riotous workers then the manufacturers would have no alternative but to bring actions against them. And in order that they should know of any such happenings they were prepared to give a reward of five guineas to anybody who would give them information leading to such prosecutions.

John Jones, on behalf of the manufacturers, was determined to do what he could to change public feeling, and on his advice the manufacturers continued to issue regular statements describing what had taken place at their meetings. Bearing in mind the fact that all these meetings were illegal, these public announcements were certainly an extraordinary method of proving the manufacturers' case, but it must be admitted that they did succeed, and from this time there was a noticeable change in the attitude of the ordinary inhabitants towards the struggle that was going on. To appeal to Parliament to prosecute their opponents for holding meetings and then themselves to hold similar ones, and issue statements about them, showed a high degree of confidence in their own case, or perhaps one should say in the capacity of the authorities to overlook its illegality. As the summer wore on the manufacturers could, however, feel that their policy had been successful, and in a statement they issued after a meeting held on 16 August they were able to report that one of them had, because of the offer of the £500 reward, been able to obtain information against several people concerned in the riots, and that in consequence several of the offenders had been arrested and were now in prison. It was confirmed that upon the conviction of any one of these people the reward of £500 would be paid out by the chairman.

At the same meeting, although this was not reported in their statement, the manufacturers appointed their chairman, with four other clothiers, to go carefully into the statutes relating to woollen manufacture and to bring a full report on them to the next meeting.

Meanwhile, plans were laid for the arrest of Thomas Helliker, a shearer's colt at the recently destroyed Naish mill in Trowbridge. The description that Mr Heath gave of the man who stood guard over him during the attack on the Littleton Mill was not unlike Helliker. The police were led to him because he had been heard, while working at Mr Naish's mill, to praise the attacks that his fellow workers had made.

When Mr Jones had received the description from Mr Heath he consulted James Read and they held an identification parade. Mr Heath then picked out Thomas Helliker. He hesitated, however, and perhaps the reason he chose Helliker was that he recognised him as being one who worked at Mr Naish's mill. He knew that all the shearmen there were opposed to machinery and doubtless he was also influenced by the fact that the mill had been burnt down there as well.

Helliker was immediately taken before the magistrates and charged with being present at the burning of Littleton Mill and of threatening Mr Heath with a gun. He replied briefly, stating firmly that he had never been there. Mr Jones retorted: 'You have been recognised and it will go bad for you.'

Helliker was sent to the county jail at Salisbury that night. James Read reported this arrest to Lord Pelham, and went on to say that he had also taken two or three other men into custody for further examination. One of these had come to the clothier who employed him, stating that he had a message from the committee of the shearmen's club. This club wished to know whether the clothier meant to carry on his business in the way the shearmen wished – in other words, whether it was his intention to introduce machinery. The manufacturer answered that he would do as other employers did. He did not particularly wish to introduce machinery, but if his competitors did so then he had no alternative. The shearman told him to keep calm and be careful of what he said, as he had promised to report to the committee everything that happened. Mr Read went on to say that this prisoner was, without doubt, a member of the shearmen's club, and that he had told the magistrates that he had had to take an oath promising to be true to the shearmen and to see that none of them was hurt and that on no account was he to divulge any of their secrets. Mr Read stated that he had learnt that the committee consisted of 13 and met every Wednesday, and that there was a chairman, a clerk and two stewards. The oath was administered to each member by the clerk, and the worker then received a printed ticket which was the same as that used by the shearmen's club in Yorkshire. With this any of the shearmen, if they were to go to Yorkshire, would be able to obtain employment; without it the Yorkshire shearmen would make certain that they did not. Mr Read also found that the tickets were changed once a year, so that shearmen's oaths were then renewed. Above everything else, the shearmen were determined that nobody without a ticket should be allowed to work. There was a shearmen's club in every town in the West Riding of Yorkshire, in the clothing towns of the West of England, and in many other parts of the country.

Mr Read reported that acting upon this information he had thought it right to advise the local magistrates to arrest all the committee and to search the houses of the chairman, clerk and stewards. It might be that they would find papers that would enable them to destroy the workers' organisation once and for all. He himself had no doubt that the committee was behind both the strikes and the riots, and he had been told that they always met just before any violence occurred. As a matter of fact they met once a week, and never altered this whatever their plans. Mr Read then reverted to an old theme, drawing attention to the fact that the shearmen's clubs in Wiltshire were closely connected with those of the same description in Yorkshire. At this point he had to admit that as yet he had not discovered that they were formed to serve any other object than that of endeavouring to obtain better terms of employment and of getting rid of new machinery. Yet, he concluded, this did not alter the fact that they could become even more dangerous. There was, in fact, no knowing what might come to be discussed at these clubs. As far as he could gather their main centre was in Leeds, and it was there that they kept their money in the bank. He had great hopes that, now he had found someone willing to inform, his knowledge would increase rapidly.

He clearly regarded the arrest he had made that morning as even more important than that of Thomas Helliker the previous day. He thought that at last he had got to the bottom of what he always regarded as a conspiracy against the state. The prisoner had told him the names of the committee, which previously he had only been able to guess even if more or less correctly. It was soon apparent to the shearmen that they were now in imminent danger. They knew that three more of their members had been arrested and that one of them was not reliable and might give away information. Several of them escaped to Yorkshire, but others, including James May, were arrested, taken before the local magistrates and charged with administering an illegal oath.

James Read was very disappointed that he had failed to arrest the whole committee. His previous report to London had suggested that he was on the point of breaking up the whole organisation – now he had to write in a less confident tone. He said he was sorry that the measures which he had adopted to capture the whole of the Trowbridge committee had failed. He had searched the premises of four of them, but his plan had gone astray because one of the informers whom he had arranged to meet had not arrived at the appointed time. He was, however, pleased to report that he had apprehended James May who was the clerk to the committee about whom Thomas Bailey had given so much information. Read went on to say he considered May was a leading figure who had done a great deal to forward the aims of the union. He had been in touch with the printer who had produced the rules for the committee, and this man had identified James May as the man who had given him the manuscript of the rules to print from. In addition, upon May's instructions he had had the club tickets engraved. James Read had found both the rules and ticket when he searched May's house, and he enclosed copies of both of them. The printer said that the tickets which he had been given had come from Yorkshire, and that the words Leeds had been crossed out and replaced by Trowbridge. That was the only difference between them. He had had orders from a man to produce a further hundred tickets exactly similar, except that Bradford would replace Trowbridge. He said that he did not know the name of the person from Bradford. James Read said, quite rightly, that he had no doubt May knew a great deal more than he would divulge. When he was examined by the magistrates he stated that he worked for Mr Waldron, who was a very honourable man, and that had the other clothiers behaved as he had done the disturbances would not have taken place. The magistrate, acting upon Mr Read's advice, considered that the Act passed in the reign of George III against the administering of unlawful oaths applied in the case of May and all the others of the committee who were present when the oath was administered. He still hoped that he would be able to arrest the remainder; he knew that normally the next meeting was due to be held the following night, and rather foolishly, despite all that had happened he still thought they might come to it. In any case, what he had done would create a sensation, and perhaps some of those who had not been arrested, realising the danger they were in, would come forward and give evidence against the rest. All this shows how far James Read had failed to understand the lives of those with whom he had come in contact. Despite all the evidence he must have had showing that these clubs, even if illegal, were serving no other purpose than attempting to maintain legal rights for the workers, he was still determined to think they had political motives. He thought they had been of relatively short life, and that they were all nationally controlled from Leeds. He had been told about the letters that had come from the North arranging for their formation, and he understood that regular reports were sent from each branch to their leader who, he had been told, was one George Palmer of Duke Street, near St Peters Street, Leeds. This information he had obtained from a well-known clothier at Warminster, and he had to admit that he had not obtained it in an honourable manner and consequently would not want any more questions asked about it at the moment.

James May and the four who were arrested with him – Samuel Ferris, George Mark, John Helliker, a relative of Thomas, and Philip Edwards – were taken to the county jail at Fisherton.

Meanwhile Mr Read, in his letters to London, continued to paint a grim picture of what was happening in the West. He kept the justices active, though he could not find anyone else to arrest. When he had arrived in the district he had expected to find the army implicated, as reports had suggested, but he was quite unable to trace any evidence of this. In the end he had to admit that this particular danger was exaggerated, and he was able to assure the Home Secretary that although the shearmen and other cloth workers were receiving considerable support from the public it was clear that neither the army nor the militia was in any way involved. They could be depended upon to carry out whatever orders were given to them.

Mr Read continued to complain that the local justices were not doing all they might, but here, as in so many other things, he was wrong. It was nonsense to suggest that they should have been more strict. There was nothing that they could be strict about until the actual burnings started, and as soon as this happened no one was more keen to make arrests than Mr Jones and his fellow magistrates. It was during this period that Mr Jones emerged more and more as a leading figure among the manufacturers. His position as a magistrate had always lent weight to his authority, but his mill at Staverton had occasioned some criticism from the older clothiers, particularly those centred in Trowbridge. They appear to have been a somewhat closed circle and many of them, linked by nonconformist religious convictions, tended to be out of sympathy with the country landowners who normally became justices of the peace. They considered that Mr Jones had broken away from what had been a cloth-making tradition, and a few of them may even have felt that he had been in some ways responsible for the worsening of the situation. Now, however, their attitudes changed. The fact that he had been the one to carry out the arrests, combined with the fact that he had been chosen as chairman of the manufacturers, brought him into the glare of public opinion. The choice of Mr Jones as chairman of the manufacturers' association may seem a little surprising when one considers his fellow clothiers' opinions; on the other hand it should be remembered that his mill was the biggest, he was a magistrate, and finally most of the clothiers who might have been chosen, having had long connections with the West, preferred to remain in the background. Throughout, Mr Jones tried to be fair, and it is difficult to instance any occasion when he definitely abused his position. Even in the case of what one might regard as the wrongful arrest of Thomas Helliker it is not easy to criticise his action on any legal ground. In this case he had only been unjust if one accepts the view that he had considerable doubts as to whether Mr Heath had been certain of the identification of Helliker at the parade. He should certainly have challenged him more carefully on this point; had he done so Mr Heath might have felt bound to admit his uncertainty, in which case Helliker would not have been arrested. It is doubtful, however, whether this really crossed Mr Jones' mind, since at that moment, one must remember, he was more concerned with his attempts to arrest the committee, and he quite rightly regarded James May as a more important person than Thomas Helliker. What certainly worried Mr Jones even more was the fact that his business was still losing money. All the comings and goings, excitement, arrest, the feeling that he was playing an important part in affairs, the letters to the Home Secretary – all this was slightly unreal to Mr Jones, whilst his business was failing. He still hoped that he would be able to check this; he could not know that before many years were out he was to be bankrupt.

Meanwhile, the rioting having died down and the strikers having for the moment gone back to work, he set his mind on the organisation of the manufacturers' case for the repeal of the statutes. It involved a considerable amount of work, and continued for several months, during which time James May, Thomas Helliker and the others were left in the county jail at Salisbury.

Mr Read, however, not concerned with any such questions, was still trying to find a means of arresting the other leading shearmen. He was prepared to bring all the forces of the Combination Acts into play, particularly now that he knew, having arrested James May and some of the committee, that there had indeed been a powerful shearmen's union at Trowbridge. He held out various temptations to any shearmen he could get hold of, hoping thereby to obtain further information, but he was completely unsuccessful. These men who had kept their secrets for so many months would certainly not give anything away now that some of their friends were in the county jail. Nevertheless, Mr Read did find an excuse to arrest a further six shearmen, though when he brought them before the magistrate Mr Jones himself pointed out that there was nothing that could really be held against them and they were allowed to go free. Mr Read considered that Mr Jones had been too lenient, but the magistrate had been quite right, for there was no case at all. At this time Mr Read's reports to London became more vague, and often he was left to give details of events that had already taken place and to state what he would have done if he had known about them earlier; for example, he reported that two shearmen who had come from Leeds with money to assist those in Trowbridge had already left the town before he had heard about it.

It was about this time that the authorities, in preparing the cases against Helliker, May and friends, began to appreciate the difficulties of their position. As long as Mr Heath maintained his identification, evidence against Helliker seemed secure, but there were signs that his uncertainty about the identification was increasing, and the supporting evidence that the authorities would have liked was not forthcoming.

The other case seemed to rest on even more uncertain grounds. The accomplice, upon whose evidence they had to depend in order to have any hope of convicting James May, was much more vulnerable to the attacks of the shearmen than was Mr Heath. He was himself a shearman, and the threats and pressures that his fellow workers could bring to bear on him were naturally very considerable.

**Chapter Thirteen**

# 'With the blessing of God and the help of Yorkshire'

THE MANUFACTURERS CONTINUED TO DO what they could to put their case before the public, and they always kept everybody well informed as to what had happened at their meetings. Mr James Read, the Bow Street magistrate, was at great pains to point out, in a letter to the Home Secretary, the public-spiritedness of the manufacturers. He explained that at several meetings held in Bath, they had passed resolutions promising to find work for all woollen workers who might lose their accustomed employment because of the introduction of machinery. These people would be given opportunities in other branches of the trade at reasonable wages. So that there should be no doubt that everybody knew this, they had pamphlets printed and circulated throughout the two counties of Somerset and Wiltshire. Mr Read therefore considered it uncharitable of the authorities in London to think that the manufacturers had not done everything in their power to provide for the workers.

He also stressed his opinion that the grievances over the introduction of machinery were being rather overdone. Only five or six of the clothiers in the area had introduced machines; indeed, Mr Jones was the only clothier in the Trowbridge and Bradford district who had done so. But of course the workers were attacking not only the gig mills but also the shearing frames. Thus when Mr Read went on to point out that in Trowbridge Mr Naish, who had suffered so much at his premises, had none of these machines in his mills, he was of course missing the point that 'machines' included these frames and that the shearmen were, if anything, more opposed to the frames than to the gig mills, although well realising that there were no statutes against them. The attack on Mr Naish's mills had been carried out simply because he had introduced frames. Mr Jones, before the erection of his new mill and the installation of the necessary machinery, had always sent his cloths into Gloucestershire to be dressed. Gig mills had always been used there, and as Mr Read pointed out, Mr Jones' use of these machines in Wiltshire could be said to constitute a new trade and could not therefore have the effect of displacing shearmen from their accustomed labour. This was, of course, correct; the introduction of gig machinery never did any shearman out of a job. The whole point was that the shearmen were fighting against the introduction of machinery of any kind, but it was the gigging machinery that gave them their best opportunity of protest as it had definitely been forbidden by law. Mr Read went on to say that Mr Hill, an important manufacturer of Malmesbury, had been the first in Wiltshire to dress his cloths by machine, but taken as a whole the majority of the clothiers still favoured dressing by hand, although they admitted that the cloths dressed by gig mills had a better finish and gained a preference in the market. Mr Read then attempted a technical explanation for all this which must have left the authorities in London rather puzzled as his knowledge of the subject was clearly not equal to the task. He continued by saying that the other Wiltshire clothiers had not introduced these mills because of the prevailing prejudice and because no Wiltshire shearmen would finish cloths that had been dressed on the gig mills. Mr Jones, at this time, had not a single shearman at his mill. He had overcome this disability, however, by introducing shearing frames as well as gigging machines, by means of which it was possible for one person to attend to four pairs of shears, and furthermore that person need not be a trained shearman. In fact, if these frames were to become generally adopted the shearmen would certainly be redundant, and then there would be no question of finding them alternative work for there would no longer be any anywhere. Indeed, in the words of Lord Fitzwilliam, such a move would entirely cut off the craftsmen in that branch of the trade. The frames that Mr Jones had introduced were working reasonably well, and another manufacturer in Trowbridge was also introducing them in order that his business should not rest on the whim of the shearmen. Read drew the Home Office's attention to the fact that when the seven delegated shearmen went to meet Mr Jones he had promised, firstly, never to use a shearing frame when shearmen were available, and secondly, to employ every man in Bradford who was out of work at that time. Mr Read said he considered that these promises made by Mr Jones ought to have satisfied the shearmen, and removed the general prejudice which existed even in those towns where neither gig mills nor shearing frames had been introduced. If Mr Jones' offer could have been trusted then the dispute might certainly have been settled, but there was so much anger and ill-feeling in the area that it had become impossible for the two sides to finalise any such reasonable agreement.

One result of the arrest of James May and the other leaders of the shearmen's union seems to have been an even closer contact with Yorkshire, which had repercussions on the preparation of the workmen's case in favour of the statutes. The shearmen in Yorkshire had been more successful than those of the West of England in preventing the use of frames. No manufacturer in the North had managed to introduce them to the extent that Mr Jones had done; when they had tried, the shearmen's refusal to use them was complete. The Yorkshire workers had also been equally successful in preventing the introduction of the gig mills which had for so long been widely used in the West.

Just as the workers of the West and Yorkshire were getting together, so there were similar attempts by the manufacturers of the two areas to do the same. This was not easy to achieve, because in both areas there were strong currents cutting across any united action. The workers were clearly fighting the bigger manufacturers, those with large mills, for it was only these who were in a position to introduce machinery. The smaller clothiers, and that group known as master shearmen who had pieces cut on commission for manufacturers, tended to support the workers, and were as keen as they to prevent the large firms getting complete control of the trade. Clothiers in both areas, however, were agreed that the Yorkshire workers' success should not be allowed to repeat itself in the West. The Mayor of Leeds, Mr Cookson, admitted that in order to keep the peace he himself had several times during the preceding months tried to prevent mill owners from purchasing gig and shearing machines as he felt certain that if they were introduced there would be riots and burnings as had happened in the West. He found that in Yorkshire all classes of workmen were prepared to make common cause with the cloth workers and were willing to support those out on strike with generous contributions. It is clear that up to the time Mr Cookson was writing, the Yorkshire workers, by keeping to strike action, had been more successful in maintaining their position than had the Wiltshire and Somerset shearers by their riots. The position in the South-west was more difficult from the workers' point of view as the gig mills were already in existence there and the workers' problem was therefore to get them out. The Mayor of Leeds stated on another occasion that the shearmen in Yorkshire were rather concerned about the manufacturers' meetings that were being held in the West. They realised that if the use of gig mills and shearing machines spread in the West it would be necessary to introduce them into Yorkshire, otherwise that area would lose trade. Mr Cookson, knowing of the troubles that had taken place, felt that if this were done then there was no knowing what would happen. He pointed out that within the past three weeks the shearmen at Huddersfield, by threatening a strike, had succeeded in stopping work in all the big mills at Huddersfield where machines were being introduced. The manufacturers in the end yielded rather than get behind with cloths which were due to be shipped abroad. Mr Cookson ended with these words: 'The law here against gig mills is now as complete in effect, nay even more so, than if enacted by Parliament.'

He must have forgotton that gig mills were actually prohibited by law. In Yorkshire the 'croppers' (as Yorkshire shearmen were called) were particularly concerned to prevent Mr Benjamin Gott, the largest of all the woollen manufacturers, from introducing machinery into his mill at Leeds. Mr Gott employed 80 croppers, who had already once stopped work when he had apprenticed two boys who were over 14. Their success on that occasion had led them to adopt an equally determined attitude regarding the introduction of machinery. The croppers there were in a strong position, and the Lord Lieutenant, Lord Fitzwilliam, summed it all up when he said: 'They are the tyrants of the country, their power and influence have grown out of their high wages which enable them to make deposits that put them beyond all fear of inconvenience from this conduct.'

There was some truth in this statement. It was because they had these funds in reserve that they were able to go on strike and hold out until the manufacturers were prepared to come to terms. Above all, the connection between Yorkshire and the West of England was a very real cause of worry to the authorities.

Down in the West odd arrests continued to be made; Samuel Baker of Warminster was committed with the rest to Fisherton jail on suspicion of being one of those who had gathered outside Mr Jones' mill at Staverton on 10 July, when shots were fired. This rather desultory firing was referred to in the indictment as an attempt to destroy the mills. Nearby in Somerset, at Wells, the grand jury considered charges arising from the destruction of Clifford Mills, Beckington.

Taken as a whole, however, everything was much quieter in the West. On 8 September two shearmen who had been arrested earlier were convicted at Warminster, one for endeavouring to intimidate and withdraw a workman from his master's employ, and the other for distributing weekly pay to shearmen who were on strike from a fund which had been collected with this purpose in mind. The following night two tenements and a stable, owned by a clothier in Warminster who had been present at the conviction of these two men, were destroyed by fire. This act of revenge was actually the last riot to take place.

In Bath the manufacturers continued their meetings to discuss the best way of getting the old laws taken off the statute book. Mr Jones was in the chair on each occasion and once he read a letter from the Blackwell Hall factors to whom so many of them sent their cloths, offering subscriptions to the fund which they had started. The manufacturers, not unnaturally, sent a letter back thanking them and a short while afterwards a list of the contributions from Blackwell Hall was given.

In all these actions the manufacturers had the full support of the Home Secretary, who sent them, nevertheless, a letter pointing out the illegality under the Combination Acts of administering oaths, etc., and holding meetings.

There were no further attacks in Wiltshire. The rather feeble outbursts of late September were not repeated. Indeed, there was no major attack after that of 3 August when the mill belonging to Mr Naish was burnt.

The firmness of the workers' decision to concentrate their efforts on the legal side of the battle was surprising. Several factors must have led to it: for instance, the fact that clothiers themselves were pressing the Government to remove the statutes controlling the woollen industry from the statute book made it clear to the men that those statutes must necessarily be protection for them as they stood. They did not realise that the statutes had only been allowed to remain in existence because no one had used them. They certainly had no idea of the difficulty there would be in any attempt to get the Government to act upon them. Perhaps, however, above all these factors was the fear as to what would happen to those of their friends who had been arrested. The solidarity of the shearmen had always been notable, and now all their efforts were turned to safeguarding their friends. They were all the more concerned with ensuring that the evidence given at the forthcoming assize would lead at least to the dismissal of the case against James May and the other members of the committee, rather than with any attempt to burn down yet another mill.

In London, however, the Government did not consider that this peace would last, and they continued to watch events with the closest attention. They were acutely aware of the close co-operation that existed between the cloth-making areas of the country. They particularly valued the opinions of Lord Fitzwilliam. He was a man of independent mind and on one occasion he wrote that according to reports he had received he did not think that the croppers committed any acts of violence. Nor did he know upon what principles the measures they adopted, which rendered them so powerful, could be restricted or even greatly disapproved of. He could not see that there was anything objectionable in groups of men laying up in days of prosperity for those of adversity that might follow. Parliament itself within the last few years had sanctioned and encouraged this principle. But he knew that the system was likely to lead to the most serious evil. The advantages that the croppers had derived from their system of combining together would be used as an example to all other branches of trade and manufacture, and the croppers themselves were at great pains to disseminate this system amongst other trades. Others would do as the croppers had done. Wages would increase all round, and subsequently the cost of manufactured goods. The question that would then face the country would be how far the foreign market would be prepared to stand this increase of price. It would encourage foreign countries to make their own goods, and this was what concerned Lord Fitzwilliam most of all. Otherwise he could see little that was wrong in the croppers' actions. This somewhat unusual point of view shows what little awareness there was in some people's minds of the power of the Combination Acts.

The Lord Lieutenant's views, however, were not shared by many others in authority in the country, and the general opinion was that the laws against combination should be made even stronger. In Yorkshire, perhaps because of Lord Fitzwilliam's point of view, the existing laws were not used to anything like the extent that they were in the West. It is clear that the Lord Lieutenant was one of the few people who felt that this attack on the workers was unfair.

During the autumn and winter months connections between the South-west and Yorkshire were closer than ever before. Delegates passed from one area to another, and occasionally information was sent by letter. On the whole the workers preferred to send delegates in person as they realised that many of their letters were still being intercepted, opened and copied before being forwarded. These meetings of workers gave all concerned a great feeling of solidarity and strength. Ever present in their minds was the fate of their friends in Fisherton jail. On one occasion James Griffin of Trowbridge, a shearman who had previously played little part in union affairs, wrote to George Palmer, one of the leaders in Leeds, thanking him for arranging for two of their members to come down to the West to give information and help. There were many difficulties facing them in the West, but they hoped that by the blessing of God and the help of Yorkshire they would surmount them all. The shearmen of the West thought that with the exception of one or two centres which were not really of great consequence the whole country would be harmonised. They had been told that something had turned up in their favour, but they could not vouch for the truth of it. Above all, they hoped that some of their friends who were in prison, and who were likely to stay there until the assizes, would not be so badly treated as they had been. If possible they would bail them out, but this was not likely. In any case, they would keep the croppers in Yorkshire fully informed of the situation.

One of the members of the shearmen's committee who had managed to avoid arrest was Joseph Warren, a nephew of James May. His sweetheart Ann Waller wrote to him when he was hiding in Leeds, saying that she knew that he could not come back to her yet unless it were to get himself into great trouble and put himself into a position where it was impossible for him to do any good for his friends. Shortly after this his mother also wrote telling him that his Uncle James (i.e. May) had been ill since he had been in jail. She concluded with the advice: 'I hope, my son, that you will think on this, that a friend in the pocket is better than to trust to another.'

Other trades in the West did what they could to help the textile workers. In Bristol assistance was organised by a Charles Thomas, who himself wrote to George Palmer saying that they had received his letter and they were sorry to hear that the West Country shearmen had so many enemies to contend with. In addition, the fact that they had so many people out of work must make it very expensive for them. They hoped that they would be able to obtain help from most of the towns in the kingdom. They themselves would be happy to make a small contribution. They hoped that it would not be long before they would receive an account of their having brought the matter to a successful conclusion, and that this would once and for all let the clothiers know that they had been in the wrong and make them ashamed of their cruel ways. They would always be happy to have news from the cloth-dressers, their brethren as they described them, of Leeds. They were a group of men who ought indeed to be esteemed by all, both in the woollen and in other trades.

Towards Christmas, 1802, William May, the brother of James, went up to Leeds himself and reported back to his friends in Trowbridge that he was much occupied on business with the members of the committee there. He had visited Huddersfield, Saddleworth and Manchester, and it had been decided to pay £50 to Mr Wilmott, an attorney at Bradford who was going to appear for the men. The members of the Yorkshire union were generous in their help, and towards the end of the year William May was able to send £100 to Trowbridge. William himself promised that, on his return to the West, he would personally collect some money towards the cost of the petition that was being taken to Parliament. Before returning, he was able to report that Mr Wilmott was making preparations to retain the necessary counsel for the trial. During that year, in Gloucestershire, the weavers revived an association with Mr Walter Hilton Jessop, an attorney, and commenced their campaign against unapprenticed weavers. Mr Jessop on their behalf issued notices of action against well over a hundred weavers for illegally carrying on their trade without being apprenticed. The action was only proceeded with in one case, against a Mr Webb, a master clothier who, it was said, employed non-apprenticed weavers. This case, which came up after the August Assizes of 1802, was later dropped on the understanding that Mr Webb would no longer employ such unapprenticed weavers. It was said that upwards of a hundred men who had been weaving gave up the occupation at this time. The workmen also threatened prosecutions under the statute that prohibited clothiers from having more than a certain number of looms, and more particularly in Wiltshire they threatened action against unapprenticed men and presented some gig mills as a nuisance to the grand jury at the Salisbury Assizes on 4 August. This was the first action of its kind that James May had planned, but he himself could not be there as he had been arrested. The jury gave no verdict and it was of course far from certain that the gig mills in question were the same as those that had been prohibited.

All these legal cases made the clothiers feel it necessary to have the statutes removed from the statute book, and in the autumn of 1802 they applied to Parliament for a Bill which would suspend them until July 1803. There were 24 statutes in all, regulating the manufacture of woollen cloth, that they wanted dealt with in this way. The Bill passed slowly through the House of Commons, and was finally passed on 8 February 1803. Its progress was checked in the House of Lords when Lord Pelham asked that the second reading be deferred for a month in order that the whole question of the repeal could be further considered. The shearmen and other workers who had been in London following the case hailed this as a great victory. One of their leaders, in a letter to a friend at Bradford, said that this meant the end of the machines and that their enemies were defeated, and that great praise was due to Mr Jessop their attorney. They had, in fact, gained a complete victory. When they were back in the West in February some of the weavers paraded in the streets of Bradford-on-Avon, waving blue cut canes, and several of the bell-ringers at Trowbridge, who were themselves workers in the woollen trade, went one night to the church and clanged the bells to celebrate their victory. One weaver named Barton who had been to London to help present the case, celebrated by coming back with his companions in a post-chaise.

**Chapter Fourteen**

# The trial of Thomas Helliker

THE NEWS OF THESE EXCITING EVENTS must have reached James May and Thomas Helliker and the others in prison. As far as Helliker is concerned there has always been a slight doubt as to whether he was actually present at the burning of Littleton Mill. He himself was quite determined not to say anything that would incriminate others. Throughout all the questioning that took place at Fisherton between the time of his arrest in August and his trial in March, he quietly maintained that he had not been there, and beyond this he refused to say anything. The authorities had felt from the start that they had a much more important member of the shearmen's union in James May than in any of the other prisoners. They appear to have made repeated attempts to shake his testimony, and without in any way physically harming him to have done everything in their power to break his resistance. They probably thought that they would succeed, for the bad condition of the prison had more ill-effect on May than on any of the others, but it would seem that his physical appearance belied the firmness of his mental capacity. He must have known that his friends outside would persuade the shearman who had turned king's evidence about the oath to recant, and if this was done all he need do was say that he knew nothing about the whole affair, continuing to maintain that he had never given an oath and that there was no combination of any sort among the shearmen.

By February 1803 the authorities began to realise that their case against James May and the other members of the committee was likely to fail, and it was probably then that they turned with increased interest to the case against Thomas Helliker. They were determined to make an example of somebody, and it was on him that the net was closing. His fellow workers, both inside and outside the prison, would have realised that this was happening and would have done anything in their power to save him, but there was in fact little that they could do. They could, in effect, only exchange Thomas Helliker for another shearman. They knew, of course, who had been at the burning of Littleton Mill, and they knew the name of the man whom Mr Heath now maintained to be Helliker. There is a traditional story that one man wished to say he had been at Littleton but was overruled by his fellow shearmen, and that many years later, on his death-bed, this man sent for the vicar of the parish church and told him that it was he who had been at Littleton and that Helliker was innocent of the charge brought against him.

The trial took place on 14 March 1803, at the County Assizes at Salisbury. The judges were Sir Alexander Thompson and Sir Simon le Blanc.

The case against James May and the other four members of the committee was taken first. They were all brought before the court together. When the five men appeared there was a spontaneous cheer from the court which was filled to capacity with their friends from Trowbridge, but this was quickly silenced. The charge was read, and it stated that the five were being tried: 'For feloniously administering and causing to be administered and aiding and assisting at and consenting to the administering to one Thomas Bailey a certain oath and engagement then accordingly taken by him intending to bind him not to reveal or discover certain unlawful combinations and conspiracies of journeymen shearmen unlawfully combined together conspiring to regulate and govern the conduct of themselves and other journeymen shearmen in their business as such by certain rules and orders established by themselves without the sanction or authority of the laws of this kingdom, they the said journeymen shearmen being workmen and artificers in the manufacture of woollen cloths within this kingdom.' When this indictment had been read, first James May then the other four (Samuel Ferris, George Marks, John Helliker and Philip Edwards) all pleaded not guilty.

The case for the prosecution was a simple one. Thomas Bailey was immediately put into the witness box and prosecuting counsel asked him whether he would confirm that the oath referred to had been sworn in the manner stated in the indictment. Bailey looked very ill, and it was only with difficulty that the court heard what he had to say. He murmured that it was not true. Prosecuting counsel immediately intervened, 'but you stated previously on oath that it was'. Bailey replied, 'That was untrue, the oath was never given'. In a loud and threatening voice prosecuting counsel then tried to maintain that he had been got at, had been threatened. Bailey merely replied that he had nothing more to say. The hearing continued for a few minutes, but it soon became clear that however many times he might have changed his story in the past on this occasion Thomas Bailey was not going to say anything to harm the other shearmen. Probably in the presence of so many he knew he dared not, even if he wished, and it is likely that he had come to regret what he had done.

Prosecuting counsel stood down and defence counsel immediately appealed to the judges that there was now no case for his clients to answer. The two judges consulted with each other, and with obvious reluctance accepted that this was so and ordered the discharge of the five men.

The whole case was over in half an hour, and James May and his friends were received with great joy by their fellow workers.

The case against Thomas Helliker followed immediately. The indictment was read and once again everything turned upon the evidence of one man. Prosecuting counsel called for Mr Ralph Heath. There was a tension in the courtroom now which had not been present before. For this was a capital indictment, and the charge, of having riotously assembled with diverse other people and having wilfully aided the setting fire to Littleton Mill, carried with it, if proven, the certainty of the death penalty.

Ralph Heath then repeated in almost the same words the account that he had given to Mr Jones in Trowbridge. He said:

I have rented for three years a cottage, fulling and spinning mill at Littleton, belonging to Francis Naish of Trowbridge, a clothier, and have carried on in it my trade and occupation as

29 *Marling & Evans Mill, Kings Stanley, c. 1812*
This mill near Stroud is architecturally the most important in the West of England, with outstanding
brickwork and decoration on the facade.

30 *Marling & Evans Mill. Exterior*
This is an earlier building than the one shown in fig. 29 and shows how important good lighting was in these early factories.

31 *Marling & Evans Mill. Exterior*
This view gives an idea of the size and extent of this fine mill. Marlings were the most important clothiers in the second half of the nineteenth century.

32 *Marling & Evans. Clothmark*
These clothmarks are found on mill buildings throughout the area.

33 *Marling & Evans Mill. Interior ironwork*
An important feature here is the iron frame. This was one of the first mills to be built in this way so as to obviate the fire risk from wooden floors.

**34  *Hand Carding and Spinning***
One of the very earliest drawings of a spinning wheel. It comes from the Lutrell Psalter of c. 1340. The hand carding is particularly well illustrated. The third object remains a mystery.

**35  *The big wheel***
Spinning wheels are divided into two types, the simple big wheel and the Saxony wheel. In this illustration the fibre is being drafted on the big wheel.

**36  *Detail of The big wheel***
The spun yarn is now being wound on to the spindle. Note the different position of the hands relative to the spindle. The big wheel was used from the fourteenth century until machine spinning in the late eighteenth century.

37 *The Saxony Spinning Wheel*
The Saxony spinning wheel was a much more complex piece of apparatus and made spinning continuous. It was invented by Jungen in 1555, and used for spinning long fibres until the late eighteenth century.

38 *Detail of the Saxony Spinning Wheel*
The main section of the Saxony wheel was the flyer, here illustrated in detail. The important point was that the bobbin ran loose on the spindle and was driven by a different-sized wheel and therefore revolved at a different speed from the flyer.

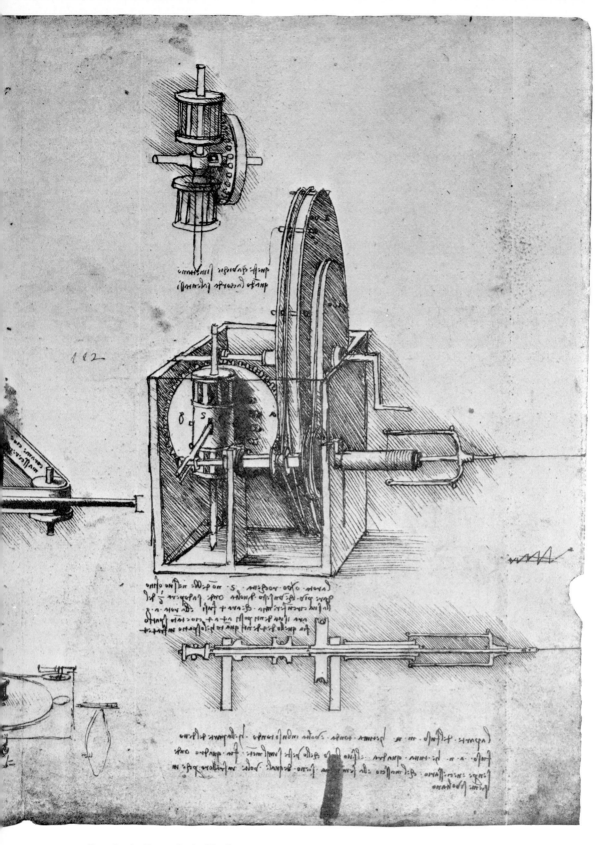

*39 Drawing by Leonardo da Vinci*
Leonardo's flyer shown here was theoretically better than the one used in practice. The flyer automatically guided the yarn up and down the spindle, whereas on the type shown in fig. 38 the hand spinner had to use the hooks on the arms.

millman and spinner. In consequence of the nightly outrages and destructive depredations which have lately been committed upon this piece of property I was under great alarm and apprehension, and had with several other persons kept watch for many nights. On Thursday morning, 22 July, I was sitting up in the said cottage to keep watch with John Pearce, Stephen Richardson and Daniel Goodship, my servants. About 1 a.m. I was alarmed to find a knocking noise without. Daniel Goodship opened the door to the house, when four or five men armed with muskets, pistols and bayonets, and their faces blackened, rushed into the room crying: 'Stand, you', and presently presenting their arms and swearing that no one should stir. A little man, about five foot six inches high, with his face blackened and having a small musket with a fixed bayonet in his hand, said: 'Is there any soldier that guards here?' After which he went out leaving the prisoner, a shearman who works for Francis Naish, in the room with some others. He had his face blackened and a pistol in his hand, which he pointed towards me and at my servants, swearing he would blow out our brains if anyone attempted to move. Soon afterwards the little man returned and said to me: 'We are come to set fire to your mill and we will.' I soon afterwards observed a light shining from the cottage, and Thomas Helliker and the other leaving we went outside where a man presented a musket at me and swore he would blow out my brains if I did not return. I immediately returned into the cottage and waited there for some time, and on going out again found the mill completely in flames. I got in through a window and saved several cloths at the hazard of my life, but the mill was completely consumed. There were many other persons who came in and went out of the cottage and stayed about the door.

Prosecuting counsel then asked Ralph Heath if he was quite certain that the man in the dock was the man who had come to his mill. He replied that he had no doubt. The question was repeated as this was crucial to the case. If there was any doubt about the identification Helliker's life might be saved. He again replied that he had no doubt. Prosecuting counsel then said that he had no more questions to ask.

Defence counsel immediately rose and pointed out that Mr Heath had said that the men who came had blackened faces: if this were so, and the men were also disguised, how could he be certain that one of them was Thomas Helliker? Ralph Heath replied that he was certain because he had seen Thomas Helliker working at Mr Naish's mill and he had two large teeth in front, slightly protruding, and the man who came to his house that night had these teeth. Defence counsel tried to argue, but Ralph Heath repeated that he was certain the man was Thomas Helliker.

Defence counsel made further attempts to shake Ralph Heath, but without success.

There were no other witnesses and prosecuting counsel then stated the Crown's case against Helliker. It was quite simple: no one doubted that Littleton Mill had been burnt, and Ralph Heath who was there confirmed the identification. The speech was brief and to the point.

Defence counsel in his speech for Thomas Helliker naturally went back to the difficulty of being certain about the identification of a disguised man. He spoke well, but it was clear that he had little chance of doing anything for his client.

The judge, Sir Alexander Thompson, summed up quickly. He referred to the burnings and stressed the evil this organisation of the workers had caused. Many, he said, had been misled, and he had no doubt that the prisoner was one of them. He was young, and he had doubtless been misled by older men, but that was not the point. The jury must not allow their sympathies for his youth to affect their verdict. They had heard the evidence of Mr Ralph Heath, and it was now up to them to say whether they accepted this evidence as being the truth. For himself he could see little

H

in the point that defence counsel had made; if one knew a person it was perfectly easy to recognise him even if his face was blackened.

The jury went out. They deliberated for about ten minutes, during which time Thomas Helliker was in a very great state of agitation. When they returned and were asked for their verdict, they replied 'Guilty'. At that point Thomas Helliker suddenly appeared as if relieved from a torturing suspense and he resumed a degree of fortitude which struck all who were present.

Judge Thompson then said to Helliker: 'This is one of those sad circumstances which arise because of the combination of workers that have become so common in this country. These combinations are unlawful, and they lead to these unlawful acts. Thomas Helliker you have been found guilty, rightly guilty of the crime for which you were indicted. Have you anything to say why I should not pass sentence upon you?' Helliker replied that he had nothing to say. The black hat was brought and the judge put it on and sentenced Thomas Helliker to death by hanging.

Later in the same Assizes, there were further repercussions and as a contemporary newspaper put it:

> There were thirteen cases entered for trial, but only two were of any importance, which were actions brought by Mr Naish the proprietor and Mr Heath the tenant of Littleton Mill at Semington, near Trowbridge, to recover from the inhabitants of the hundred of Whorlesdown the damage which they respectively sustained in July last from the destruction of the factory with the stock and goods therein. It appeared that about twenty persons, armed and disguised, came to the mill in the night; the latter part of them entered the dwellinghouse adjoining the mill and kept guard over seven persons who were protecting the premises, and that the other persons forced open the door of the mill and set fire to the same. Mr Sergeant Lens on the part of the inhabitants of the hundred made an ingenious speech in which he contended that words in the riots and subsequent acts of parliament were confined to the demolishing or pulling down, and that the premises in question, being burnt, did not come within the meaning of the several acts, and particularly that act which was passed about three years since relating to mills. Justice le Blanc was clearly of the opinion that the plaintiffs were entitled to recover the damages which they had sustained, and that whether the premises were pulled down or burnt or blown up with gunpowder it would equally be a demolishing; and his Lordship accordingly instructed the jury to find for the plaintiffs, which by consent of the parties were the amount of the sums mentioned by the declarations.

Meanwhile Helliker went back to Fisherton jail. Fisherton is on the outskirts of Salisbury, and so close to the city as in fact to be part of it. While he was there Helliker is said to have written several letters to his relations and also some verses. They were printed later by Mr Sweet of Trowbridge. He had, he said, slightly altered them, and the originals were never found. Indeed some of Helliker's friends protested that he had never actually written them, and probably this was the truth. However, they are perhaps worth quoting. First of all there was a letter to his mother dated 13 March 1803:

> Alas my distressed state: but I thank the Almighty God I am more composed than I was when I saw my brothers last. Dear father and mother, I wish you and my brothers and sisters to come here to see me before the 22nd of March. Dear father and mother I have been troubled with a very bad headache, but thanks be to the Almighty God that I think I never found myself better than I have been for these two days past, both in mind and body, and I hope it will continue

until the fatal day, when I hope the Lord will receive my departing spirit. I hope that my brothers will be there for I have something to say to them, so God Almighty bless you all. So no more from your unfortunate son, Thomas Helliker.

A few days later, on the 21st, he wrote:

My dear brothers I hope this will be a warning to you all to consider my untimely fate (being cut off in the prime of life) which I hope will be a warning to all young men like me, and for the love of God Almighty let my fate be always in your memory to think that before I knew what life was was called off to everlasting I hope happiness; I thank God I find myself very happy in mind and I hope the Lord God will receive my soul and so no more. Remember my last fate, Thomas Helliker.

It is thought that his brother saw him in prison the day before his execution, when he is said to have given them the following letter to his father and mother:

Dear Father and Mother, brothers and sisters and all relations, this is my last night; in the middle of the night I wrote this letter; give my love to my Uncle Elsworth and all the rest of the family. Dear Father and Mother, I think that some of the principle shearmen have been the ruin of my body (but I hope the Lord will receive my soul) and that they will put this on my tombstone to be a warning to all young men; to be a warning against bad advice and for my brothers to be good to you both, for it is a bad thing to forget you when you read this I hope my soul will be at rest for ever and ever. Dear Father and Mother, give this to my brother Joseph and think of me when he swears and I hope in God he will leave it all. Farewell for ever and ever, Yours, Thomas Helliker.

Helliker also, it was claimed, wrote the following verses:

> To thee my God and Saviour I,
> By day and night address my cry,
> Vouchsafe my mournful voice to hear,
> To my distress incline thy ear
> For seas of trouble me invade
> My soul draws nigh to death's cold shade
> Like one whose strength and hope are fled
> They number me among the dead.
> Removed from friends I sigh alone
> In a loathed dungeon laid were none
> A visit will vouchsafe me
> Confined past hope of liberty
> My eyes from weeping never cease
> They waste but still my grief increase
> But daily God to thee I pray
> With outstretched hand invoke thy aid.

Such, according to Mr Sweet's pamphlet, were the last words and letters of Thomas Helliker, though their authenticity is extremely doubtful. More probably they represented a kind of early nineteenth-century attempt at moral uplift.

Thomas Helliker was executed in front of Fisherton jail on Tuesday, 28 March 1803. A great crowd of workers in the woollen trade had come from Trowbridge and the other cloth-making towns nearby, and there were representatives from Gloucestershire and even, it was said, a few from Yorkshire. They came, strange as it may sound, to pay homage to the man who was being hanged. It might seem to some that a better way to pay homage to the young martyr would have been to have stayed away and let the state pursue its vengeance alone. This, however, was not the view generally held at the time.

There were about three thousand people crowded round the scaffold. At the due hour Thomas Helliker was brought out. He was calm and collected, and acknowledged his friends who were standing below him, but he made no attempt to speak to them. An official addressed him and asked him whether he did not wish, at this last moment of his life, to confess that he was guilty of the crime for which he was to be executed. Thomas Helliker replied, as he had always done, that he was not at Littleton when the mill was burnt. The rope was placed around his neck, the black cap was put over his face, the cart was pulled away from under him, and poor Thomas Helliker was soon hanging there in his last agony. Still he uttered no word, and fortunately he died quickly.

Even those who had thought he should die appear to have been struck by his bravery, and one Bath newspaper which reported the execution made the following remarks:

> He was one of that great body of men among the working clothiers who have associated to over-come the manufacturers and compel them to abandon the use of machinery, and in pursuit of this object he had joined the riotous assembly by whom the mill in the parish of Steeple Ashton was wilfully set on fire and property destroyed to the amount of several thousand pounds. He was only about nineteen years of age, and bore a good character in the ordinary relations of life. In spite of his conviction, his behaviour was resigned and decent and when brought to the scaffold he betrayed neither unmanly fear nor audacious daring. Having discharged his devotional duties before mounting the scaffold, he was detained there a very short time during which he looked round at the crowds, noticing among them some of his former friends he threw his hat to them; the cap was then drawn over his face and he was launched into eternity.
>
> The youth of the criminal and his falling a victim of a party occasioned some commiseration of his fate, but the recollection that he and his associates were engaged in offences, the pursuit of which was attended with violence, anarchy and misery, prevented all applications to the fountain of mercy on his behalf, this severe example is necessary to restore a due reverence of the law.

The other Bath paper was less sympathetic:

> Tuesday. Thomas Helliker was executed in front of Fisherton Jail. He was one of that mistaken body of men among the working clothiers who have associated to overthrow all the manufacturers and compel them to abandon the use of machinery, and in pursuit of this object he joined the riotous assembly while the Littleton Mill was wilfully set on fire and property destroyed to a large amount. He was about nineteen years of age, of orderly character in the ordinary relations of life.
>
> It is sincerely hoped that the fate of Thomas Helliker will operate as a useful caution to all workmen against unlawful combinations and riotous proceedings, especially to those persons in the manufacturing district of this neighbourhood, who must feel conscious of having been concerned in the outrages committed last year; for although they have hitherto escaped that justice which their crime deserved and they imagine themselves to be unknown and in security, and yet they ought to be thankful that they cannot take confidence in their apparent safety and

that it behoves them to be most circumspect in their future conduct. A rigid observance of their duties to assist may be considered as a small reparation for the injuries committed and as some atonement to the offended laws of their country. It must afford much satisfaction to the manufacturer whose property had been attacked and destroyed by Helliker and his accomplices that in his last moments he fully confessed his guilt of the offence for which he died and made an acknowledgement that his sentence was just.

When the execution at Fisherton was over and Thomas Helliker was dead, his fellow shearmen put into action the plan that they must have decided upon a while before. When the body was taken down from the scaffold and was about to be removed by the prison authorities some of them moved towards these authorities and quietly took the body of their friend from them. There is nothing in contemporary accounts to indicate that they met with any resistance.

They laid the body on a cart and started back on their long journey to Trowbridge. The procession must have stretched for nearly a mile as it wended its way up the road which led from Salisbury to the Plain, past Old Sarum on the right, and it would have been dark by the time they reached the villages of the Plain itself. In the early morning they would have come down off the Plain by the old road through Tinhead and very near to Littleton where the burning had taken place. When they finally reached Trowbridge they took the body straight to the church. There, rather surprisingly, the funeral service was carried out with full Church rites by the curate, for which he was subsequently reprimanded by the absentee vicar, Mr Berisford.

# Chapter Fifteen

# *To Parliament*

THE EVENTS OF MARCH 1803 CONVINCED the shearmen that in future they should pursue their legal rights rather than resort to violence, and the delegates who finally went to London for the Parliamentary Enquiry into the wool trade laws represented a real cross-section of the woollen trade of the South-west. There was Thomas King of Stroud, a rather superior sort of weaver who sometimes called himself a clothier but who in practice seems to have been a master weaver employing three other weavers to help him. He was one of those who in times of expansion might have passed from the side of the workers to that of the clothiers. There was in Thomas King a certain innate conservatism which had kept him to the old type of loom, and he had never used the flying or spring shuttle, which had been invented many years before by John Kay.

Another of the weavers chosen from Stroud was John Clayford. He represented the typical hand-loom weaver who was for the moment reasonably secure in his occupation but who was during the coming years to find conditions increasingly difficult. Another weaver from Stroud, William Clement, appears from his evidence as a natural delegate. He had realised that only by uniting could the workers obtain a fair reward for their labour, and despite all the numerous impediments that had been put in the way of such combinations he seems to have led his fellow workers well and done his utmost to give them a real sense of solidarity. It was probably due to his efforts that a payment of ten shillings a week was made for as long as 12 weeks when any member of the union fell sick. This was certainly one of the really important moves that he introduced, and if payments were made for sickness it was easy to use the same system when strike action became necessary. William Clement played a similar part in organising the weavers of Stroud as James May appears to have done at Trowbridge, but we know more about him due to the fact that he was one of the delegates who gave evidence before Parliament. We do not know why James May did not go – possibly because of ill-health following his months in prison. The West of England workers owed a great deal to William Clement, clearly a man of individuality and ability, though his one fault was perhaps a tendency to be dogmatic in the statement of his views. As these were usually correct it did not greatly matter, but on one occasion there was a somewhat unfortunate controversy between him and John Clayford, who claimed it was not true that the weavers received ten shillings a week as stated by Clement: he said that when he had been sick he had only received six shillings, and he demanded an explanation of this. He seems to have been a very forthright character, as dogmatic in his way as William Clement, and he said he would not be satisfied until this had been cleared up. Although it should have been a simple enough matter it was never settled and the two unfortunately continued their argument before Parliament. John Clayford did, however, make one good point. He said that the weavers should now admit that they had an association. He argued that they should maintain that this association had only been started in order to bring their case before Parliament – in his own words: 'our case that we might not be sent to the factories'.

Another representative from Stroud was John Niblick. He was a rather strange man, and it is difficult to understand how he had obtained a position of trust in the union movement. He had been a weaver, but was now employed as a wool loft man, supervising the handing out of the wool for one of the clothiers, which suggests that he ought really to have been on the other side. But he always maintained that the clothier for whom he worked was sympathetic towards the weavers and had no objection to his coming to the meeting. John Niblick was inclined to talk at considerable length about his good relations with the clothier who employed him. He referred to him as 'the master' and on one occasion confidentially told the others present that 'the master for whom I superintend is in the Russian trade'.

There must have been many meetings between the representatives of the workers of Trowbridge and Stroud while preparing their case for the parliamentary enquiries. Many of these meetings were attended by Mr Jessop of Stroud, the attorney whom the Gloucestershire weavers had appointed to state their case. He was to fight hard and well for the workers, and later when asked in the Commons if he knew that he was to have an annuity in place of fees he said: 'No.' When further asked if he would accept pay, he promptly replied: 'Yes, indeed I would.' Mr Jessop from the start felt that the woollen workers had a strong case under the law, and he was prepared to do all he could to assist them.

Of the Trowbridge area representatives at the enquiry one was Joseph Bailey of Rode. He was to describe the Bill as being one intended to make it law that all working should be done in a factory, which in effect was what the Bill meant. He was a likeable man who stated the case for the workers clearly and well, and on one occasion when questioned about his occupation he said he thought broadcloth weaving was really a ridiculous sort of business.

The other representative for the area was James Jones of North Bradley, a rather more difficult choice to understand. However, he was a weaver, and as the legal case being prepared concerned the weavers to some considerable extent the choice of one of them was reasonable. He was a well-known character, and at the enquiry when asked, 'You stood against the spinning jenny at Shepton Mallet?' he answered that he had, but admitted that the spinning jenny was now in general use. In this way in many meetings the weavers and shearmen of the West of England prepared their case. Likewise their opponents, the clothiers, simultaneously did the same, and eventually the time came for both sides to place their cases before the House of Commons.

The first witness to be called was the famous clothier Mr Sheppard, of Uley in Gloucestershire. He stated that he had been a clothier for upwards of 15 years, and if the statutes were carried into effect a very great part of the trade of the county of Gloucestershire would be lost. A considerable proportion of the weavers at present employed had never been apprenticed; the majority of these were men, although a few were women. In his own mill, at one establishment, he employed about

75 weavers, of which only five had been apprenticed according to the statute. Of the other men he employed there were about 83, and of these 16 had been apprenticed. He stressed the point that, with all due respect to the cloth workers, apprenticeship had largely died out and he had not one amongst all of his workers who had been apprenticed for a legal term of seven years. If none but legal workers were employed he would lose a major part of his trade. Notwithstanding the introduction of spring looms, which had of late much increased and which would in the end replace the old type, there was not at the present time any surplus of competent and good weavers in Gloucestershire. Mr Sheppard thought it desirable that the number of weavers should not be decreased. Weavers who produced good work should not be prevented from continuing their occupation because they could not produce proof of their apprenticeship. The coarse woollen trade had already been largely lost to Yorkshire. He thought it took several years to learn to weave, and owing to the introduction of machinery it had been necessary to set up manufacturing establishments in villages which possessed the advantages of water-power. If there were in any such areas apprenticed weavers without work he would be pleased to meet them. He gave no preference to apprenticed workers – in fact rather the reverse, for they were usually the older men and not as good.

The second manufacturer to give evidence was Mr Jones of Staverton, who said he had been a clothier for 20 years. It would be a very bad thing if apprenticeships were enforced, as the art of weaving was by no means difficult to learn, and it was customary for young children to be brought to the loom to learn weaving from their parents. Most of his workmen came from different parishes to his mills, and they returned to their homes to sleep. There had, he said, recently been plenty of work, especially for broadloom weavers, whilst the trade in narrow cloth had improved. On the subject of the workers' attempts to prosecute those whom they maintained were breaking the statutes, he said he had seen a public notice in the newspapers signed by Mr Frank Frampton, solicitor, which stated that all unapprenticed weavers in Bradford, Trowbridge and neighbourhood would be prosecuted if they did not stop working within a month of the date of the notice.

Another clothier was Mr Thomas Joyce of Freshford, who said that it was essential for the manufacturer to have the power of moving workmen to different places where business was conducted. Many of his friends in the woollen trade agreed with him regarding this. All the workpeople in the neighbourhood from the age of seven years to seventy, both men and women, were at present in employment. He himself had employed as many women as men. He went on to state that children were now employed at an earlier age than they should have been, under the existing law. This was one of the results of machinery. He did not use the spring shuttle, but it had been introduced in the area about two years before by a weaver who had gone to the North of England to find work. He used it for a few weeks and then, because of the riots it caused, gave it up.

Thomas Joyce was followed by a Mr Daniel Lloyd, also of Uley, who used the gig mills. He maintained that it was quite impossible to say whether the gig mills now in use in Gloucestershire were the same as those which had been proscribed by the earlier statutes. The important point was that cloths were better made than before thereby allowing the wider introduction of gig mills. He himself made fancy cloths, and it was very noticeable that trade was good at those mills where gig mills were used.

John Warrington, clothier of Stroud, who had been in business for 30 years, said that he himself knew of only one gig mill now in use and this was not used for the purpose which was proscribed in the statute. It was not, he stressed, used for perching and burling the cloth. The gig mill in Gloucestershire was only used for the purpose of rowing and dressing the fabric. If it was used for burling the cloth it would cause damage to the fabric, but it was found to be very beneficial if used for rowing and dressing. The gig mill was in every way a very great advantage over the hand method. He then said that although gig mills were not now used for perching and burling, yet it was possible to use them in this way. Perching and burling, however, meant different things in different counties. Occasionally the term was used for dressing the cloth after fulling. Cloths before fulling were open and loose, resembling flannel. After being fulled they were firm like felt, and therefore able to resist any impression necessary for the dressing of the cloth. It was certainly not in the interest of any manufacturer to perch and burl cloth by the gig mill. This was in fact the very thing that they would wish to avoid. Mr Warrington continued his praise of the gig mills, saying that it did not necessarily strain the cloth more than was done when hand dressing took place. The machine, he tried to explain, had power in itself capable of regulating the force so as to dress cloths of a most delicate kind. Cloths made on the gig mill were not damaged unless the mill was applied for the purpose of burling. In conclusion, however, he rather confused the issue by admitting that he could be liable for prosecution under the statute if he himself used a gig mill.

Mr John Wansey, a manufacturer of London and relative of the well-known Warminster clothier, was the next to give evidence. He had bought cloths for 30 years. Those dressed on the gig mills were by far the best, being softer and more mellow, and he greatly preferred them both for the home and the foreign markets. He had, only a day or so before, made a check on his Russian trade, and found that his customers there had chosen those dressed on the machines, and he often had to send hand-dressed cloths back to be done again on these machines.

Mr Henry Dyer, a clothier from Wotton-under-Edge, said that he had been a manufacturer of medley cloths for 20 years. He used gig mills and they were, without question, much better than hand dressing. Trade was good at the moment, and there was no unemployment and no discontent. Everything, so far as he could see, was all right in the cloth trade. This statement must have occasioned considerable surprise amongst all present at the enquiry.

Mr Abraham Lloyd Edridge repeated the advantage of machine dressing, and said that the cloth was bound to be strained during the raising to the extent of about one yard in 20. He stated that trade had increased since the introduction of the gig mills, and that he could not now supply all that was asked for by the London market.

Edward Sheppard was then re-examined, and he admitted that he used gig mills but stressed that it was for neither perching nor burling. He said that trade had increased where gig mills were used. Gloucestershire had gained particularly at the expense of Somerset. He admitted that he was liable to prosecution under the statutes respecting gig mills.

John Jones was also re-examined. He said that he used gig mills and had little doubt that their wider introduction in Wiltshire would have the same effect as in Gloucestershire. He did not think that gig mills would throw people out of work, and in any case the manufacturers of Wiltshire and Somerset had, in Bath on 16 August 1802, at a meeting they held at the White Hart Inn, promised that anybody so put out of work should be re-engaged. He went on to say that the Gloucestershire cloths were more popular because they were dressed by machine. Many a Wiltshire clothier sent cloths there for finishing. The gig mills had only just been introduced into Wiltshire. Having described the meeting he had had with the shearmen, he referred to the question of shearing frames, and stated that they had not been generally introduced. He described one of these new machines. There were a number of hand shears in a frame and these worked together by means of a crank. Mr Jones said that he had seen these machines at work, but he had himself always felt that it was impossible to get the clear-cut skin-like finish so desired with them. He added, however, that he had heard reports recently of a new type of frame which had been invented in

America and this was on an entirely different principle. He understood it was based on a kind of circular blade which traversed the cloth. He had not seen the machine himself, but from accounts given to him it looked as though this invention might well be the answer to the clothiers' problem.

John Wansey of Warminster, another member of the clothing family of that name, said that he had made cloth for 20 years but had recently given up business. He had, he said, listened carefully to all that Mr Jones had said, and he agreed entirely with his remarks. Rather unnecessarily he then referred to the riots, and until the committee stopped him, gave an exaggerated picture of how guns had been fired at night into the houses of many of the clothiers of the district, particularly those who had antagonised their workers by threatening to introduce gig mills. The committee, although naturally deploring this, felt it was not the question being considered at the moment.

William Sheppard, a clothier of Frome and one whose business was expanding rapidly, said that there was a very great preference for cloths finished on the gig mills. He had himself sent cloths eighty miles away for finishing, and now during the last few months had introduced machines himself. Mr Sheppard went on to make a plea to the workers to accept the innovation, saying that unless the industry was prepared to try everything new it would fall behind in the years of close competition that he foresaw.

Edward Sheppard was then called for the third time. He made the point that although weaving was still mostly done in cottages the clothiers had to guard against thieving which took place to an enormous extent in the homes of the workers. He himself agreed that there were a lot of problems in bringing the workers together; in fact it was bad, but not, he firmly believed, as bad as when they were each on one loom and not working together like the shearers. Generally speaking, he felt that the coming together in factories of workers led to a great increase in honesty, and this would, he thought, outweigh any disadvantages. He himself had always found work was worse done in the villages farthest away from the centre of the business.

Mr Sheppard then went on to deal with the statutes regarding length and breadth inspection and the prohibition of the use of lambswool. He said that he wished to make his position here quite clear. He did not obey the statutes regarding measurements, nor did he obey the others. He and all the other clothiers had to make the cloth their customers required. Some cloths, for example, were better made from lambswool than from fleecewool. He concluded by saying that he had never known of such a person as a searcher or an overseer. There was no inspector in Gloucestershire although he had heard of one in Somerset and Wiltshire. He wished, above all, to stress that it was in the highest interest of the clothiers to maintain a reputation for the fairness of their fabric, otherwise their trade would disappear, and they would go out of business.

Thomas Joyce confirmed the account given by Mr Sheppard. He had never had a cloth measured or inspected by any inspector, although a man did call twice a year to receive his two pennies per piece and he himself annually went to the Quarter Sessions and swore that he had done his duty. The man who was now receiving the money was actually a shoemaker.

John King of Freshford said that he had been a millman for years, and had seen an inspector in the villages of Lullington and at Clifford Mills, Beckington. About 33 years before, these mills had belonged to the same person, and he himself had been apprenticed there for seven years. The inspector used to come to measure and seal all the cloths. He had finished his apprenticeship 20 years ago, and had been in business ever since except for about seven years. He had duly given an inspector details of cloths fulled so that he could collect his two pence per piece but whether he came or not made not the slightest difference to the way the fulling was done.

William Sheppard of Frome confirmed it was quite impossible to lay down any laws regarding the stretching, the measurement and other aspects of manufacture. Today, for example, the Turkish trade took the finest and the thinnest cloths, the ladies a degree thicker, the East and West Indies a degree thicker still, the Russian trade more so. Superfines were thicker still and double-milled superfines were thickest of all. Finally he pointed out that the statutes had been made years ago when the trade was entirely different.

The parliamentary fight was long and involved – much longer than the workers of the West had ever imagined. The clothiers, however, were probably better prepared. They had realised when they first met to prepare their case that the proceedings were likely to be long and difficult. They had made their first petition to Parliament, asking that the old statutes regulating the woollen trade should be repealed, in March 1803, at almost the same time that Thomas Helliker had been tried and executed. They appealed for the repeal of the Acts dealing with apprenticeship, gig mills and the limitation of looms, and the merchants in London who bought their cloths joined them in this appeal.

On the other side, all the workers in the woollen trade were combined together. They were described as the weavers and the shearmen living in the clothing towns of Wiltshire, Somerset and Gloucester. They were supported by the shearmen of the West Riding of Yorkshire, and as the case in Parliament developed they were joined by all the other workers in the cloth trade in this area, and increasingly this section of the trade took the leading part.

A Bill giving the clothiers what they were seeking passed through the House of Commons, but rather surprisingly when it came to the House of Lords it was reduced to one that simply suspended the statutes for one year. After a considerable amount of discussion it was stated that an understanding had been reached and the whole question was to be brought up again the following year, when an attempt would be made to bring it to a final settlement.

As is often the case in such circumstances, the two sides did not agree as to what had been the basis of their talks. The shearmen later stated that the master clothiers had obtained the passing of the Suspending Act by promising that they would, early in the next session, bring forward a Bill for the general revision of the statutes regulating the woollen trade.

Whatever the intention, the following year brought instead a new ministry, and there was far too little time available to go into the details involved in the revising of these woollen statutes. If the master clothiers on the one hand and the workers on the other had been able to introduce an agreed Revision Bill it would have been accepted, but the Government were certainly not ready to introduce one themselves. After some discussion, however, everybody agreed that the clothiers were breaking the law and the Government therefore felt it necessary to introduce a further Suspending Bill to legalise their position for a further year. The Prime Minister, Pitt, said when doing this that it was then too late in the present session to give sufficient time to discuss so complicated a subject. Once again the shearmen stated that they had, at the time, been promised that the matter would be introduced again early in the following session.

The following year brought a determined effort, this time led by the small clothiers of Yorkshire, who were really themselves workers, to obtain a Bill that would settle the matter in their favour. The riots and discussions of 1803 mark a very real division, and the events which centred around the death of Helliker were the last occasion when the woollen workers of the West led the way – indeed, they played a very small part in the discussions that took place in the autumn of 1804 and the winter of 1805. The initiative came almost entirely from the small working clothiers of Yorkshire. These men had their own looms in their own homes, worked by their own families, and they took the woven cloths to the cloth halls in the Yorkshire towns and there sold them to the merchants who finished the cloths and then sold them wherever they could. These working clothiers took an active part in all the negotiations, and although it appeared at first that their interests were the same as those of the workers of the West, this was not in fact quite the case. Those people who were anxious to destroy what they regarded as the pretentions of the woollen workers of the West of England were able to take advantages of this difference to the great detriment of those workers. At the time, however, it must have appeared that something was to be gained by allowing the initiative to come from these small Yorkshire clothiers. Many conservative figures in the Government, who had been frightened by the combination of workers they had witnessed in the West, were prepared to look with sympathy upon the struggles of the small Yorkshire clothiers against the important merchants to whom they sold their cloths and under whose influence they appeared to be falling.

A Bill was prepared on their behalf, and as it originally stood it would have gone a long way towards preventing the introduction of machinery in the woollen trade. The Government realised this was the case, and they had come to see clearly that such a step was impracticable. They therefore opposed this part of the suggested Bill and, following discussion, it was changed. But they were prepared to accept the other section, which they thought would safeguard the position of the small Yorkshire clothiers and at the same time destroy the defences of the workers who had organised themselves into unions. Once again it was too late to do anything in the current session, and yet another Suspending Bill was put through.

On this particular occasion the workers tried very hard to prevent the passing of this suspending Bill, and they received some support from a few Members of Parliament who realised that this continual whitewashing of the clothiers was unfair. The Government, however, perhaps realising the weakness of their case but nevertheless seeing the necessity of keeping the master clothiers in business, held to their view that the Suspending Bill must be passed.

Pitt died in 1805 and a new ministry was installed. Once again there was so much to do during the first year of office that it was impossible to tackle the complicated issue of the woollen statutes and yet another Suspending Bill was introduced.

Finally, in 1806, yet another Parliamentary Committee was set up to consider the matter, and evidence was taken on an even larger scale than had been done in 1803. On this occasion, furthermore, most of the people questioned came from Yorkshire; the West of England clothiers and workers played a very small part. The report of this committee ended all the hopes the woollen workers, particularly the shearmen, still held that machinery would be prohibited.

Although the report of the Parliamentary Committee of 1806 had shown that the workers' attempt to put new life into the statutes was bound to fail, yet two more years passed before Parliament introduced measures clarifying the position. Two more Suspending Acts had to be passed before all the old laws were wiped off the statute books in 1809. The woollen trade was then free to introduce whatever machinery it wished, and by this time workers of the West appear to have lost interest. Most of them probably felt that it had all been a waste of time and money: they had certainly spent a great deal of both in taking their case before Parliament, where it had been held up for so many years. The Stroud attorney who had fought so hard for them said on one occasion that he had used £1,500 of the weavers' money.

**Chapter Sixteen**

# Decline of the hand workers

THERE IS LITTLE MORE TO SAY ABOUT THE shearmen. They had for long been reckoned the aristocrats of the trade. Their strength had been typified by such men as James May and Thomas Helliker. With conditions turning increasingly against them, there was nothing they could do. When the old statutes had been repealed the gig mills increased rapidly, and soon new shearing frames appeared. The hand shearmen were no longer wanted. Their job simply disappeared, and in most cases they were left to starve.

The Trowbridge committee of the shearmen's union, which had been so powerful, disintegrated. Indeed, as the parliamentary enquiry dragged on and the Suspending Acts were passed, the shearmen came to realise that there was little they could hope for from Parliament. Once they became disunited, whatever power they had once had was lost, and their last efforts were some rather futile petitions sent to such unlikely people as the Prince Regent. They told him they had hoped that when peace came trade would get better, and that there would be jobs for all, but this had not happened and there were many unemployed woollen workers wandering about the streets of Trowbridge and Bradford-on-Avon. When the war had started there had been no gig mills or shearing frames, but now they were appearing in all the factories. The petition brought no response and no sign of sympathy.

As already indicated, the final blow came in 1815 when Mr Lewis, of Brimscombe, near Stroud, further improved the rotary cutting machine and this type of cutter became widely adopted in the West Country. With it a comparatively untrained operator accomplished 20 times what had previously needed the skill of the handicraft shearmen. Indeed, clothiers, when they brought in these machines, found they could use boys instead of men. The tyrants of the country had certainly met the fate that had been forecast by Lord Fitzwilliam in 1802 (see Chapter Thirteen). He had said that they would be superseded, and then their importance would simply melt away. The ban which they had for so long exercised would be effective no longer, their dreaded combinations would disappear, and then, he concluded with a sigh of relief, no more would be heard about their meetings. It had all come true, and never again was one to hear the shearmen referred to as a distinct group in the woollen trade.

James Read had given his final verdict on the events in the West in a letter he wrote to Lord Hawkesbury. The struggle, he said, between the workers and the clothiers had begun many years before because of the prejudice of these workers against the introduction of machinery, which they pretended, as far as the gig mills were concerned, was prohibited by statute. Mr Read should have known by 1805 that there was no pretence about this. He went on to say that this discontent had continued for a time, culminating in 1802 when there had been a great many riots in the cloth manufacturing areas of Wiltshire; some of the ringleaders he had himself arrested. Mr Read obviously remained well satisfied with the work he had done. The riots, he concluded, had stopped, and the man who had been the ringleader had been hanged. Perhaps he thought this was true, though more likely he did not care. Thomas Helliker was not really executed because he had been thought a ringleader but because he was the one man against whom the authorities could just scrape together a case. They probably thought it was necessary to make an example of someone, and Thomas Helliker was there at hand, though in fact there was no need for a scapegoat at all. The workers had been quite prepared for their case to go to the House of Commons, and the Government, although it never recognised that such things as workers' organisations could exist, had, in so far as it admitted there was a case for the House of Commons to discuss, admitted that the workers' unions were being reasonable. The workers could not hope to win their case, but to get as far as they did was, in fact, a very great achievement.

Thomas Helliker had therefore perhaps not died entirely in vain, and those leaders of the union whose names we know, and whose views we can perhaps still see and appreciate, had not worked in vain in all they had done to fight the issue on so many grounds. The work bore fruit many years later when the trade unions were able to give back to the workers some of the dignity they had lost when they finally had to forsake the hand methods which they had used for so long in their own homes and go to the new machines in the factories.

Very few people today visit the mill at Littleton where Thomas Helliker was said to have been on that fateful night. The mill is still there, not greatly changed although now a corn mill, and the river that drove the water-wheel still runs under the mill, now however driving a turbine. The house where Mr Heath lived is also little changed. Here, hidden from view on a by-road of a main route from the West of England to London there is a corner of history, a place one would have thought worthy of an occasional pilgrimage. The mill had been used for cloth-making from the fifteenth century, but it ceased to be so used soon after the burning described in this section. Apparently it was repaired after the attack and was used again as a cloth mill for a while, perhaps as late as 1840. Certainly somewhere about this time the increasing difficulties of the West of England cloth trade led to the owner turning to flour milling.

It was about this period, of course, that many small mills in the West of England area closed down, and many of the workers who could remember the great days of the early years of the century then made their last cloths.

Historical events sometimes ripple out in waves of different strength. The riots in Wiltshire led to the debates in the House of Commons. The attack on Littleton led to the death of Helliker, and the epilogue on the burning of Littleton Mill was a rather pathetic and trivial attempt of the people round about to avoid paying certain fines which had been imposed on the tything of Hinton at the same assize where Thomas Helliker was sentenced to death. The overseers of the poor of the parish were appointed to assess the damage that had been caused. They ordered the inhabitants to meet them at the New Inn at Steeple Ashton, so that the assessments due according to the law should be made. The inhabitants of the Hundred of Whorlsdown were, however, in no hurry to find the money. Six months later the solicitor acting on behalf of Mr Naish wrote to the parish officers to ask when the money would be paid.

The solicitor, Mr Clutterbuck, was not unnaturally being pressed by Mr Naish, and had received a letter from him saying that it was nearly three months ago that he had been told that the principal paymaster in the Hundred of Whorlsdown had requested six weeks or two months to collect and pay the money. He had consented to this, and he did not wish to put anybody to any inconvenience, but the extent of the delay had been a considerable loss to him and he was now obliged to say that the money must be paid immediately.

Mr Naish, by this time, had gone to live at Twerton. Perhaps this led to no notice being taken, for in November he was still unpaid. The solicitor tried again, threatening this time that unless the money came he would call the Sheriff in. At this point the inhabitants of Great Hinton felt they had stalled as long as they could and the sum of £161 7s was paid to Messrs Naish and Heath. So Mr Heath and Mr Naish got their money, and it should be noted that the total damage was far less than the thousands of pounds which Mr Read had mentioned in his letter to London.

By 1820 all the processes except weaving – admittedly a very important exception – were now done in the factories, and in most cases by machines. Weaving remained a hand-loom operation, a large percentage of the pieces still being woven in the cottages.

In so far as there were further strikes in the West, they centred around the attempts of the hand-loom weavers to retain a reasonable standard of living.

In the 1820s, probably as a result of the repeal of the Combination Acts, there were two series of strikes, one in Somerset and one in Gloucester. Their course can again be followed from the Home Office papers. The Revd Henry Sainsbury, J.P., writing from Frome in 1822 to Robert Peel, reported that there was considerable agitation in the town in consequence of the weavers having gone on strike demanding higher wages and refusing to work until they had obtained them. Local justices had acted strongly to suppress these workers, so much so that Sainsbury and another justice, Henry Edgill, received a rebuke from the Home Secretary, in a letter which deserves to be quoted fairly fully:

I am directed by Mr Secretary Peel to acknowledge receipt of your letter, from which he understands that you have convicted eight weavers for neglect of their work and committed them to jail in addition to those who were committed on the first. You likewise state that at the instance of some of the masters you had been induced to issue warrants authorising the peace officers to take measures for the preservation of the masters' property which was in the homes of the weavers, although such warrants were not authorised by the law; at the process being resisted the constables opened the houses by force and executed the warrants from whence some riots ensued, which were not terminated without the interference of the Yeoman Cavalry.

Upon this statement, Mr Peel directs me to remark however desirable it may be to preserve the property from deterioration, it is vastly more important that the magistrates should act strictly within the limit of their authority; and without meaning to cast any reflection on the motives which induced you to act as you have done he thinks the tendency of the measure you adopted is rather to ferment than to allay the existing discontents.

To one of the reasons adduced by the clothiers for requiring your interference in regard to the restoration of the yarn, namely that if it were withheld the weavers would in some degree triumph,

Mr Peel can attach no weight. The propriety of such interference must depend upon other considerations, and the triumph of the weavers will be the most certain if, at the instance of their employers, an authority is assumed with regard to them which the law does not warrant.

The justices were taken aback and, in their own words, regretted 'to find that our proceedings, which originated in the best intentions, do not appear to have met with your approbation. But we are confident that although the law may not strictly sanction what we have done, our acting on the emergency of the case and under its peculiar circumstances, was the means of preventing any outrages on the second list of commitments which took place, and we have the satisfaction of knowing that no personal injury was intended.'

It is not clear what the justices would consider to be a personal injury; one might have thought that being committed to jail illegally would be so reckoned. The justices' letter concluded: 'The clothiers have applied for other warrants, but we consider ourselves restricted from interfering in consequence of your letter. They (the clothiers) are therefore resolved to send a deputation to London and have requested us to give them this introduction.'

The justices must have exaggerated the danger, as a week later they were able to report that everything was now perfectly quiet. They attributed this happy result to several causes: first of all to the arrival of a troop of regular cavalry, which they said had tended to convince the disaffected people that the magistrates supported by the Government were determined to put a stop to their practices; secondly to the starving state of the weavers and their families, after their having been so long out of work and having so little support; thirdly to the circumstance of 18 weavers being sentenced to hard labour, and of those remaining at liberty feeling conscious that a similar fate awaited them.

As a final cause of the improved state of affairs, they added: 'And also to the weavers finding that they could not satiate the vindictive feeling of leaving their work to rot on the looms while they went to jail as the clothiers in all cases have recovered the possession of their property where the wives or friends of the weavers refused to complete their work.'

The justices' grammar may leave something to be desired, but their sentiments are clear; and, as is often the case when respectable men hurt their fellow citizens, they were careful to point out how noble they had been. 'We hope Sir', they wrote, 'that you will give us credit when we assure you that our duties have been far from enviable on this occasion. We have a very delicate as well as a very painful part to act.'

'We have', they concluded, 'weighed our justice impartially, eighteen weavers in jail, one master fined £20 for breaking the law relating to truck.'

The Home Office was impressed, and withdrew from its earlier somewhat critical attitude. 'Mr Peel', they wrote, 'is well aware that your duties have been arduous, but he is convinced that they would have been more so if you had not taken the determination to pursue the straight path of administering the law equally to all parties.' Was there a touch of irony here?

Three years later, in 1825, the Gloucestershire weavers struck for increased rates, saying that the new twilled cloths which were being introduced took longer to weave. The manufacturers in the Uley district, where broadcloths were still mainly made, increased their rates and then joined forces with the workers to make the Stroud clothiers do likewise. After a struggle lasting four weeks their efforts were successful. This action of the weavers revived all the apprehensions of earlier years, and as though confirming them a further strike began in 1829. The strikers had chosen their ground well, refusing to work for two clothiers who paid partly in truck. Most of the clothiers

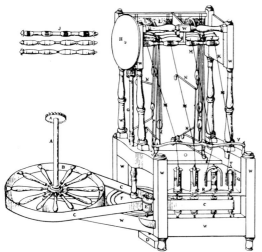

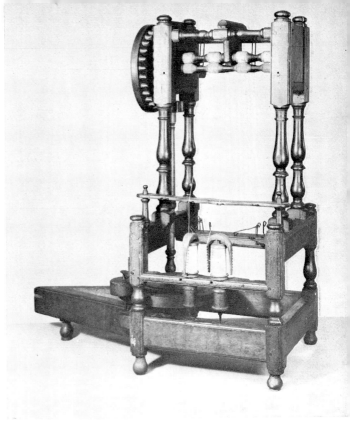

40 *Arkwright's Water Frame. Technical details*
This sketch illustrates the technical background to
the machine.

41 *Arkwright's Water Frame, 1769*
The first practical development of roller drafting.
The rollers can be clearly seen, also the differences
in covering between the top and bottom rollers.

42 *Hargreaves' Spinning Jenny* (below)
This was a model of the developed form of the
spinning jenny. Hargreaves' original machine,
*c.* 1764, was much smaller.

43 *Hand Winding*
These winding wheels are sometimes confused with spinning wheels.

44 *Hand Loom*
A typical narrow hand loom, as used for weaving cassimeres, *c.* 1850.

were reasonable, and at a meeting held at Stroud, while expressing abomination and horror at what they called secret societies – their name for the early trade unions – they passed a strong resolution against truck payment. The workers also demanded the abolition of shop looms, but they failed to carry this point; Mr Sheppard of Uley said that about half the weaving in Gloucester-shire was done on them, but this proportion probably did not apply to the whole of the West Country. Mr Sheppard, in a letter to the Home Office, appears to have painted a grim view of what was happening. He said: 'Nine out of ten of the whole body of operatives in every department of the woollen trade were sworn and entered and a very considerable number of shopkeepers, trades-men, artificers, etc. in all twenty thousand persons in this county'. Later that year the Government sent down Francis Fagan from Bow Street to enquire into the whole business, and he sent back a vivid description, complete with swords, masks, scarves and turbans. But taken as a whole, this later series of strikes never worried the Government as did those in the first years of the century.

The next ten years finally subdued the last traces of any fighting attitude in the weavers, and the workers interviewed by the two commissioners, Miles and Austin, were so downtrodden that not even a nineteenth-century Government could feel that they were dangerous.

The monumental report of the Handloom Weavers Commission, 1839–40, can bring this account of the Industrial Revolution in the West of England to a fitting close. The Assistant Commissioners for the South-west were A. Austin for Wiltshire and Somerset and W. A. Miles for Gloucestershire. Miles gives more details, but Austin's reports make the more interesting reading. He explained that having arrived at any particular town he first called on one or more of the most influential manufacturers, whom he noted were sometimes magistrates, to consult with them as to the best mode of conducting his investigations, so as to obtain the greatest quantity of information with the least disturbance to the tranquillity of the district. He found that great ignorance prevailed as to the object of his enquiry and, except among the weavers of Trowbridge and Bradford, a consider-able amount of apathy regarding it. In the end he overcame this, and his remarks were wise and just, and without departing from his position the presentation of his evidence suggests that he sympathised with the hand-loom weavers. He certainly did not accept at face value the stories of those who, like the relieving officer at Westbury, complained of the extravagances of the weavers, saying that they were bad managers who 'when they bring in their work are apt to drink'. He had known, he said, of instances of the wife working by day and the husband by night to get the work done quickly, but when they were in work they were not provident: the female spent too much on finery, the young men dressed smartly, thought of nothing but drinking and sweethearting, married very early, and, to cap all this recklessness, 'On Sundays some of the young men dress very gaily and have watches'. All this, it should be remembered, was accomplished on six shillings a week, which suggests they may have been extremely good managers.

Austin questioned one weaver about the early marriages. Why marry so young? The weaver said that he was compelled to do so in consequence of company keeping, as it was called. Company keeping was the custom of the place, and the result was generally a marriage.

The destitution of the hand-loom weavers was well illustrated by one piece of evidence given by Austin: 'That there is considerable suffering, and that many families are in a worse condition as regards food and clothing than the inmates of the workhouses, and they would willingly receive relief if it could be obtained as formerly at their own homes. The master weaver is worse situated in this respect than the generality of workmen are. He would not be received until he had sold his loom, and having done so his means of obtaining a living are gone and he becomes an inmate for life. That they have made great efforts to keep out, and have only been driven there by actual starvation, the following statement which was made to me by the master of a workhouse will amply prove. He was regretting that the nature of the food, its scantiness, or some other causes produced great mortality in the workhouses, but as for the poor weavers he verily believed that their children in some instances died of repletion. They had previously been brought so low that the workhouse allowance was too good for them.'

Austin concluded his report by saying that the weavers were worse paid, allowing for the hours they worked, and the great strength and activity required for the more laborious sorts of weaving, than were any other group of workmen. He had little to suggest by way of mitigation, but stressed the desirability of repealing the corn laws.

Mr Miles' evidence from Gloucestershire confirmed Mr Austin's. He was more detailed, and his many tables give valuable information concerning the cloth made and the size of the firm, all of which is of considerable technical interest. He was inclined to favour emigration as a cure, but most of the hand-loom weavers opposed the idea. As one of them put it, he 'preferred to live and die in old England but wished trade was better'. A few parishes, notably Uley and Bisley, both very badly hit by the depression, borrowed money for the purpose of organising emigration, and Miles gives an interesting statement of the cost of taking 60 people from Bisley in 1830. But emigration was never widely accepted and could not be taken up sufficiently to have any real effect on the position.

The state of the hand-loom weavers was one facet of the new way of life that was spreading over England. One of the few imaginative writers who realised something of what was happening was the poet Crabbe, and it is interesting to recall that he was vicar of Trowbridge for many years, dying there in 1832. But it is not to the poetry he wrote then that one has to turn to understand something of what the old hand-loom weavers suffered, but rather to his early Suffolk work. His account of the decline of the farm labourer might, with a few alterations, stand for that of the hand-loom weaver:

> He once was chief in all the rustic trade;
> His steady hand the straightest furrow made;
> Full many a prize he won, and still is proud
> To find the triumphs of his youth allow'd;
> A transient pleasure sparkles in his eyes,
> He hears and smiles, then thinks again and sighs;
> For now he journeys to his grave in pain;
> The rich disdain him; nay, the poor disdain:
> Alternate masters now their slave command,
> Urge the weak efforts of his feeble hand,
> And, when his age attempts its task in vain,
> With ruthless taunts, of lazy poor complain.

The only possible end, as for the hand-loom weaver, was the parish poor-house:

> Theirs is yon house that holds the parish poor,
> Whose walls of mud scarce bear the broken door;
> There, where the putrid vapours, flagging, play,
> And the dull wheel hums doleful through the day;
> There children dwell who know no parents' care;
> Parents, who know no children's love, dwell there!

> Heartbroken matrons on their joyless bed,
> Forsaken wives, and mothers never wed;
> Here, on a matted flock, with dust o'erspread,
> The drooping wretch reclines his languid head;
> For him no hand the cordial cup applies,
> Or wipes the tear that stagnates in his eyes;

The doctor arrives:

> All pride and business, bustle and conceit.
> A potent quack, long versed in human ills,
> Who first insults the victim whom he kills;
> Whose murd'rous hand a drowsy Bench protects,
> And whose most tender mercy is neglect.

But by the time he came to Trowbridge this kind of theme no longer attracted Crabbe, and in its place we have the carefully observed social theme as when the rich Danvers goes to visit his old love Phoebe Rayner:

> Meantime there rose, amid the ceaseless din,
> A mingled scent, that crowded room within,
> Rum, and red-herring, Cheshire cheese and gin;
> Pipes too, and punch, and sausages, with tea,
> Were things that Richard was disturb'd to see.

No writer deserved success more than Crabbe, and one likes him whether he is enjoying ministerial claret with Canning, flirting with Caroline Lamb or receiving a fat cheque in John Murray's office in Albemarle Street. Yet one cannot help regretting a little that all the events at Trowbridge – the riots, the strikes, and the poverty of the hand-loom weavers – did not excite his imagination and so give us a poet's version of the theme. We know that he was friendly with several of the leading clothing families, the Clarks, for example, and the Waldrons. One wonders whether he talked much to his poorer parishioners. Perhaps he felt he had done all that before, and poverty was much the same whether in Suffolk or in Wiltshire.

Considering the deplorable conditions described by Austin and Miles, it is surprising that hand-loom weaving still lingered on for another thirty years. In his young days in the factory the present writer often talked to old people who could remember their parents working at the hand-loom. His own great grandparents were among the last at Broughton Gifford, where the final decline has been described by the vicar there, Mr Wilkinson. A Stroud clothier has also memorably described a hand-loom weaver: 'His battered old beaver top hat, which he almost invariably wore when coming to the mill in his best clothes, a truly pathetic figure, and I can to this day remember the keen disappointment on his face when told there was no yarn for him to take home.'

**Postscript** *The nineteenth century*

DURING THE EARLY YEARS OF THE NINE-teenth century conditions in the woollen trade were dominated by the economic tension generated by the Napoleonic wars, best illustrated by the physical difficulties of obtaining adequate supplies of raw material. Otherwise trade was good, profits relatively easy, and as prices rose there was a great demand for cloth – in short, everything built up for the inevitable slump that was to come. Prices of Spanish wool certainly rose sensationally. The next decade, 1812–20, was different, with raw material coming down in price.

It was during the period after 1825 that the West of England trade really began to decline. Bradford, for example, was badly affected, and the large mill at Staverton was continually having trouble. In Trowbridge, however, trade continued to expand a little. It is a minor mystery why Bradford, where the cassimere trade began, never made real progress with these cloths, but instead allowed Trowbridge to take them over, as it were. They were lighter-weight cloths, more approaching the worsteds of the future, if only the clothiers had read the signs. It should have been clear to all that the days of the old broadcloth, whether made from British or Spanish wool, were numbered. Men were no longer going to wear the heavy, long, broadcloth coats decorated with embroidery that were so fashionable in the eighteenth century. A lighter-weight cloth was needed, preferably one which showed some sign of design in its structure. For a time, therefore, the cassimere with its neat twill effect was popular. The West Riding also made these cloths, and, in particular, increased the design appeal by printing on them, an idea the West rarely adopted. The firm of Clark's have patterns of a few printed cassimeres, but they are not very attractive. It is possible to draw obvious comparisons between the position here and that in East Anglia two centuries before. To some extent the comparative success of the cassimere trade in the West was itself misleading because it only needed the successful development of fine wools to show clearly that fine cloths of this nature were better produced as worsteds. As yet, however, the fact that fine wools were mostly short and early attempts at machine combing were unsuccessful, strengthened the view that the future of fine woollen cloths remained bright.

122

As late as 1825 the general position of trade in the West of England was rather confusing. Its failure to survive in north Wiltshire had brought about a very definite division between the Gloucestershire and the Wiltshire section of the trade. In Gloucestershire conditions remained static, without either progress or decline. In Wiltshire one had the contradictory position of good and expanding trade in cassimeres but dwindling business in the traditional broadcloth. Trowbridge illustrates this point well: nationally it was, and indeed remained until 1850, quite an important town, ranking about fiftieth in population rating, which means that it could compare with, say, Rochdale or Oldham today. It was, incidentally, for a period, the largest town in Wiltshire, having overtaken Salisbury where a long-established wool textile trade was in its final decline; but it was itself destined before long to be overtaken by the new railway town of Swindon. Bradford, on the other hand, had declined considerably. After 1850, under pressure from the new worsted cloths all fine woollens, whether derived from the cassimere or the newer fancies began to decline. Contemporary pattern books show how desperate was the search for new cloths.

As yet there were comparatively few signs of the competition from the new low woollen trade, which was soon to be a dominant theme in Yorkshire, and it was only a little later that some mills in the West attempted to compete in this field. Bearing in mind the important part the low woollen trade played in the history of wool textiles in the nineteenth century something more should be said about it, for it still awaits its historian. As worsteds came increasingly to dominate the picture as far as the finer types of cloths were concerned, the woollen manufacturer who wished to retain a bulk business had to attempt to bring the price down, which was particularly difficult before 1850 because there was a continual scarcity and consequently high-priced fine wool. Prices rose steadily, and in 1850 wool was very expensive. Afterwards the Australian supply really caught up with demand, conditions changed, prices came down, which of course was of equal benefit to both worsted and woollen manufacturers, and after 1870 wool was a very cheap commodity. In the meantime, however, the low woollen fabrics made from torn-up rags had become established. All types of rags were used – the first was unfortunately called shoddy, and a later type was mungo. Several firms in the area, including the mill at Staverton, tried to make a success of this type of trade, but all of them failed and low woollens were never manufactured successfully in the West of England.

Technologically, the fifty years between 1800 and 1850 saw the final switch in imported wool, the Spanish being replaced by the German which dominated the trade between 1820 and 1840 – giving a new name, Saxony Suiting, to one of the area's cloths – and finally Australian. No English wool, except perhaps an occasional fine Rylands, could compete with these wools.

As far as yarn-making was concerned the switch to the factories did not produce the technical advance that might have been expected. Important changes did take place: the jenny was slowly replaced by the self-acting mule, which derived from Crompton's crucial invention as improved by Roberts, but in its woollen form made no use of roller drafting. But the break in continuous production after the carding machine still remained. The 48-inch wide slubbings were still laboriously pieced together by hand before being drawn out on the billy ready for the mule. There is no sign of the use of any form of condenser before 1850.

Tradition has it that the first power-looms were introduced into the area at Staverton Mill in 1830, and this may well be true as this firm was always among the first to introduce new machinery. If so, it does suggest that the owners there probably introduced the power-loom too soon. The Sheppard family at Uley in Gloucestershire may well have done the same.

Many attempts had been made in the Lancashire cotton trade of the first decade of the nineteenth century to produce power-looms that would bring about the same revolution in weaving as the work of the great early inventors had done for spinning. It is not always appreciated that it took a long time to make a success of power-loom weaving, and any attempt to maintain that power-loom weaving and the Industrial Revolution in Lancashire were closely connected is a mistake. Machine spinning, not machine weaving, created the Industrial Revolution in the textile trade. None of the later attempts to produce a power-loom warrant a description in an essay of this kind. There was no inventor of the first order in the field. The most significant for the future was the power-loom made by William Horrocks of Stockport, but it did not contain anything really new. However, by means of this loom and other adaptations and variations, the number of power-looms used in the Lancashire cotton trade slowly increased. There were two thousand in 1813 and fourteen thousand in 1820. There were, as yet, hardly any power-looms in use in the woollen trade. Woollen yarn was much weaker than cotton yarn, and the greater strain arising from the use of power meant that there was no real gain in changing from the hand-loom. Indeed, there is evidence that some woollen firms who attempted to use power-looms at an early date found them a financial embarrassment. Some manufacturers attempted to bring the weaving into the mill so that they could have closer control over it. But they still continued to use hand-looms.

After 1820, improvements in power-looms in the cotton trade continued, and one of the main inventors making their wider use possible was the distinguished engineer Robert Roberts, whose work on the mule was the culmination of mule spinning development. Roberts was a great engineer rather than a great inventor, and the fact that it was he that did so much towards the final development of the loom meant that when it finally replaced the hand-loom the power-loom tended to be a power-driven hand-loom rather than a really new invention. Roberts introduced several new details. He had two shafts, the main one driving the beat-up while the other drove the shaft, but this idea was not retained and later looms went back to having one main shaft. More important was Roberts' successful development of an automatic weft stop motion which stopped the loom when the shuttle was caught in the shed, or when the weft was missing. His loom spread fairly quickly and was widely used in France, where there had been several earlier but unsuccessful attempts to make a power-driven loom.

Other improvements followed but none involved matters of real principle, all being simply improvements in detail. They resulted in a reasonably efficient power-loom for the plain trade and these slowly ousted the hand-looms in the cotton industry, thus the monumental reports of the Parliamentary Commission on Hand Loom Weaving in 1839 showed the financial plight of the hand-loom weavers of Lancashire. The woollen trade followed behind, and at the time of the enquiry a considerable amount of woollen weaving was still being done by hand although it was clear that here also the future lay with the power-loom. Hand-loom weaving continued for woollen cloths to a limited extent as late as 1870, but the period 1850–70 really marks the final decline of the hand worker.

There are from this time onwards various new kinds of evidence about trade and the lives of the work-people, not least the personal accounts of the last hand-loom weavers themselves, whose difficult last days remained a vivid memory for some who were still in the trade. My own grandmother often described to me her childhood days when she would quilly wind for her parents. When there was work the father would weave during the day and the mother at night, or *vice-versa*, so that the piece would be woven quickly and their turn, after the traditional waiting, would come round again that much sooner. My grandmother herself went into the factory, but her parents never did.

Certainly the hard conditions of the hand-loom weavers, with the drudgery of the early factories, left a permanent mark on their children. I remember in particular my grandmother's fear of becoming a pauper, though with her various skills and continual hard work there was never much risk of this for her or her family. But to go to Semington Workhouse was the final despair, an idea doubtless partly based on the hand-loom weaver's knowledge that he could never receive poor relief unless he had sold his loom. Equally vivid is the occasional report in the local paper, and one in particular stands out in my mind of a hand-loom weaver who committed suicide in Trowbridge: his son, at the inquest, described how he had become depressed because he was always being given bad work, in other words difficult warps that would not go into the power-looms.

Even at this late date there is little to suggest that the West of England really lagged behind the West Riding in introducing new machinery. In any case there were comparatively few important developments in the second half of the nineteenth century. In attempting to assess whether an area was keeping itself relatively up to date in this way various lines of research can be adopted, but perhaps three are particularly valid at the period. Firstly one might look into the question of how far any particular firm had gone in introducing the condenser. The condenser did away with the awkward hand-piecing of slubbings. There were two types, the ring doffer and the tape; the former had been invented in America around 1825 but it was never widely used elsewhere until a much later date. The other type, the so-called tape condenser, was a continental invention. Both types were satisfactory and finally made the whole woollen spinning system continuous. When Salter's of Trowbridge rebuilt in 1862 they claimed they were one of the first three firms in Great Britain to introduce condensers. The old hand-piecing methods had certainly lingered on. Secondly one might take the question of the power-loom, though as already indicated there appears to be nothing to choose between the West Country and Yorkshire in this respect. Finally, there is the question of the steam engine, and in this aspect it is at least arguable that the West was as advanced as most. There had, for some time, been a considerable number of them purchased from Mr Haden, who had come to Trowbridge as a representative of the well-known firm of Boulton and Watt. He was so struck by the possibilities of introducing steam engines to the woollen industry of the area that he stayed and went into business on his own account and greatly prospered.

The more one considers these questions, however, the less it appears justifiable to infer that there was any real difference in the rate at which machinery of any kind was introduced in the two areas. And it is worth noting that at the time there were in the West a number of machine makers with good reputations, some of whom were responsible for introducing new ideas. Among them mention may be made of Moore's wool dryer which is often photographed in early technical books as being the best machine available. Among carding machine makers the firm of Apperly in the Stroud area had a high reputation, and the work they did on the intermediate feed that went by their name is well known in the trade; it was used in the West of England until recent times. Earlier, Lewis of Brimscombe had been a distinguished maker of cutting machines. Ferrabie and Clissold made good carding sets; Rawlings of Frome were well known for their card wire and remain so today. Most of the other firms have not survived, but this is due to the decline of the cloth industry and not to the quality of the machines.

All the firms of importance purchased steam engines from Haden. Clark's, for example, used one for years and still possess a model of it. Salter's had one, and in the Stroud area Marling and Evans operated another.

Hand-loom weaving was still used for a few very difficult cloths, for example the trousering and vesting, which remained a speciality of the area, but the power-looms were used for the more easily woven cloths. For a time looms made by West Country machine makers, notably Millwards, were widely used, but they had disappeared by the end of the century to be largely replaced by looms from leading Yorkshire loom makers, such as Hattersley and more popularly Dobcross, a great favourite in the area.

A clear recollection among the textile workers of the West was the long walks that the final moving to the factories involved. Much of the hand-loom weaving, particularly of the last survivors, had continued to be done in the villages, whereas the new factories were mainly in the towns. My own great-grandparents were living at Broughton Gifford when the final end came to hand-loom weaving. They had to walk along the canal towpath to Bradford, a well-recognised route which meant five to six miles and the same back each morning and evening. As the working day began at 6.0 a.m. and ended at 8.0 p.m. their hours at home were certainly very limited, and some of the workers slept during the week on the factory floor beside their machines, only going home at the week-end.

The great technical change of the second half of the century was the complete mechanisation of yarn-making already mentioned. One result of this development was that it became possible to take the condenser sliver from the carding set much smaller – that is, less weight per unit length – than had previously been the case, and as a result drafting in spinning was reduced by something like 50 per cent. In the case of the older cardings, as supplied to the slubbing billy, ratios had been different. And here sliver might be 2s or 3s to give a final yarn of 16s, whereas now under the new arrangement the sliver would be about 9s.

Incidentally, yarn sizes were and are reckoned in terms of the number of hanks of a unit length that will weigh one pound. In the West of England the basis was the number of hanks of 320 yards that weighed one pound. Each woollen area had, and still has, a different system. On the other hand the worsted trade had only one, the number of hanks of 560 yards that weighed one pound, and the importance of the worsted trade is clearly indicated by the fact that this numbering system was transferred back, as it were, and used for describing wool. To say wool is 64s quality means that its limit spinning range is to a yarn of the fineness that 64 hanks of 560 yards would weigh one pound.

The new spinning routine considerably reduced the production of the carding set, but it also reduced the processes by cutting out the billy and was therefore quite acceptable. It was fiercely attacked by leading technical writers who said that the basic structure of the woollen thread was changed. Vickerman, who wrote with a vigour unusual in textbooks, said: 'Our present condenser thread is utterly unworthy of its name, it is a tissue of fibres that are not half formed into a thread, indeed it has only received a quarter of the drawing necessary to constitute a thread; it is only a crude conglomeration of fibres without form or void'; and more moderately: 'we cannot produce the finer super West of England broadcloths as in days gone by, from our present condenser thread'.

There was a certain justification for what Vickerman wrote, because the system previously used meant that the wool fibres in the sliver were, to a large extent, laid at right angles to the lateral direction of the yarn. With the new system of condensing there was a large degree of straightening. There is no doubt that Vickerman is correct in saying that heavily fulled cloths could not be produced so well with the newer type of yarn, but as heavily fulled broadcloths were out of fashion this did not really matter.

Consequently by 1875 the West of England cloth trade was at last entirely mechanised and the old cottage industry had finally disappeared. Everybody worked in the factories, but in many departments, notably the carding and spinning, and above all the finishing, the high degree of craftsmanship remained.

The final decades of the nineteenth century were depressing years for the West of England trade. Many times the industry virtually vanished. In Bradford, for example, by 1900 only one mill was left, and this last survival of a once prosperous industry closed shortly afterwards. During the same period several mills closed down in Stroud and Trowbridge, where at the end of the century only six were left. One of these shut down shortly afterwards. The Staverton mill also finally ceased to be a woollen mill. Gloucestershire did rather better than Wiltshire.

Generally speaking, these years marked the final success of fine worsteds. Even the last standard produce of the West Country mills, the striped trousering, was no longer in great demand. A few fancy cloths, such as vestings, remained the chief trade.

Some experiments were made with worsteds, and Laverton's of Westbury had some success. They bought worsted yarn but secured an excellent name for their cloths by good designing and excellent finishing. Further South, in the old Somerset–Devon border area, Fox of Wellington made a complete change and introduced both worsted combing and spinning machinery. They became in fact one of the few completely vertical worsted mills in the country. No other West Country mill followed their example.

Elsewhere in Wiltshire the last Melksham mill, Matraver's, an immigrant from Westbury, shut down in 1899, and by 1900 only one mill was left at Chippenham, Pocock's, which continued until 1930. Similarly down the Wylye Valley the once-important mills at Heytesbury closed, and the last one was at Upton Lovell owned by Walker of Trowbridge. It ceased working after a fire in the early 'nineties.

Essentially the Wiltshire trade had become centred on Trowbridge, and the Gloucestershire on the Stroud area, and we are reasonably well informed about this. The local press naturally dealt with it fully, and there are many surviving business records. In 1886 the US Consul made a full report which showed factory life in a very favourable light. His wage figures are interesting. He gave the average for a man at 23s a week and for women 12s 6d. Where both husband and wife worked, which was certainly common practice, he found the highest family earnings between 29s and 32s. These last figures seem rather high and my own impressions, from what I have heard from men working then, was that 16s would have been more accurate. Yorkshire workers would have been doing rather better.

There is hardly any sign of trade union organisation, but this was common to the whole woollen industry. Occasional strikes occurred, usually in response to individual grievances at individual mills, and they were settled locally with the chances loaded against the workers. There were occasional attempts to organise a more united trade-union system. Lady Dilke came down and spoke. After a strike in 1863 there was talk of a general organisation of the weavers.

1900 is perhaps a reasonable period at which to make a final survey of the changing pattern of the raw materials and manufacturing processes. With hardly any exception West of England manufacturers no longer used native English wool. Leominster wool, now the established Rylands, was not what it had been and no longer approached the Australian. Spanish wool, which for so long had dominated the fine wool scene, had likewise disappeared. For the very finest cloths, particularly the superfine billiards, German wool was preferred even to Australian. These fabrics were mainly manufactured in the Stroud Valley, and these wools continued to be used until 1939, when they came from Hungary. A few bales of this wool still appeared in the 'fifties, and the fibre, particularly the crimp development, was still different from the Australian. However, for every-day purposes, certainly for the trouserings, vestings and coatings, the Australian Merino was at least as good, and indeed had the advantage of being less dirty. Both wools have, of course, to be scoured, but yields of

German wools were exceptionally low mainly because the Saxony and Silesian sheep were often stud sheep and consequently kept closely confined.

Most leading West of England manufacturers therefore used mainly Australian wool, and this was a time when a great deal of it was bought in the London wool sales, which during the second half of the nineteenth century were the greatest wool market the world had ever seen. Visits to the London wool sales were regularly made, and prices were reported in the local paper. Never before or since have wool textile manufacturers had such an excellent spot market available on their own doorstep. And this position was maintained certainly until 1914 and even between the wars, although of course by this time considerable quantities of Australian wool were being sold in Australia.

Although all the processes had been mechanised their basis remained the same as before, and the underlying technique with a few exceptions remained as it was when done by hand. Indeed, the complete failure by the designers of the power loom to invent a really new piece of mechanism stands out as one of the main failures of the textile trade as a whole. One of the main curses of the trade has been that the power loom was only a hand loom driven by power. It contained no really new ideas at all. Similarly the mule, in its finally developed self-acting state, consisted simply of more and more processes being, as it were, piled on top of the other. In the end a machine was obtained which its defenders rightly claimed would spin anything and would also produce some remarkably fine yarn. It was equally a machine that could produce a great deal of bad yarn. The cop, which was the name given to the form in which the yarn was taken from the mule, shows it as a very ingenious and complex winding machine, but the very complexity causes considerable trouble.

It was still in the finishing that the West of England cloths really excelled, and as far as raised cloths were concerned no area produced anything to equal them. The high degree of craftsmanship in this respect continued for another 50 years.

Several of the larger mills were as well equipped as any in the country. Salter's, Clark's, and Palmer & Mackay in Trowbridge, and Marling's and Playne's in Stroud, certainly kept abreast of the best machinery that was being produced – not, it may be pointed out, a very difficult task, as the introduction of new ideas making a rapid replacement necessary certainly did not occur. There were many other firms, however, that were out of date and had changed little for many years. Machinery 30, 40 or even 50 years old was still being used. But one should add that this was equally true of other areas.

Mill buildings were at least as good as the West Riding. The early spinning mills had been rectangular, but the new mills that were built, the Home Mills of Salter's, Studley Mills of Clark's, Ashton Mills of Palmer & Mackay's in Trowbridge, the Abbey Mills of Bradford-on-Avon, and the Stroud mills of Marling's, Apperly's and Strachan's, were square solid buildings which architecturally appear more attractive than the contemporary, mainly square, building of Yorkshire.

To turn finally to the many and varied problems of the closely connected subjects of marketing and design, it is clear that when one looks at the woollen trade of Britain as a whole the dominating theme is the growth of the low woollen section of the industry. The increasing dominance of the worsted trade, particularly the way in which men switched to wearing worsted cloths, meant that the woollen trade either had to make speciality fabrics or turn to the cheaper cloths that could be made from wools that were not suitable for the worsted type of manufacturing. The woollen trade therefore, when it found itself losing so much of its trade to the new worsted industry, looked around for new methods and new markets, and in what some might consider an evil moment it decided that the answer lay in tearing up old cloths and respinning the short fibres into yarn from which a fabric of sorts could be made.

To some extent this development was the result of two quite distinct trends. First of all the greatly increased population of the country was demanding ever increasing quantities of cheap cloth, and in addition the middle of the nineteenth century saw the beginning of the ready-made garment industry of Leeds which, in the twentieth century, was to play such an important part in the wool textile industry. Relationships between the low woollen trade of Yorkshire and this new clothing industry have perhaps been rather overlooked by writers. On the other hand, when the low woollen trade first began there was another economic reason for its growth, namely the shortage of raw material. Actually the shortage of wool, which had indeed been a dominating theme in the first half of the century, disappeared during the second half when the vast growth potential of Australia was realised.

The comparative glut of wool during the later years of the period considerably affected prices. Wool had been expensive in the middle years, then began to fall during the last years of the century, when the wool growers certainly had a difficult time. Continually falling wool prices meant stock losses for most manufacturers, particularly as falling prices usually meant short order books, and the impossibility of avoiding an under-sold position. With rising prices the reverse, of course, applied.

Whether any connection can be traced between wool prices and the fortunes or misfortunes of the area is, however, doubtful. Many fortunes have been won and lost in wool dealing, but the really risky occupations are those like wool marketing, where the merchant buys wool in, say, Australia and brings it to Britain hoping to sell at a profit, or the top maker, who carries out one single process and is consequently very much in the hands of raw material prices. A manufacturer of woollen cloth, unlike the worsted trade, usually effected all the processes in one mill. His wool would cost about a third of the total selling price, and therefore a 10 per cent. movement in raw material prices could hardly ruin him unless he continued to make miscalculations. On the other hand, rising prices, like those of the early decades of the century, were particularly useful for a successful (i.e. busy) manufacturer. Long order books allowed him to keep both his workers and his plant fully employed.

As indicated, the worsted trade, where several people handle the material during cloth-making, was and remains more vulnerable. But during the nineteenth century, price movements, although considerable, were hardly drastic or of the dramatic nature of the 1922 and 1952 movements, and did not have any great effect, although this does not mean that the long-term effects of raw material prices and their reaction upon the liquid resources of an industry should be ignored.

The low woollen trade brought a real prosperity to some sections of the Yorkshire trade, and the mills of Batley and Dewsbury were famous for their low-priced cloths. Such firms as J. & T. Taylor of Batley and Mark Oldroyd of Dewsbury were founded about this time, and their reputations became world wide. The West of England manufacturers, struggling to maintain a high class trade, were naturally inclined to look with envy at what appeared to be the real prosperity of this new woollen trade and were often inclined to enter the field themselves. Some tried, but with little success, and as a whole the West of England never really made much headway in manufacturing this type of fabric. In 1865 a group of businessmen raised money to start a rather similar type of business at Staverton. Their prospectus suggested that they had very revolutionary ideas and were intending to by-pass both spinning and weaving by making felts. All who have studied the wool trade know that a fabric of sorts can be made in this way, but in the past it has certainly not been suitable for wearing apparel.

The difficulty with felt-making has been obtaining uniform thickness in comparatively light-weight fabrics. For this reason pure felts are only used where a really thick felt is needed – felt hats, for example. Elsewhere a so-called woven felt is used, the cloth being woven and then very heavily fulled or milled, so that a kind of felt is obtained. These cloths have wide individual uses, and it is surprising that the West of England has not been more successful in capturing a larger proportion of this trade.

The success of the low woollen trade as compared with the fine section is sharply demonstrated when one sees how much more the former would spend on new machinery. The finest carding plants in England in the late nineteenth century were in the low woollen section.

Meanwhile, in the West of England the majority of firms continued to keep to their traditional cloths, but they had a difficult time. They managed to maintain certain markets, for example overcoatings are better made from woollen than from worsted yarns but as they are heavier in weight and call for much raw material they were ideal for the new low woollen trade. A useful trade was done in trouserings and vestings, but a study of the outstanding pattern books of J. & T. Clark shows clearly how many patterns and designs had to be made to keep the factory busy.

It is worthwhile digressing at this point to look at the one branch of the woollen trade that was able to keep relatively busy and prosperous without resorting to manufacturing low woollens. The growth of the high-class woollen trade of Scotland during the nineteenth century was certainly one of the most unexpected developments and the new history promised by Mr Gulvin is keenly awaited.

Woollen cloth had been made there for many years, but only for local consumption, and the trade as we know it began only in the second quarter of the nineteenth century. The early years were not particularly successful: in 1830 there is a report from Galashiels, which can be taken as the centre of the more important section of the trade, stating that the town was in a most disastrous state, at least twenty mills having been reported as failed, with a total loss of £30,000.

The sudden burst of life that came to this industry originated away from the actual mills, and this may have some relation to the West Country problem. A group of London merchant tailors, some of them Scottish, realised that there was a need for a new fashion in trouser cloths. Perhaps the West Country was showing nothing new in this field, which for so long had been their traditional trade. At that time the standard product of the Border trade was a black and white check worn by the shepherd. A claim is sometimes made that this standard check, now known throughout the world as the Shepherd's Check, received its name from the West of England firm of that name which manufactured at Frome, but in fact the name derives from the traditional Scottish use. It was also popular as a travelling rug. At the same time Sir Walter Scott, who was making all things Scottish fashionable through his Waverley novels, often wore a pair of checked trousers. He was much in the public eye as Sheriff of Selkirk and his home at Abbotsford was right in the centre of the Scottish tweed country. Other fashionable gentlemen, notably Lord Brougham, followed Sir Walter's lead, indeed Lord Brougham is said to have been called to the Bar wearing a pair of check trousers. All these influences helped the movement forward, and it later received an additional impetus from the Queen's liking for anything with a Scottish flavour.

There was certainly a well-concerted effort to launch the new idea. In the North, as in London, the merchants played a leading part. In 1830 Alexander Craig of Edinburgh received a definite enquiry for a coarse woollen black-and-white check stuff expected to be wanted for trousers by James Lock of London who owned a fashionable tailor's shop in Regent Street. It was probably due more than anything else to Lock's energetic promotion of it that the taste for shepherd's check trousers became so much the rage in London. It was a pity the West Country did not have a James Lock to popularise their products and, perhaps more important, advise them on what was going to be fashionable, but relations between West of England manufacturers and London merchants often appear to have been strained. In the Border trade variations in design were supplied as needed, and they were quickly adopted. Colour and weave were successfully combined and the word 'tweed' was happily coined – not incidentally from the beautiful river that runs through the border country but due to a mis-spelling of the word twill. It is worth noting that both the cassimere, which had done so much for the West of England, and the new Scottish cloths were made in the two-and-two twill weave. From London the demand spread to the provinces and soon no well-dressed man was without a Scottish tweed suit. Closer connections were established between manufacturers and London merchants, providing the continual interchange of ideas that is so necessary.

The growth of the Scottish tweed trade indicates the priority that must be given to design and colour. It will be suggested later that this was one of the main factors overlooked by the West. Not that insufficient designs were made, rather there were too many, but that they were made in the wrong type of fabric.

The modern concept of range-making and the consequent practice of selling before manufacture probably dates from the rise of the Scottish tweed trade. Too little consideration has been given to this question in the past. Did Stumpe, in Tudor Wiltshire, have his orders placed before he made the goods? And it is not clear what happened later. The evidence of Salter's pattern books is that cloths were often manufactured first and then sold, which must surely have been the case at Bristol Fair.

To revert to the new developments in Scotland, at first no ranges were made; new patterns were conceived by the merchants and tailors using ribbons, leaves, stones and heather for information – the idea that Scottish tweeds in their colour resembled the native heather has remained a living tradition. These designs were then made into pieces about forty yards long. Although some turned out quite well, it is not surprising that many of them were unsaleable. Apparently it was James Lock who suggested that patterns might be woven before pieces were actually put into work. Modern cloth manufacturers would certainly feel that he started something. Pattern and range making is today one of the curses of the trade. Nevertheless, some such development was obviously necessary, since design and its attempt to meet the need of fashion became the dominating theme with the wool textile trade. It is said, and understandably so, that Lock's suggestion met with little enthusiasm, but it was adopted and ranges several yards long became the normal way of showing patterns.

Because of native talent, or perhaps because they were first in the field, Scottish designs and therefore Scottish designers became accepted as the best in the country, even in the world. They were the envy of other areas, and many Scottish designers went to other mills, in both Yorkshire and, later, the West of England.

In local West of England newspapers, when bad trade is being reported, one meets more complaints about Scottish competition than about that from the Yorkshire low woollen trade.

Lock himself, advertising the new trend well on his invoice, 'tweeds in heather and granite colouring for shooting and deer stalking', combined snobbery with real demand to that degree we have come to know so well in the modern advertising world. Scottish manufacturers gave good support, combining quality and design: 'Spare no expense' a Hawick manufacturer advised in 1857: 'Resist all attempts to compromise'. And most firms were heedful of this, although towards the end of the century the temptation to compromise and lower standards was as pressing in the Scottish trade as in the West of England. It is possible that the Scottish manufacturers gained something by making a fabric from their native wool. The name Cheviot was slowly introduced, and without doubt the wool from the Cheviot sheep was one of the most attractive non-Merino wools developed during the nineteenth century. The West Country badly needed a similar new look.

In the West of England the proportions of home and export trade did not greatly change. There was a useful export trade with America despite all the problems caused by the tariff system there. But there is no doubt that, generally, the years between 1875 and 1900 were very bad, and the memories of various people from the cloth-making towns of the period are chiefly of weavers waiting – that is, playing for work, as they described it, and not knowing when the next warp would be available.

During these years the worsted trade continued to prosper. Laverton's of Westbury, even after buying their yarn, did reasonably well. Looking back, one is impressed by the way the worsted trade overcame the difficulties that had beset it during the earlier part of the century. There had been all the many problems connected with finding a satisfactory machine comb. The answer here came with a rush about the middle of the century. Lister produced his comb, and fought with great skill his legal battles. Holden followed with his invention; Lister, as with so many others, purchased it. Meanwhile, at Mulhouse the Frenchman Hielmann discovered a different method of combing which proved very successful with shorter fibres. But Lister dominated the scene. He was an outstanding entrepreneur using inventors like Donisthorpe and Noble for his own purposes. The modern structure of the worsted trade owes nearly everything to him. This success in machine combing fitted in excellently with the arrival in the country of the longer, slightly straighter, Merino wools of Australia, and the two led to the great success of the worsted trade with the consequent progress of Bradford and Yorkshire to dominance in worsteds. As a result, the men's suiting trade was irretrievably lost to the West of England, and has never been recovered. The ladies' trade, which later became an important factor in saving the industry from extinction, was not then available, few women wearing the type of fabrics that they do today.

It was during these long and difficult years between 1875 and 1900 that several long-established manufacturers finally dropped out of business. In Wiltshire, for example, the Stancomb family gave up in 1903, as had earlier the Webbs, the Waldrons and the Haywards, who had previously been in partnership with the Gouldsmiths at Salter's. And in all these cases the mill buildings passed to other uses. The Gouldsmith family, who had been particularly successful, found it possible to sell their mill. The Clarks continued to manufacture but, as the records show, made little money during these years. Brown & Palmer, who later changed their name to Palmer & Mackay, also prospered, whilst the newer firms of Kemp & Hewitt and McCall's began relatively successful careers. As a result, although the cloth trade declined it remained in 1900 the main trade of Trowbridge. At Bradford-on-Avon, however, there was no real success to set against the general decline, and the last mill closed in 1905. Five were then left running at Trowbridge, but all attempts to re-establish the Staverton factory failed and it finally, after a long and chequered career, began a new life working for a successful firm of milk converters.

From what has been said it is clear that by the end of the century the West of England played a relatively small part in the wool textile trade of Britain. It was no longer even second to Yorkshire, for Scotland had taken over that position. Inside the West Country the final extinction of Bradford as a cloth-making town left Trowbridge rather isolated, and the Stroud Valley area was at the time, with about 12 mills still running, of more importance.

# PART IV

## *Documents of the West of England Clothing Trade*

The selection of documents that follows is
intended:

(1) to illustrate certain facets of the West
of England clothing trade which have
not been covered in the text, and

(2) to print in part or whole, certain documents that are either difficult to obtain
or have before not been printed.

45 *Fulling Stocks*
Detail of heavy wooden hammer used for beating the cloth, which was placed in the pit below the hammer.

46 *Fulling Stocks*
Detail of gearing system which raised and lowered the hammer.

47 *Powerloom, weaving shed, c. 1900*
This complicated system of belting clearly illustrates the problems of power transmission experienced in mills of the period.

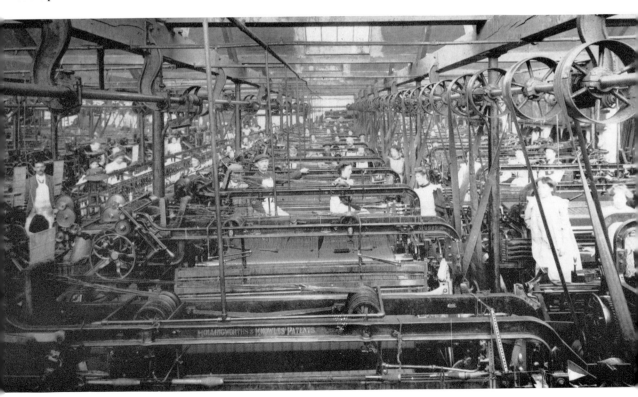

**48** *Cutting Shears*

The illustration clearly shows the wooden hand lever and the table with the curved top, usually called the 'horse', on which the cloth was placed. Although the shears were four ft. in overall size, they were operated by one man. The principle of the cutting shears had been in use since Roman times; early in the eighteenth century shears were replaced by cutting machines.

**49** *Cutting Machines, c. 1900*

These machines were a development of the early circular principle, from which the modern lawn-mower is also derived.

### The Guild Regulations of Bristol
(From: *The Little Red Book of Bristol*, ed. Bickely, 1900)

These regulations give the clearest picture we possess of the wool textile industry organised under the guild system.

#### Ordinances of the Weavers

Firstly that no drapery be made except it has six bondes in width. And if any one shall be convicted of less that drapery, whatsoever it be, be taken before the Mayor, and for every stone let him be amerced in forty pence for the use of the Commonality, and let the instruments of the weaver be amerced in five shillings and one penny to the Mayor and forty pence to the Alderman.

Also that no woof which is called abb be in the place where the thread which is called warp ought to be. And if it be found the cloth and the instrument on which it is worked ought to be burnt.

Also if the threads are deficient in the cloth, or are too far apart which the weavers called 'tosed', that cloth and the instrument on which it is worked ought to be burnt.

Also if the cloth be worse in the middle that at the sides, that cloth and the instrument on which it is worked ought to be burnt as before, or at the discretion and assent of the Mayor and other good men of the town he shall pay a fine therefore.

Also, if any of the weavers work at night let them be amerced in five shillings and one penny to the Mayor and forty pence to the Alderman, and if he be found so doing a second time let him be so amerced a second time, and if he be found a third time working at night he shall abjure his trade for a year and a day.

Also, if any instrument of the weaver, i.e. a Webenlam [loom], be newly made, although it be just there shall be paid for the Mayor's fee five shillings and one penny and for the Alderman's fee forty pence.

(The preceding ordinance is annulled on Wednesday, the Feast of the Apostles Symon and Jude – October 28th – in the Twenty-ninth year of the reign of King Edward III after the conquest – by Thomas Babbecary, Mayor, and all the commonality of their common assent).

Also that no weaver's instruments shall stand in solars (i.e. upper rooms) or in cellars only in halls and shops next to the road in sight of the people and if it be found otherwise let it be amerced in forty pence and notwithstanding let it be removed within fifteen days.

Also that the Mayor of Bristol cause all the weavers to be summoned before him and they ought to elect four aldermen who ought to supervise all that craft on their oath. And if they shall find anything contrary to the prescribed ordinances, so often as they shall find it they ought to show and faithfully present it to the Mayor.

Also that no weaver's instruments, to wit, a Webenlam [loom], coming from foreign towns remain in Bristol except they pay the fee to the Mayor and Aldermen as noted above.

Also that no weaver remain in the craft of weavers in the town of Bristol unless he become a burgess and be received into the liberty.

Also it is agreed that the instruments for making 'Osetes' in future be allowed provided they stand in the halls and shops next to the road in sight of the people. Likewise that they receive no woollen thread i.e. yarn, from any one but only from husbands and wives: and if it be otherwise found let it be amerced in forty pence. And nevertheless let it be removed within the next fifteen days. And if he offend again let him be amerced again as is aforesaid. And let such weavers be sworn before the Mayor to do these things faithfully.

Also that no woollen thread be sent out of the town to be woven except it first be seen in chain by the aldermen that it be of the width above said, that it is made in no other manner.

Also it is ordained and agreed that if henceforth any cloth be found in the town to be made of woollen thread called thrums he who shall be convicted of this shall lose the cloth for ever. And let the said cloth be burnt.

Also that each weaver make his own mark on each kind of cloth that he works that it may be known as his as well on his own cloth as on the cloth of others. And if anyone be convicted of this let him be amerced in forty pence for each cloth.

#### Ordinances for the Dyers

It is ordained and agreed that no cloth of pers be dyed otherwise than in the wool on the pain of forfeiting forty pence for each stone.

Also that no alum be used anywhere in the town except Spyralum, Glasalum and Bokkan. And that no Alum de Wyght or Bitterwos be used or employed in working, and that no one harbour any such kind of alum or purchase it. And if any be found with such kind of alum let him be amerced accordingly to the discretion of the Mayor and the other good men.

#### Ordinances for the Fuller

It is ordained that no man cause to be taken out of

K

the town any kind of cloth to be fulled which is called 'Raucloth' on pain of losing forty pence for each cloth.

Also that each fuller who receives cloth to full cause it to be well and properly dressed without any defect. And if the cloth be damaged by his fault let him thereupon make amends to the owner; and let him be amerced in forty pence (half a mark interpolated) the moiety to be paid to the commonality and the other moiety to the surveyor of the cloth appointed for that work. And if default be found more than three times that he forswear that work for a year and a day.

Also that no fuller cause or suffer any cloth to be taken to the mill before it be washed and dressed in the manner that is called 'wranghalved' on pain of forfeiting five shillings each time to the Mayor.

[There are a number of ordinances of a more general nature]:

No man dwelling in the town send outside the franchise of the town woollen thread to be woven elsewhere on the pain of the forfeiture of all the cloth without any pardon. (1381).

No one cause to be sent or taken out of the town oiled wool to be spun or combed except he suffer it to be fetched by those who ought to spin and comb it.

*Ordinances newly made for the fullers (1346)*
[Mainly concerned with the wages the master is to pay them]:

First that no man who is a master of the said craft pay any stallager, or to any other man working in the stocks but 3d. a day as well in summer as in winter and no more.

. . . The work men who work on land, to wit, at the perch, take 2d. a day.

Also it is ordained when a man goes to the stocks to the work which is called fulling that he take 4d. (altered to 6d.) a day.

No master to pay any women, who is called a 'Wedestere' nor may she take from any master but 1d. a day and for the half day a ½d. as well in winter and in summer.

[Further regulations attempt to guard against bad workmanship and are rather puzzling].

Also it is ordained that no master give any kind of cloth called 'Raucloth' by night or day to any workman of the craft for piece work except his own cloth on the pain of aforesaid.

Also it is ordained that no man send any cloth to the mill which is called 'Raucloth' and afterwards receive the said cloth from the fullers to finish on the pain abovesaid, and on the pain of paying to the surveyor of the said cloth half a mark.

Also that no fuller of the said town receive cloth which is fulled on 'oppelande' for rekkying, pleyting, or amending on the pain afore said.

(Oppelande = upland, i.e. the country as opposed to the town.)

(Rekkying is racking, i.e. tentering. Pleyting is folding or perhaps pressing.)

[There follows a further set of ordinances for the fullers dated 1381.

The stallager's wage is increased to 6d, those who work on land, to wit, 'at the perch', from 14 October to Ash Wednesday 3d, 4d, else. It is not clear why the separate rates are given, they had apparently been refused before.

The regulations relating to work being done outside the town are repeated – 'that no fuller receive cloth which is fulled outside the town for rekkying, pleyting or amending.']

*Ordinance of Weavers in the time of William Canyinges, Mayor of the said town 1389-90*
No master of the said craft shall give to his servant by way of covenant more than the third part of the cloth as has been customary before this time.

No one shall employ any servant in the said craft except it be by covenant for a whole year.

No master shall retain or employ any servant being claimed by or in covenant with, any other person in any way after that the master be warned and forbidden thereof by the said four aldermen.

*Ordinances as to the sale of cloth: Temp: Richard II*
Whereas before this time the petty custom of our lord the King of this town had been concealed in so much that cloths, half cloths and remnants have been sold in inns, chambers and in other places in secret, so that the offices of our lord the King cannot have notice or knowledge for demanding the customs and duties due thereof to our lord the King: It is ordained, agreed and assented by the Mayor, sheriff and good men who have the government of this town that all kinds of people bringing cloth to the town to sell shall put their cloths in a house within the court place of Thomas Danyell in Baldwin Street, which is appointed for the sale of cloth, and that the said cloths which may be offered for sale shall be openly exposed for sale twice a week that is to say every Wednesday and Friday in the said house and no where else.

*Ordinances of the Fullers: (1406)*
[A revision of the previous ordinances with the usual statement that the laws are not being kept, then]:

Also whereas certain merchants of Bristol have

before now been accustomed to full parcels of their cloth in divers parts of the country round about, the which merchants after the said cloths are so fulled seeing well that they are not able to be exposed for sale on account of the defaults in them without great amendment and labour of the fullers of Bristol, wherefore it is ordained and assented that henceforth no man of the said craft cause any such defective cloth so fulled outside the town to be fulled and amended on pain of paying . . .

. . . Saving always that the said masters have agreed at all times to be ready to amend with all pain and diligence all the cloths which shall be purchased between merchant and merchant to their satisfaction.

[This is an interesting ordinance, who were the merchants and what does the last sentence mean?]

*Ordinance for the Weavers: (1419)*
[To confirm the previous ordinances that are good and annul those that are bad. They seem to have confirmed them all but for the first time we find fines imposed for not attending processions and what may be called the civic duties of the craft guild.]

## The Laws of the Weavers and Fullers of Marlborough and Winchester.

(From: 'The Weavers and Fullers of Marlborough': Ponting, K. G., in *Wilts. Arch. Society Mag.*, volume LII, June 1949.)

The laws of the weavers and fullers of Marlborough and Winchester appear with those of Oxford and Beverley in the Liber Custumarum, The London Book of Customs, and were first printed in *Monumenta Gildhallae Londoniensis* edited by H. J. Riley, in 4 volumes. They appear in the Liber Custumarum immediately after an ordinance made in Edward I's reign, first the law of the fullers and weavers of Winchester, then those of Marlborough, finally those of Oxford and Beverley. It has since been shown that these were all taken from a much earlier manuscript now in the British Museum (additional manuscript 14252) which gives a great many documents dealing with the laws and customs of London, none later than 1209. The nature of the handwriting is of the last quarter of the twelfth century. In the Liber Custumarum the headings have been changed from Norman French to Latin, and the text is in some cases more intelligible.

It is easy to see the object of these so-called laws; that London Municipal Government in one of its many contests with the weavers and fullers thought it would be a good thing to have details of the way in which the craftsmen were treated elsewhere, and asked the authorities of these four towns for copies of their rules.

All four laws are similar in tone, and represent the weavers and fullers as being in a very oppressed condition. Marlborough is even stricter than the rest; there if they wished to forswear their craft and become freemen they must wait two years, and only in the third year if they have the wherewithal to satisfy the town authorities will they be allowed to forsake their craft and become freemen. At Winchester it was only necessary to forswear your craft, put your instruments out of the house, and pay for the freedom of the city.

All the laws have the same object in view; their aim is to keep the workers distinct from the merchants of the town. They can only weave or work for those in their own town. They are not allowed to build up a stock of cloth and thereby become a merchant. The point in the Marlborough laws about paying 3d or more for food is obscure. Mr. R. B. Pugh has suggested that the 3d limit may have been intended to prevent the richer weavers outbidding the freemen in some sort of black market. Was it, he suggests, a case of the medieval crime of forestalling?

Economic historians have differed considerably about the reasons for these diabilities. The early ones, Riley, Gross and Cunningham, thought it was because the weavers were aliens, but there is no evidence for this. Indeed, the more the cloth trade is studied the smaller the part that aliens appear to play in its growth. Especially is this the case in the West of England. Miss Bateson, in an often-quoted but surely unnecessarily harsh review of Leach's book on the Beverley documents, thought that the weavers and fullers already had their own powerful guild organisaion before the town received a charter, and therefore preferred not to take up the new franchise, thinking that they were already well enough safeguarded; later, however, when the town organisation became more powerful it began to impose these disabilities on the weavers and fullers because they had maintained their own old organisation. Professor Heaton, in his well-known study of the Yorkshire woollen and worsted industry (1920) rather agreed with this, but more recent research has tended to hold with Ashley in his pioneer work, and Leach in his introduction, that the town authorities tyrannised over the weavers and fullers as the first industrial proletariat. If this is the correct interpretation, it brings the position in England more in line with that in Flanders as explained by Professor Pirenne.

Probably the best explanation of these laws is given by Professor Carus-Wilson in *The Economic History Review*, volume XIX – 'The English Cloth Trade in the 12th and 13th centuries' – and here the stress is laid on the industrial status of the weavers and fullers:

'A close analysis of these laws shows that the majority of the clauses refer not to the legal but to the industrial status of the weavers and fullers, and that they are principally concerned with the economic organisation of the industry and reflect the subservience of the wage earning craftsman to the capitalist entrepreneur.'

Although we may not be certain how this occurred, there is little doubt that it was so in the late twelfth and early thirteenth centuries.

The late H. C. Brentnall, editor of the *Wilts. Archaeological Magazine,* was responsible for the translation. The Marlborough law was published but the Winchester translation was a private communication to the writer.

*The Laws of the Weavers & Fullers of Marlborough*
Be it known – that none may bear witness against any freeman. And if he buys his victual at the cost of three pence or more he shall pay his custom . . . for as much as he shall buy or for more. Nor may any one weave or work except for the good men of the town or have anything of his own to the value of one penny but what shall pertain to cloth making save as much as amounts to five ells of cloth for clothing himself each year. And if any one of them should become so rich as to covet the freedom of the town one year shall pass to see how he would make good without his crafts. And the second year he shall tender the whole of his years earnings. And the third year he shall forswear his craft to become a freeman if he does what is necessary for the good mens consent. And that they may engage in any trading he must remove all his tools out of his house.

*The Laws of the Weavers & Fullers of Winchester*
Namely; that no weaver or fuller may dry or dye cloth or go outside the town to effect the sale. They may not sell their cloth to any stranger but only to the merchants of the city. And if it happened that any weaver or fuller in quest of gain wished to go out of the city to make a sale, it is permissible for the goodmen of the city to take all his goods and bring them back into the city and deal with those goods as with goods that are forfeit, by view of the sheriffs and goodmen of the city.

And if any weaver or fuller sells his cloth to any stranger, the stranger loses the goods and the others remain in the mercy of the city for all that he possesses. Nor may the weaver or fuller buy even that which pertains to his trade unless he satisfy the sheriff each time. Nor may any freeman be impleaded by weavers or by fullers, nor may they bear witness. And if any of them grow rich so that he would fain quit his trade let him forswear it and all his tools he shall remove from his lodgings and so let him do all that the city requires that he may be of the freedom. And this law they have of the freedom and custom of London as they do affirm.

## From John Leland's Itinerary

(From: *Wilts. Arch. Society Mag.*, Vol. I, p. 132, etc.)

*Malmesbury* [of a small church not the abbey]. Weavers have now looms in this little church, but it standeth and is a very old piece of work . . . some say John the Scot was killed there.

The whole lodgings of the abbey now belong to one Stumpe, an exceeding rich clothier that bought them of the king. This Stumpe's son hath married Sir Edward Baynton's daughter. This Stumpe was the chief causer and contributor to have the abbey church made a parish church. At this present time every corner of the vast office that belonged to the abbey be full of looms to weave cloth in, and this Stumpe intendeth to make a street or two for clothiers in the back vacant ground of the abbey that is within the town wall. There be now made every year in the town 3,000 cloths.

### Bradford

Hall dwelleth in a pretty stone house in the east end of the town on the right bank of the Avon. Hall, alias de la Sale, a man of £100 lands by the year. There is a very fair house of the building of one Horton, a rich clothier, at the north east part by the church. This Horton's wife yet liveth. This Horton buildeth a goodly large church house at the east end of the churchyard without it. This Horton made diverse fair houses of stone in Trowbridge town. One Lucas, a clothier, now dwelleth in Horton's house in Bradford. Horton left no children. All the town of Bradford standeth by cloth making.

### Trowbridge

The town standeth on a rocky hill and is very well builded of stone and flourishes by drapery. Of later times one James Terumber, a very rich clothier, builded a notable fair house in this town and gave it at his death with other lands to the founding of two chantry priests in Trowbridge church. This Terumber made also a little almshouse and in it be six poor folks having three pence apiece by the week towards their finding. Old Bayley builded also of late in the town and also two miles out of it at a place on the way to Farley Castle. One Alexander is now a great clothier in this town.

### Steeple Ashton

Robert Long, clothier, has builded the north aisle, Walter Lucas, clothier, builded the south aisle at their proper cost . . . a very fair church builded in the mind of men now living.

## William Stumpe

[The development of the West of England broadcloth trade during the sixteenth century is excellently illustrated by the career of William Stumpe of Malmesbury. There are several references to him in contemporary literature; indeed, he almost rivals Jack Winchcombe of Newbury as the typical example of a successful businessman during Henry VIII's reign. The best-known account as given by Leland has already been quoted.

For his deeds at Malmesbury, Stumpe has been unfairly attacked by many scholars and antiquaries. If every rich man who bought monastic property from the king had preserved at least part we should be more fortunate than we are. The antiquary Fuller is an exception, and praises Stumpe for saving part of the church, characteristically wishing for more branches from such Stumpes who, by their bounty, 'may preserve the monuments of antiquity'. Stumpe's influence in seeing that the old abbey church became the parish church deserves more credit than it is often given. It is more difficult to forgive his destruction of the precious library, which had been started by Aldhelm a thousand years before.

The clothier's use of the abbey buildings as a loom shed was an innovation. He also negotiated an agreement with the city of Oxford to utilise similar buildings at Osney Abbey. Nothing came of this scheme, and it seems that government policy was becoming increasingly opposed to these new developments in the clothing trade, but Stumpe who was now looking more towards land investment, decided against expanding his clothing business. At Malmesbury his abbey house survives, a good example of sixteenth-century domestic architecture, but he does not seem to have carried out his plan for building a street or two for clothiers.

His other main appearance in English history comes from Fuller, who describes how Henry VIII, while hunting at Braden Forest, came with all his court to dine with him. The dinner was a great success, for as the antiquary remarks, 'great housekeepers are so seldom surprised with guests as vigilant captains with enemies. Stumpe commanded his little army of workmen which he fed daily in his house to feast on meal until night, which they might easily do without endangering their health, and with the same provisions did give the king and his court company, though not so delicious and various most wholesome and plentiful entertainment'. Fuller, alas, is not always an accurate writer, and we cannot rely on the truth of his statement, but the whole episode is typical of the Tudor monarchy, and shows how near in spirit Henry VIII was to the English people.

Some background to these picturesque accounts of Leland and Fuller is given by Canon Manley's researches contained in *Wilts. Notes and Queries,* volume 8, page 385, etc., but the material for Stumpe's biography remains scanty. According to Aubrey, his father had been the Parish Clerk at North Nibley, and was also a weaver until he at last grew up to be a clothier. William Stumpe was at Malmesbury before the dissolution, being a tenant of the monastery. During these years there are records of him buying land extensively, and he frequently appears on commissions; obviously a rising man, he was exactly the type that would be ready to profit from the dissolution shareout. Malmesbury Abbey surrendered on 15 December 1539, some of the buildings were appointed to remain undefaced, and of these Sir Edward Baynton had charge. Others considered superfluous were committed to the custody of William Stumpe deputy to Sir Edward. The clothier had already decided to get possession for himself, and would therefore have prevented the destruction of anything likely to be useful. Leland's visit was between 1540 and 1542, and Stumpe was licensed to use the abbey church as the parish church dated 20 August 1541. Four years later Stumpe's title to the old abbey buildings was secured by a grant which cost him £1,516 15s 2d. We do not know how much he had paid previously.

He married, in 1518, Jocoses (Joyce) daughter of James Berkeley of Bradley, and they had two sons, James and John. Later, towards the end of his very successful career, he married again, a widow Catherine Mody. They had a son William before the old clothier died in July 1552. His will is still in existence. He was M.P. for Malmesbury from 1529 to 1536 and possibly later.

His eldest son James married a daughter of Sir Edward Baynton and he was knighted a few years before his father's death. He was M.P. from 1555 to 1556, and in 1561 presented Queen Elizabeth with two greyhounds. He does not seem to have had any connection with the clothing trade, and his father left him considerable property in the nearby Cotswolds and surrounding country. After his first wife's death he rather strangely married her step-mother Isobel, the widow of Sir Edward Baynton. He died in 1562, leaving a daughter Elizabeth. She was a very wealthy heiress and married Sir Henry Knivett, an interesting man who fought for his country in France and Spain, and later became M.P. for Malmesbury between 1584 and 1587. Lady Knivett was mentioned in the midwife's deposition concerning the famous child murder at Littlecot, and there is a letter from Sir Henry referring to it. He was often in conflict

with Wild William Darrell and was very active in preparing for the Spanish Armada. Later he wrote a pamphlet on the defence of the realm in which he advocated conscription. They had three daughters who each married into noble families, those of the Earls of Suffolk, Lincoln and Rutland. Their grandfather might well have felt that they had completed his attempt to rise into the highest class in the kingdom.

The second son John probably intended to follow the clothing business, but there is little information about him. Perhaps the connection with the trade declined fairly quickly. It is clear that whereas until the middle of the century the dividing line between the wealthy clothiers and the country gentlemen was tending to blur, it afterwards widened and became quite distinct again. The Stumpe family, having become well established in the higher heirarchy may well have decided to forget the clothing trade.

Of the third son, the infant William, little is known; but if Aubrey is right, and he usually is, there was a William Stumpe, Rector of Yatton Keynell, 1621–66 who was the grandson of the great clothier. He must have been descended from the third son. Aubrey tells how he stopped the bungholes of his wine barrels with manuscripts from Malmesbury Abbey; presumably they were a legacy from his grandfather. His son Thomas had some extraordinary adventures in the Orinoco Valley, splendidly described by Aubrey. All this has no connection with the clothing trade, but suggests that something of the old clothier's spirit of adventure came out in a different way in the fourth generation.]

## Peter Blackborough

(From: Privy Council Records, Elizabethan, and Tawney and Power: *Tudor Economic Documents*)
[Blackborough's name first appears in Privy Council records in August 1575 when the Council wrote to the sheriffs and justices of the peace in Somerset saying that they had seen a letter written by them to the Lord Treasurer telling how Blackborough 'upon a statute made in the time of the late Queen Mary molested certain clothiers, whereof some inconvenience was like to ensure, they should call the said Blackborough before them and command him in their Lordships name not to proceed further, but at the end of the next term in the Star Chamber appear before them and inform them of the state of his cause, against the which time they should also command some of the clothiers to be there present to show what they can say to the contrary.'

Peter Blackborough was clearly a mischief-making fellow, probably a small clothier of Frome, who thought that spying on his more successful rivals might be a better proposition than following his own occupation. He certainly aimed his attack at the big men, and among the clothiers he indicted were Edward Horton of Bradford and Westwood and two members of the Long family.

In January the Council sent another letter to the local justices ordering them to examine fully Blackborough's complaints and 'to consider what is possible and convenient to be done, and what imperfection is to be amended in the statute that the same may be corrected at the next parliament'.

As a result of this enquiry, the Western clothing counties were exempted from the Act, but it is what follows that makes Blackborough's adventure particularly interesting. He seems to have satisfied the Council that he meant well.]

*8th May 1566* 'A letter to Sir John Thynne and Mr. Sherrington, with a petition enclosed to one Peter Blackborough, clothier, complaining against the abuses of clothworkers contrary to the laws of the Realm and for that the said Blackborough did desist from persecuting his suit against the said clothiers by their Lordship's letter and commandment, whereby he hath now lost that advantage of law against them by reason of Her Majesty's General Pardon, which, if he had followed his suit, he might have had, and for that the poor man had sustained great charges and expenses in following the said suit they are required to deal with the said clothiers of that country and to use all persuasions that they can to induce them to contribute some reasonable relief to the said poor petitioner, that such sums as they shall agree to pay must be put down in writing and to give order for the collection thereof at such time as shall be appointed, and after it is collected to deliver the same to the said Blackborough; and to cause a perfect book to be made and sent up to their Lordships of the particulars of such sums as every clothier of them shall so contribute that they may thereby know as well how he is recompensed, as what they be as do so contribute unto him'.

This ingenious idea appears to have been ignored in the Western counties, and the Council wrote repeating their instructions. The justices replied by asking whether all clothiers were supposed to contribute to the fund, or only those that Blackborough had had in suit. To this perhaps ironical question the Council answered that as all clothiers were really rogues all should contribute. Nothing else happened and several months later the Council complained that the matter must be attended to at the next Quarter Sessions or explanation sent giving the reason why not.

Meanwhile Blackborough, feeling his chances of getting anything from the clothiers were negligible, returned to the attack. He cleverly seized on the way the aulnagers neglected their duty. Since the fourteenth century they had been responsible for sealing cloths as being the correct weight and width. Their position had always been open to abuse. The Government was to blame because, from the start, it farmed out the post, consequently the aulnager regarded his job as one where, at all costs, a profit must be obtained. As the clothiers were prepared to pay handsomely for the opportunity of sealing their own cloths, the result was that by the early sixteenth century hardly any proper inspection was taking place. Blackborough's attack throws considerable light on the state of the trade and also shows that he was thoroughly acquainted with the position. He wrote a memorandum for the Council headed '*Objections Against the aulnager sealer, keeper of seale within the counties of Wiltes and Somerset and Gloucestershire ready to be proved.*,' which was printed in Tawney & Power: *Tudor Economic Documents*, Volume I, pp. 190–1. Blackborough pointed out that the aulnagers:

'1. Be not expert in cloth making (according to the statute), but contrary to the law do let the seal ferme unto clothiers that have mylles in their own hand. Whereby infinite abuses and deceits in cloth making are permissive.

'2. The aulnagers and sealers neglect the execution of their office in that they do not make due search of every cloth made to be measured both length and breadth being wet from the mill and before they be set upon the rack to be dried, but having the seal to farm and in their own custody to set to the seal before the cloths be measured accordingly, and thereby great defects in cloth making increaseth.

'3. The aulnager executed not his office, in that he causeth clothiers to set to his seal of lead into every of their cloths and kerseys in which seal the true and just length of every cloth and kersey should be contained. But suffered the clothier to permit the aulnager's seal without controlment or survey of the cloth be ordered accordingly to the text of the laws whereby such letting the seals to farm deceit in cloth making aboundeth and the aulnager forfeited his office.'

But the real gem comes at the end:

'Therefore Peter Blackborough desireth (in recompence of all his charge, time and trouble sustaineth) to be aulnager and sealer in the said three counties. Who being expert will not only execute the office duly but also pay £20 more in yearly rent for every county than heretofore has been paid.'

Comment on this perfectly worded application is quite unnecessary. The information given could hardly have been news to the council but they were interested in the scheme. The idea of satisfying Blackborough and adding £60 to the revenue was at first irresistible, but they hesitated before finally committing themselves. In any case Blackborough had not exhausted his resources for there is a later letter from the council to one of the local justices saying, 'that where there was attached by Peter Blackborough to Her Majesty's use 50 cloths belonging to Robert Howse and Henry Phippes he is requested to inform himself of their goodness and if they shall be found subject to forfeiture being not made according to the statutes of the realm in that behalf provided that then he call information to be given unto the exchequer to be there followed on Her Majesty's behalf upon the eviction of the owner then that the said Blackborough may according to the law obtain that portion of the said cloths as in such case is allowed.'

It seemed that even if his attempt to become aulnager failed that Blackborough might make a profitable career as an informer. For the moment he certainly enjoyed the council's confidence, and in September they were again writing to the local justices stating, 'that Her Majesty is informed that through not obeying the statutes trade is declining and thereby the workers are impoverished and Her Majesty defrauded of her custom. Her Majesty therefore wants them to call before them people who understand the trade, especially one Peter Blackborough who is trying his best to have things reformed, to examine the abuses and say how they can be mended'.

A report was to be sent quickly to the council. Once again, the local justices stalled; whatever they may have thought of the clothiers' honesty, however jealous they may have been of their prosperity, they had no use for Peter and resented his approach over their heads to London. This, indeed, was a point that anybody connected with or sent down by the central authorities always found difficulty in surmounting. The justices and the clothiers forgot their own squabbles in the face of what they thought was outside interference. The council repeated their request but in the face of local intransigence they were powerless. They tried again, saying it was really too bad nothing had been done for Peter, adding that he had told them that Sir John Thynne, Sir Walter Hungerford and Mr Sherrington had all read the letters but said nothing. The council protested that they could not understand this, and repeated their demand to know exactly what had happened. And there, as far as we know, the matter ended. Whether Peter did get anything is uncertain. Perhaps the clothiers in the end bought him just as they had the aulnager, regarding it as a legitimate trading expense. Whatever the case, one can still be grateful to Blackborough for throwing so much light on the detailed working of the clothiers' businesses.

## Letter from Charles 1 to Prince Rupert, 1642

(In possession of Messrs Strachans of Stroud)
Charles R.

Most trusty and entirely beloved Nephew Wee greet you well Whereas we are credibly informed that at Cirencester, Stroud, Minchinhampton, Tetbury, Dursley, Wootton underedge and Chipping Sudbury great quantities of cloth canvass and Locherame are to be had for supplying ye great necessities Our Souldiers have of Suits. Wee have thought good to advertize you thereof And doe hereby pray you to send a competent party of Horse under ye command of some able person to visit those several places wch lye not farr asunder, and to bring from thence all such cloth canvass and Locherame as they shall find there to Cirencester. Giving a Ticket to ye Owners for all ye parcells they shall take up and keeping a perfect Accompt thereof, and from what persons ye same was taken with this intimation that every one of them shall upon his repaire to Oxford receave such Security for his comodity as hee shall have noe cause to except against. For ye better ordering and managing of this Service Wee shall expressly send Mr. Nevill, Mr. Bradburne and Mr. Ball, men of experience, to take order for receaving and putting of ye cloth where of Wee intend ye best shall be reserved for ye service of our Troopers and ye rest for ye Dragoons and Foot of our Army. In this wee pray you to use you wonted diligence. And bid you heartily farewell, Given at our Court of Oxford ye first day of February 1642.
P. Rupert.

## J. Aubrey's Notes on Cloth-making and Economic History

(From: *The Natural History of Wiltshire* (ed. Britton, 1847; *Wiltshire Collections,* ed. Jackson, 1862; and an unpublished section from MSS. in Bodleian)

Slowly but surely John Aubrey, one time regarded as little more than a gossip, has become recognised as a first-rate archaeologist, and, an even greater claim to fame, as a great master of English prose. The manner in which nineteenth-century writers were inclined to take his best stories and then condemn him as a gossip is quite extraordinary. As far as his archaeological work is concerned, recent excavations have shown how accurate he was. As an economic historian he is, of course, less important, his interest consisting in the fact that his keen eye for the odd fact often helps us to understand some facet of the economic background which would otherwise have been obscure.

I have allowed myself the liberty of including a few of Aubrey's remarks about agriculture, though they have little if any relevance to sheep, and therefore to cloth-making.

### Agriculture

The wheat and bread of this county, especially South Wilts, is much indifferent; that of the Vale of the White Horse is excellent. King Charles II, when he lay at Salisbury in his progress complained that he found there neither good bread nor good beer. But for the latter 'twas the fault of the brewer not to boil it well; for the water and the malt there are as good as any in England.

### Inclosing

Anciently, in the Hundreds of Malmesbury and Chippenham were but few enclosures and that near houses. The north part of Wiltshire was in those days admirable for field sports. All vast champian fields as now about Sherston and Marshfield. King Henry VII brought in depopulation and that, inclosures; but after the dissolution of the abbeys in Henry VIII's time more inclosing. About 1695 all between Easton Pierse and Castle Coombe was a campania like Cotswold upon which it borders; and then Yatton and Castle Coombe did intercommon together. Between these two parishes much had been inclosed in my remembrance, and every day more and more. I do remember about 1633 but one inclosure to Chipnamfield, which was at the north end, and by this time I think it is all inclosed. So all between Kingston St. Michael and Draycott Cerne was common field and the west field of Kingston St. Michael between Easton Pierse and Heywood was inclosed in 1664. Then were a world of labouring people maintained by the plough as they were likewise in Northamptonshire. 'Tis observed that the inclosures of Northamptonshire have been unfortunate since, and not one of them have prospered.

### Sheep and Shepherds

As to the nature of our Wiltshire sheep, negatively they are not subject to the shaking. Which the Dorsetshire sheep are. Our sheep about Chalke do never die of the rot. My cousin Scot does assure me that I may modestly allow a thousand sheep to a tything, one with another, Mr. Rogers was for allowing of two thousand sheep, one with another, to a tything, but my cousin Scot says that it is too high.

The Britons received their knowledge of agriculture from the Romans and they retain yet many of their customs. The festivals of sheep shearing seem to be derived from the Parilia. In our western parts I know not what is done in the north, the sheep masters give no wages to their shepherds but they have the keeping of so many sheep pro rata; so that the shepherd's lambs do never miscarry.

### Cloth Trade

Query, if it would not be a better way to send our wool beyond the sea again, as in the time of the staple? For the Dutch and French do spin finer, work cheaper and dye better. Our clothiers combine against the wool masters and keep their spinners but just alive: they steal hedges, spoil coppices and are trained up as nurseries of sedition and rebellion.

This nation is the most famous for the great quantity of wool of any in the world; and this county have the most sheep and wool of any other. The down wool is not of the finest in England, but of about the second grade. That of the common field is the finest.

When Henry VII lived in Flanders with his Aunt the Duchess of Burgundy, he considered that all or most of the wool that was manufactured there into cloth was brought out of England; and observing what great profit did arise by it, when he came to the crown he sent it to Flanders for clothing manufacturers whom he placed in the West, particularly at Seend in Wiltshire, where they built several good houses yet remaining: I know not any village so remote from London that can show like. The clothing trade did flourish there until about 1580, when they removed to Trowbridge by reason of (I think) plague; but I conjecture the main reason was that the water here was not proper for the fulling and washing of their cloths; for this water, being impregnated with iron, did give the white cloth a yellowish tincture.

Memorandum: – In this country here about are several families that still retain Walloon names, as Goupy, etc.

The best white cloths in England are made at Salisbury, where the water running through chalke becomes very nitrous and therefore abstersive. These fine cloths are dyed black or scarlet at London or in Holland.

Malmesbury, a very neat town, hath a great name for clothing.

Sutton of Salisbury was an emminent clothier: what has become of his family I know not. John Hall, I do believe, was a merchant of the staple at Salisbury, where he had many houses. His dwelling-house, now a tavern [1669] was on the ditch where in the glass windows are many scutchions of his arms, yet remaining, and several merchant marks. Query, If there are not also woolsacks in the panels of the glass?

The ancestor of Sir William Webb of Oddstock, near Salisbury, was a merchant of the staple in Salisbury. As Grevill and Wenman bought all the Cotswold wool so did Hall and Webb all the wool of Salisbury Plain, but these families are Roman Catholics.

The ancestor of Mr. Long of Rood Ashton was a very great clothier. He built a great part of that handsome church as appears by the inscription there between 1418 and 1500.

William Stumpe was a wealthy clothier at Malmesbury at the time of Henry VIII. His father was the parish clerk of North Nibley in Gloucestershire, and was a weaver, and at last grew up to be a clothier. This clothier at Malmesbury, at the dissolution of the abbeys, bought a great deal of the abbey lands thereabouts. When King Henry VIII hunted in Bradon Forest he gave His Majesty and the Court a great entertainment at his house (the Abbey). The King told him he was afraid he had undone himself; he replied that his own servants should only want their supper for it. Leland said that when he was there the dortures and other great rooms were filled with weavers looms.

Mr. Paul Methwin of Bradford succeeded his father-in-law in the trade and was the greatest clothier of his time [Charles II]. He was a worthy gentleman and died about 1667. Now [James II] Mr. Brewer of Trowbridge drives the greatest trade for medleys of any clothier in England.

Stroud Water in Gloucestershire is a little commonwealth of clothiers and cloth workers not like in the nation. The water here is found by experience to be very proper for red or scarlet dyes, also black; in both which they do drive a mighty trade. The water here is run through an iron mine which is the reason it dyes red the better. Whereas the water at Seend was neglected because it burnt their cloths yellowish, let them consider the improvement and follow the example of the clothiers at Stroud.

Sherston Magna. On a tomb in the churchyard: Here lieth the body of Samuel Millard, clothier, who deceased the 27th day of June, 1667, aged 48.

Here lieth one who left his art
(First having sought the better part)
Although he made both red and white,
Yet in his own did not delight.
There are white robes of righteousness
His Savours works, this was his dress,
And though his own were ready made,
Yet none to those that will not fade
Now heaven crowns him, where all labours cease,
He long endured pain, but died in peace.

Melksham: – In the chancel is an inscription for Isaac Self, a wealthy clothier who died in 1656 in the 92nd year of his age, leaving behind him a very numerous offspring, 83 in number.

Fullers Earth, which they use at Wilton, is brought from Woburn in Bedfordshire, and sells for ten groats a bushel.

Old Mr. Broughton of Herefordshire was the man that brought in the husbandry of soap ashes. He lived at Bristol, where much soap is made, and the haven there was like to have been choked up with it considering that ground was much meliorated by compost, etc., did undertake this experiment and having land near the city did accordingly improve it with soap ashes. I remember the gentleman very well. He died about 1650, I believe near 90 years old, and was the handsomest well limbed, straight old man that ever I saw, had a good wit and a graceful elocution. He was the father of Bess Broughton, one of the greatest beauties of the age.

[As Aubrey's account of Bess Broughton is one of the masterpieces of his prose, it may perhaps be permissible to quote it]:

Mrs. Elizabeth Broughton was daughter of Broughton in Herefordshire, an ancient family. Her father lived at the Manor House at Canon-Peon. Whether she was born there or no I know not: but there she lost her maidenhead to a poor young fellow then I believe handsome but in 1660 a poor old weaver, clerk of the parish. He had fine curled hair but grey. Her father at length discovered her inclinations and locked her up in the turret of the house but she gets down by a rope; and away she got to London to set up for herself.

She was a most exquisite beauty, as finely shaped as nature could frame; and had a delicate wit. She was soon taken notice of at London and her price was very dear – a second Thais. Richard, Earl of Dorset, kept her (whether before or after Venetia I know not, but I guess before). At last she grew common, and infamous and got the pox of which she died.

I remember thus much of an old song of those days, which I have seen in a collection – 'twas by way of a litany – viz:

*From the watch at 12 o'clock*
*And from Bess Broughton's button'd smock*
*Libera nos', Domine.*

[Aubrey notes in the margin of his manuscript at this point] Barbara C.C. (that is the Countess of Castlemaine and mistress of Charles II) had such a one: my sempstresse helped to work it.

In Ben Jonson's execrations against Vulcan he concludes

*Pox take thee Vulcan! may Pandora's pox*
*And all the ills that flew out of her box*
*Light on thee. And if those plagues will not do*
*Thy wife's pox take thee and Bess Broughton's too.*

In the first edition in octavo her name is thus at length. I see that there have been famous women before our time.

I do remember her father (1646) near eighty. The handsomest shaped man that ever my eyes beheld, a very wise man and of an admirable elocution. He was a committee man in Herefordshire and Gloucestershire. He was commissary to Col. Massey. He was of the Puritan party heretofore; and had a great gift in praying etc. His wife (I have heard my grandmother say who was a neighbour) had as great parts as he. He was the first that used the improvement of land by soap ashes when he lived at Bristol, where they then threw it away.]

In King James's time Mr. Chaloner (of Hankerton, near Malmesbury) who was an ingenius gentleman who had been a traveller and had seen the alum works in Germany, driving and hunting in Yorkshire, discovered by the herbage and nature of the ground and of the taste of the water, that alum might be made there, whereupon he got a patent of the king and this work was worth £2,000 per annum or better; but in King Charles I time the profit was thought too much for him and notwithstanding the said patent the king granted a moiety or more to another, a courtier, which was the reason that made Mr.

Chalenor so zealous for the parliament and to be one of the king's judges.

The falling of rents as a consequence of the decay of the Turkey trade; which is the principle cause of the falling of the price of wool. Another reason that conduces to the falling price of wool is our women wearing so much silk and indianwear as they do. By these means my farm at Chalke is worse by £60 per annum than it was before the civil war.

*Fairs*

The most celebrated fair in North Wiltshire for sheep is at Castle Coombe on St. George's Day (23rd April) where the sheep masters do come as far as from Northamptonshire. Here is a good cross and market house; and heretofore was a staple of wool as John Scrope Esq., Lord of this Manor affirms to me. The market here now is very inconsiderable.

At Wilton is a very noted fair for sheep, on St. George's Day also; another on St. Giles' Day September 1st. Graziers etc., from Buckinghamshire come hither to buy sheep.

At Chilmark is a good fair for sheep on St. Margaret's Day, 20th July.

Burford, near Salisbury, a fair on Lammas Day: Tis an emminent fair for wool and sheep, the eve is for wool and cheese.

At the City of New Sarum is a very great fair for cloth at twelfth-tyde called Twelfth Market. In the parish of All Cannings is St. Ann's Hill, vulgarly called Tan Hill, where every year on St. Ann's Day (26th of July) is kept a great fair within an old camp called Oldbury. The chief commodities are sheep, oxon and finery. This fair would be more considerable, but the Bristol fair happens at the same time.

At Devizes several fairs, but the greatest is at The Green there, at Michaelmas; it continues about a week.

*Bradford-on-Avon*

This is a market town.

I would have the prospect taken of Mr. John Hall's house which is very fine. It is the best built house for the quality of a gentleman in Wilts. It was of the best architecture that was commonly used in King James I reign. It is built all of freestone, full of windows, hath two wings, the top of the house adorned with rails and balusters. There are two, if not three, elevations or ascents to it: the uppermost is adorned with terraces on which are rails and baristers of freestone. It faces the river Avon which lies south of it about two furlongs distant: on the north side is a high hill. Now I do conclude that if one were on the south side of the river, opposite to the elegent house, that there must, of necessity, be a good echo returned from the house; and probably if one stands east or west from the house at a due distance the wings will afford a double echo.

In this town is a fair old built house of the family of Rogers of Cannington, here are many old escutcheons which see; now it is the seat of Mr. Methwyn the clothier.

On the top of the north hill above Mr. Methwyn is the finest hermitage I have seen in England; several rooms and a very neat chapel of good freestone. This high hill is rock and gravel, faces the south and south west, and therefore is the best site for a vineyard of any place I know; better in England cannot be.

*Eminent Clothiers of the County*

Chivers of Quemberford, near Calne, whose racks remain yet in 1680, left an estate of at least £100 per annum. Was sheriff in 1642.

Benedict Webb of Somersetshire was the first that made medley cloth (before they were blues, greens, etc., coloured cloths) who improved the art and got a great estate by it (Charles I) His great grandmother, a sister to Whitely the last Abbot of Glastonbury. He was the greatest clothier in the town.

[Aubrey has a story about Henry II coming to Salisbury, and being presented with a piece of very fine broadcloth by Sutton, the clothier. Then follows a poem which is difficult to make sense of.] 'There was fine weaving in this prophecy which I cannot yet unfold'.

Aubrey further adds:

'He Sutton made his parliament robes, and the first parliament that ever sat in England (at Clarendon) was graced with the king's presence in these robes, in requital whereof His Highness afterwards granted Sutton many princely favours. This Sutton did much good at his death and did give £100 to be yearly lent to the poor weavers of the town to the worlds end.'

## Trowbridge Wage Rates

These commence with a copy, on paper, of an agreement proposed by the weavers and spinners of Trowbridge for their trade at the close of the year 1602, which was confirmed by the justices, and in 1605 was reconfirmed in a list in which the only noticeable variation is the insertion 'of cloths of 800' of the line: 'For weaving of a broad listed white of this marking 9/–.' This is followed by the first (on a parchment roll) of a series of orders signed by the justices, fixing the rates of wages of weavers and articificers in each year in which series, however, various years are wanting. In this first table, dated 3 May 1603, which will be seen to be specially full and minute in its particulars, a few lines in the heading have become entirely indecipherable through the wear of time. In 1605 the table is completed by the next item given below, which settles the wages of weavers not found in 1603. The annual order appears to continue the same rates unaltered up to the year 1654, except that in 1653 there are alterations in the husbandry wages. In 1655 a new table altogether is drawn up.

*1602*

'Trowbridge 30th December.'

The just proportions of the several works usually put forth by the Clothiers of the county of Wilts, both to the weavers and spinners with the valuation of the wages according as every sort of work do deserve by reason of the fineness of the wool and spinning of every sort of work. As also by reason of the hard working of every sort with the usual numbers of hundreds, beers and abbs, which is commonly put forth to weave every cloth, which is the best rule by which we can keep apportion, set down by us the clothiers of the said county.

| | | |
|---|---|---|
| **700** | Imprimis we think a weaver is worth to have for the weaving of a cloth of seven hundred. | 7 shillings. |
| | And for every beere above seven hundred and under eight hundred. | 2 pence. |
| | The spinning of these sorts of warp is worth per pound. | 2 pence. |
| | And the spinning of the abb is worth per pound. | 1½ pence. |
| **800** | Item one of eight hundred of white work is worth the weaving. | 8 shillings. |
| | And for every beere above eight hundred and under nine hundred. | 2½ pence. |

| | | |
|---|---|---|
| **800** | The spinning of these sorts of warp is worth per pound. | 2½ pence. |
| | The spinning of the abb is worth per pound. | 1½ pence. |
| | These sorts of broad lists are more worth than the narrow lists by the cloth. | 12 pence. |
| | The hanking is worth. | 12 pence. |

Scales also for nine hundred, a thousand, eleven hundred, twelve hundred.

A graduated rise in price varying from twelve pence in the case of a cloth weighing nine hundred pounds to two shillings for a cloth of eleven to twelve hundred pounds is awarded; for every beere one penny up to six pence and for every pound of abb above fifty four, and not above sixty, – eighteen pence and above sixty, twenty pence.

Clothiers signing were William Yerbury, Nicholas Phippe, John Usher, Walter Yerbury, John Yewe, Edward Cogswell, Richard Dycke.

Weavers signing were Hughe Watts, Henry Cappe, William Rundell, Henry Prior, Thomas Lavington, Batholemew Sleegge.

*1603*

Wages paid by the year for the journeymen of these occupations following with meat and drink. (Includes)

For a dyer, for a brewer, for a tanner, for a linen weaver. The cheapest to take by the year of wages not above fifty shillings and all other common work men of the same occupation of wage by the year not above forty shillings without livery.

| | |
|---|---|
| A woollen weaver. | |
| A tucker. | The cheapest of these to take by |
| A fuller. | the year of wages not above |
| A shearman. | forty shillings. |
| A cloth worker. | |

And every common work man of the same occupation to take by the year of wages not above twenty six and eight pence.

Further lists 1605. Similar.

*(Wilts. County Record Office)*

## Trowbridge Work-men Parade for more Wages

The information of William Brewer of Trowbridge, clothier, taken upon oath the 25th day of June, 1677.

Who sayeth that being in his house in Trowbridge the day aforesaid he heard an uproar in the street and going forth he saw a great company of men following after a fidler, and one of them made a kind of proclamation that;

'whosoever was of their side should follow them'.

Afterwards, hearing that they were at an alehouse near the bridge he went thither with the constables, where he heard Aaron Atkins say that he was the man that made the proclamation, and that the intention thereof was to engage as many as he could to combine for the raising of their wages 6d per week, and that Samuel Bowden and others affirmed the same and were with him in the street upon the same design, and Atkins said that he had a sword and wished that he had it with him.

Taken before William Brewer.

Samuel Bowden confessed that he was amongst the others today, and being demanded for what reason so many were assembled in such a manner, with a fidler before them and calling those that were on their side to come, sayeth it was to raise their wages to 6/6d. for working twelve hours in a day.

Signed J. Hall.<br>(Cunnington, pp. 259–60)

## The Westbury Weavers

1647 – 'The humble petition of the ancient weavers of the parish of Westbury sheweth that notwithstanding the manifold wholesome and good laws and statutes, which hath formerly been established for the preservation and ordering of the trade or occupation of weaving as that none should have liberty to exercise the same himself unless he hath served an apprenticeship therewith the full term of seven years and attained to the full age of twenty four. So it is now that divers who formerly hath been bound apprentices either to parents or masters hath in these disordered times contrary to their duty forsake their parents and masters under the colour of following the wars, which being ended they do not only refuse to serve out their time, but before they come to the age of eighteen or twenty years they be take themselves to marriage and gaining a loom work for themselves, the ancient weavers are many times (by this put out of their work) and some time the master under crept by him who should be his servant by reason whereof the trade is like to come to utter ruin.'

Similar complaint from Devizes. Marked says Cunnington 'No order'.

(From Cunnington, pp. 189-90)

1657 – The inhabitants of Westbury send in a petition on behalf of certain poor people, who had obtained their living by burling of broad medley cloths, three of whose daughters have now been indicted by certain persons desirous to appropriate the said employment to themselves. The petitioners say that 'they presume humbly to certify this session that the said employment of burling hath not been known to be practiced amongst us as any prentice trade, neither hath any been apprenticed to it as such, but the clothiers have ever put their cloth to burling to any who would undertake the same as they do their wools in spinning. Also that the same said employment of burling is a common good to the poor town and parish, conducing to the relief of many poor families therein and the setting of many poor children to work.

(Cunnington, p. 153)

**A Tour Through England and Wales,** Daniel
Defoe, (ed. Cole, Everyman, 2 vols.)

[Defoe's notes on the West Country trade are most
interesting, although it must be admitted that there
is nothing to compare with the fascinating account he
has given of the market on the bridge at Leeds.]
I come now to that part of the country which joins
itself to Wiltshire, which I reserved in particular to
this place in order to give some account of the broadcloth manufacture, which I several times mentioned
in my first journey and which is carried on here, and
that to such a degree as deserves a place in all the
descriptions or histories which shall be given of this
county.

As to the east and south part of Wiltshire are, as I
have already observed, all hilly, spreading themselves far and wide in plain and grassy downs for
breeding and feeding vast flocks of sheep and a
prodigious number of them: and as the west and
north parts of Somerset are, on the contrary, low
and marshy, or moorish, for feeding and breeding of
black cattle and horses or for lead mines etc. So all
the south west part of Wiltshire and the east part of
Somersetshire are low and flat, being a rich enclosed
country, full of rivers and towns, and infinitely
populous, in so much, that some of the market towns
are equal to cities in bigness, and superior to them in
numbers of people.

This low flat country contains parts of the three
counties of Somerset, Wiltshire and Gloucester, and
that the extent of it may be easier understood by those
who know anything of the situation of the country,
it reaches from Cirencester in the north to Sherborne
on the edge of Dorsetshire in the south, and from
Devizes east to Bristol west, which may take in about
50 miles in length where longest and 20 in breadth
where narrowest.

In this extent of country we have the following
market towns principally employed in the clothing
trade, that is to say, in that part of it which I
am now speaking of; namely fine medleys, or mixed
cloths, such as are usually worn in England by the
better sorts of people; and also exported in great
quantities to Holland, Hamburg, Sweden, Denmark,
Spain, Italy, etc. The principle clothing towns in
this part of the country are these:

Somersetshire:
 Frome
 Pensford
 Phillips Norton
 Bruton
 Shepton Mallet
 Castle Cary
 Wincanton
Wiltshire:
 Malmesbury
 Castle Coombe
 Chippenham
 Calne
 Devizes
 Bradford
 Trowbridge
 Westbury
 Warminster
 Mere
Dorsetshire:
 Gillingham
 Shaftesbury
 Beaminster
 Beer
 Sturminster
 Sherborne
Gloucestershire:
 Cirencester
 Tetbury
 Marshfield
 Minchinhampton
 Fairford

These towns, as they stand thin, and at considerable
distances from one another; for except the two towns
of Bradford and Trowbridge the others stand at
unusual distance; I say these towns are interspersed
with a very great number of villages, I had almost said
innumerable villages, hamlets, and scattered houses
in which, generally speaking, the spinning work of all
this manufacture is performed by the poor people;
the master clothiers who generally live in the greater
towns, sending out the wool weekly to their houses
by their servants and horses, and at the same time
bringing back the yarn that they have spun and
finished, which then is fitted for the loom.

The increasing and flourishing circumstances of
the trade are happily visible by the great concourse
of people to, and increase of buildings and inhabitants in these principle clothing towns where this
trade is carried on, and the wealth of the clothiers.
The town of Frome, or as it is written in our maps
Frome Selwood, is a specimen of this, which is so
prodigiously increased within these last twenty or
thirty years that they have built a new church and
so many new streets of houses, and these houses are so
full of inhabitants, that Frome is now reckoned to
have more people in it than the City of Bath, and
some say than even Salisbury itself, and if this trade
continues to increase for a few years more, as it has

done for those past, it is very likely to be one of the greatest and wealthiest inland towns in England.

I call it an inland town because it is particularly distinguished as such, being, not only no sea port, but not near any sea port, having no manner of communication by water, no navigable river at it or near it. Its trade is wholly clothing, and the cloths they make are, generally speaking, all conveyed to London; Blackwell Hall is their market, and thither they send up the gross of their clothing products; and if we may believe common fame there are about ten thousand people in Frome now, more than lived in it twenty years ago, and yet it was a considerable town then too.

Here are also, several large meeting houses, as well as churches as there are, generally, in all the manufacturing trading towns in England, especially in the western counties.

The Devizes is, next to this a large and important town, and full of wealthy clothiers; but this town has lately run pretty much into the drugget making trade; a business which has made some invasion upon the broadcloth trade and great quantities of druggets are worn in England, as also exported beyond the sea, even in place of our broadcloths, and where they usually were worn and exported; but this is much the same as to the trade still; for as it is all a woollen manufacture and that the druggets may properly be called cloth, though narrow and of a different make, so the makers are all called clothiers.

The river Avon, a noble and large fresh river, branching itself into many parts and receiving almost all the rivers on that side of the hills waters this whole fruitful vale; and the waters of this river seem particularly qualified for the use of the clothiers; that is to say for dyeing the best colours and for fulling and dressing the cloth so that the clothiers generally plant themselves upon this river, but especially the dyers as at Trowbridge and Bradford, which are the two most eminent clothing towns in that part of the Vale for the making of fine Spanish cloths and of the nicest mixtures.

From these towns south to Westbury, and to Warminster, the same trade continues, and the finest medley Spanish cloths not in England only but in the whole world are made in this part. They told me at Bradford that it was no extraordinary thing to have clothiers in that county worth from £10,000 to £40,000 a man, and many of the great families who now pass for gentry in these counties have been originally raised from and built up by this truly noble manufacture.

If I may speak here from the authority of the ancient inhabitants of the place, and who have been curious observers upon this subject, the country

which I have now described as principally employed in, and maintained by, this prodigy of trade contains 2,330,000 acres of land, and has on it 788 parishes and 374,000 people. It is true that this is all guess-work; but I confess myself very willing to believe that the reckoning is not far short of the account, for the county is exceeding large and populous.

It may be worth enquiry by the curious how the manufacturers in so vast a consumption of wool as such a trade must take up can be supplied with wool for their trade; and indeed it would be something strange if the answers were not at hand.

1. We may reasonably conclude that this manufacture was at first seated in this country, or as we may say planted itself here at first because of the infinite numbers of sheep which were fed at that time upon the downs and plains of Dorset, Wilts and Hampshire, all adjoining, as a trading town is seated or rises gradually upon some large river because of the benefits of navigation; and as gentlemen place the mansion houses of their estates and seats of their families as near the pleasant rivers, woods and fine prospects as possible, for the delight of their living; so the first planters of the clothing manufacture doubtless chose this delightful vale for its seat because of the neighbourhood of these plains which might be supposed to be a fund of wool for the carrying it on. Thus the manufacture of white cloths was planted in Stroud Water in Gloucestershire for the sake of the excellent water there for the dyeing scarlet and all colours that are in grain which are better dyed there than in any other part of England, sometimes near London excepted. Hence therefore, we first observe they are supplied yearly with the fleeces of two or three millions of sheep.

2. But as the numbers of sheep fed on these downs is lessened rather than increased because of the many thousands of acres of the ground being of late years turned into arable land, and sowed with wheat; which by the way has made Warminster a market town on the edge of Somersetshire as it now is without exception the greatest market for wheat in England with this exception only, viz: where none of it is brought to send to London.

I say, the number of sheep, and consequently the quality of wool decreasing, and at the same time the manufacture, as has been said, prodigiously increasing the manufacturers applied themselves to other parts for a supply, and hence began the influx of north country wool to come in from the counties of Northampton, Leicester and Lincoln, the centre of which trade is about Tetbury and Cirencester, where are the markets for the northcountry wool, and whereas they say several hundred packs of wool are

50 *Cloth Hall*
From Walker's *Costumes of Yorkshire 1885*. A typical cloth hall.

51 *Raising*
From Walker's *Costumes of Yorkshire 1885* and of particular interest because
of the good drawing of the preemer boy who cleaned the teasels.

**52 Bishop Blaize's Festival**
From Walker's *Costumes of Yorkshire 1885*. This shows the festival of the hand wool combers;
and there are many accounts in Yorkshire literature of these meetings.

sold every week for the supplying of this prodigious consumption.

3. From London they have great quantities of wool, which is generally called Kentish wool, in the fleece which is brought up from thence by the farmers since in the late severe acts against them selling it within a certain number of miles of the sea, also fell-wool for the combers bought of the wool staplers in Barnabyfleet, and sent back by the carriers which bring up the cloths to market.

4. They have also sometimes large quantities of Irish wool by way of Bristol or of Minehead in Somersetshire; but this is uncertain, and only on extraordinary occasions. I omit the Spanish wool as being an article by itself.

Thus, in short, as those that see the number of sheep fed on the downs and plains as above, and that see the quantity of wool brought into the markets of Tetbury and other towns, and the quantity sent from London all into this one vale would wonder how it was possible to be consumed, manufactured and wrought up; so on the other hand those that saw the number of people employed and the vast quantity of goods made in this part of England would wonder where the whole nation should be able to supply this with wool.

(Defoe, Volume I, pp. 279–84)
[Defoe has other valuable information regarding the West of England trade.]

### Exeter

From here we came to Exeter, the city famous for two things which we seldom find united in the same town, that is full of gentry and good company and yet full of trade and manufacturers also; the serge market, held every week, is very well worth the stranger seeing, and next to the Brig Market at Leeds in Yorkshire is the greatest in England. The people assured me that in this market is generally sold from 60 to 70 to 80, sometimes 100,000 pounds value in serges in a week. I think it is kept on Mondays.

This city drives a very great correspondence with Holland, and also directly to Portugal, Spain and Italy; shipping off vast quantities of their woollen manufacture, especially to Holland, the Dutch giving very large commissions here for the buying of serges, perpetuanas and such goods; which are made not only in and about Exeter, but at Crediton, Honiton, Culleton, St. Marys Autry, Newton Bushell, Ashburton, and especially at Tiverton, Cullompton, Bampton and all the north east part of the county, which part of the county is, as it may be said, fully employed, the people made rich, and the poor that are properly so called well subsisted and employed by it.          (Defoe, Volume I, pp. 222–23)

### Tiverton

Next to Exeter, this is the greatest manufacturing town in the county, and of all the inland towns is next to it in wealth and in numbers of people; it stands on the river Exe.

But the beauty of Tiverton is the free school at the east entrance into the town, a noble building but a much nobler foundation; it was erected by one Peter Blundell, a clothier, and a lover of learning, who used the saying of William of Wickham to the King when he founded the Royal School at Winchester, viz: That if he was not himself a scholar he would be the occasion of making more scholars than any scholar in England; to which end he founded the school.

(Defoe, Volume I, p. 288)

### Newbury

This town of Newbury is an ancient clothing town, though now little of that part remains to it; but it retains still a manufacturing genius, and the people are generally employed in making shalloons, a kind of stuff which, though it be used only for the lining and insides of men's cloths, for women's use but little of it, nor the men anything but as above, yet it becomes so generally worn, both at home and abroad, that it increased to a manufacture by itself and is more considerable than any single manufacture of stuffs in the nation. This employs the town of Newbury as also Andover, another town on the side of Wiltshire about twelve miles from it, and abundance of other towns in other counties of England of which I shall speak in their place.

(Defoe, Volume I, p. 189)

### Andover

But the chief reason of my making this digression is to mention that within a mile or thereabouts of this town at the place where the open down country begins is Weyhill, where the greatest fair for sheep is kept that this nation can show. I confess though I once saw the fair yet I could make no estimate of the numbers brought thither for sale; but asking the opinion of a grazier who had used to bring sheep there he boldly answered there were many hundred thousands. This being too general, I pressed him further; again he said he believed there were 500,000 sheep sold there in one fair. Now though this might, I believe, be too many, yet 'tis sufficient to note that there are a prodigious quantity of sheep sold here; nor can it be otherwise if he considered that the sheep sold here are not for immediate killing but are generally used for store sheep for the farmers, and they send for them from all the following counties: Berks, Oxford, Bucks, Bedford, Hertford,

Middlesex, Kent, Surrey and Sussex: the custom of these farmers is to send one farmer on behalf of perhaps twenty, and so the sheep come up together and they part them when they come home. These ewes have also the property that they generally bring two rams at a time. What wethers are bought here are carried off by the farmers who have feeding grounds in order to fat them for killing; but they are few compared to the ewes.

(Defoe, Volume 1, p. 289)

*Dorset Sheep*

The downs around this town are exceedingly pleasant, and come up on every side even to the very street end; and here it was that they told me that there were 600,000 sheep fed on the downs within six miles of the town; that is six miles every way, which is twelve miles in diameter and thirty-six miles in circumference. This I say I was told, I do not affirm it to be true; but when I viewed the country round I confess I could not but incline to believe it.

It is observable of these sheep that they are exceedingly fruitful, and the ewes generally bring two lambs and they are, for that reason, bought by all the farmers through the east part of England who come to Burford Fair in this country to buy them, and carry them into Kent and Surrey eastwards, and into Buckinghamshire and Bedfordshire and Oxfordshire, north even to Banstead Down in Surrey.

(Defoe, Volume 1, p. 210)

## Francis Yerbury's Patent 858–1776

(From Patent Office Records)
There are two species of the cloth distinguished by the name of cassimeres, one is quilled in the weaving with a flat whale, the other with a round one which may be directed to any point, the threads of both chain and shoot crossing each other in a traverse manner, either to the right or the left; or it may be whaled on one side and not on the other, either of which are equally useful. The chain of both sorts are spun in the same manner, either of warp or abb warp. The woof or shoot must not be spun in the same manner as for common cloth, but drawn out into a much finer thread, mostly about the same degree of smallness, weight and twist that chain is, whether it goes to the right or the left.

[This is the introduction of twill weaving in the South-west. It is obscure. What is the point about one being quilled with a flat and the other with a round one? Is he referring to different types of twills? The latter phrase, 'it may be whaled (?twilled) one side and not on the other' might suggest he could have been using some weave like a venetian or doeskin, which does not show a twill on the back. There is nothing to indicate the use of a herringbone. Flat might be an ordinary twill, round a venetian. The last paragraph confirms that the older cloths used a thick weft.]

## Rudder's New History of Gloucestershire (1779)

The trade is centered in Bisley, Hampton, Stroud, Painswick, Woodchester, Horsley, Stonehouse, Stanley, Uley, Dursley, Wotton-under-Edge,

'It is there the master clothiers live and the most curious operations of the manufacture are performed under their immediate inspection, but the women and children all over the country are chiefly employed in carding wool and spinning the yarn.' (pp. 60).

Trade has increased gradually during the past century. Helped by war because our fleet stopped the French merchants, also less smuggling then. ('The smugglers and owlers of wool'.)

[Rudder says he has collected an account of the trade from the most intelligent manufacturers.]:

### The Inland Trade:

In the language of the manufacturers it must not be strictly taken as if confined to our own Kingdom for that is not the fact. It may be so called for its furnishing the sorts of cloth usually worn in our country consisting of superfines, seconds, forests, drabs, naps, duffels and all that variety to be found in a well stored draper's shop. The trade is governed by the fashion and fancy and has been introduced into Gloucestershire within the last fifty or sixty years. Great part of the goods are dispersed by means of travelling though Great Britain and Ireland by the manufacturers themselves or their servants. Many of them are likewise sold to merchants, who send them to our colonies and other foreign markets; and some go to the warehouse in London from whence they are dispersed in like manner. This branch has been supported with such spirit and industry as from small beginnings to become very valuable. Being less subject to fluctuation than the other branches, it employs more regularly and uniformerly a number of hands perhaps than most of any of them. Many persons have succeeded in it, and some large fortunes have been made; but at present through the dearness of provisions, the disagreement with our colonies, and other discouraging circumstances common to most, trade at the time is in a languid condition though the returns in it are estimated at £250,000 per annum.

### The trade with London:

The second branch of the trade is with drapers in London, who take a variety of goods for their retail customers, and the cloth for the army, the marines and the militia passes through their hands. The demand in this part of the clothing trade at different times is very disproportionate. In times of war it is very great, but not very considerable at present, the share which this county has of it being estimated at £100,000 per annum.

### The Turkey trade:

The third branch of the trade to Turkey, which is much declined. The French by reason of their political connections with the Porte, the situation of this country, the price of labour, and the method of conducting this trade have gained a great superiority over us at this market. But I am told that our superfines still support their credit there, and that the share of this county in the Turkey trade cannot be less than £50,000 per annum.

### The East India Trade:

The cloth made for the East India Company is the last and most considerable branch of our foreign trade, yet for the present method of conducting it is far from being advantageous to the clothiers. [Rudder has a long section describing the snags to this trade. It was done through the Blackwell Hall Factors.] They show it to the company who impartially choose the best cloths according to price. The trouble is the factor who from being a mere agent now dominates the trade. He even sets up (i.e. finances) clothiers and by his infamous activity has pushed down the price of these cloths to there is now no profit in them. [One feels that Rudder, or rather the clothiers who informed him, have rather overdone the case. Probably the market was falling off, and that caused low prices.] Value £200,000.

[Rudder gives a valuable contemporary picture of the Stroud Valley district in what was perhaps its greatest period.]

### Alderly

Leland says clothing village but business now largely declining.

### Avening

Cloth trade furnishes employment. Edward Sheppard has lately built a handsome house at Gatcombe.

### Bisley

The traveller sees the houses intermixed with rows of tenters along the side of the hill on which the cloth is stretched in the process of making. In the bottom are eight fulling mills and in the village above the hill called the Luichers a large number of people employed in the trade reside. But the trade has lately much declined.

### Cam

'Here are no antiquities whatsoever'. The river 'feeds no kind of fish, on account of the great quantity of dyestuffs thrown into it' (p. 313). The poor are employed in clothing by masters at Dursley and Uley, but about thirty years ago there were three or four considerable clothiers residing in the parish who are since died or who have declined business.

### Cheltenham

No manufacture but women and children of the poor sort spin woollen yarn for Stroud.

### Dursley

Leland says pretty clothing town. Rudder remarks still is, also business of making cards for clothiers.

### Horsley

Clothing employed many here, but now much declined. The poor are very burdensome 'but much of their wretched conditions due to idleness and bad habits.'

### Painswick

Prosperous.

### Rodborough

Mr. James Winchcombe, an eminent clothier, has built a fine house at Bownham.

### Chipping Sodbury

One master clothier employing a few hands. But women have spinning brought from outside.

### Kings Stanley

The poor work for clothiers.

### Wotton-under-Edge

Chiefly fine cloth. Very ancient (see Leland). Seven or eight master clothiers now, still flourishing but not equal to what it was. Sir Jonathan Davies was a clothier, also Robert Webb.

### Stonehouse

Clothing trade flourished for many years.

### Stroud

Population scattered through the parish 'the clothiers do not reside in the town but generally near the riverlet where their respective mills stand.' The so-called 'bottoms' which from the hills exhibit a most pleasing view of a populous country. Trade is considerable but fluctuating. Broadcloths for home and abroad from those of low value to the finest Spanish. Sent away either white (that is undyed) or dyed, many scarlets 'for which branch of the trade the place is noted'. 'The beauty of the colour is very great, to the perfection of which the Frome water has been erroneously supposed to contribute, for it is most assuredly owing to the skill of the artist.'

Clothiers send their wool twenty miles away for spinning. There are about 18 clothing mills and about 30 master clothiers, value £200,000. One clothier makes 3,000 cloths.

An idea of making the river navigable from the Severn (1730) turned down by pressure of the clothiers. Another idea of having boats working between each mill (a crane at each to move the chests) tried but not practicable.

### Tetbury

Formerly some woollen cloth made but declined for want of constant water to run the fulling mill. Now wool combing employs fifty people.

### Uley

This village, though not large, is very populous for the manufacture of fine broadcloth long established here. It is still carried on by several persons in a very extensive manner and furnishes employment for the lower class of people. But idleness and debauchery are so deeply rooted in them by means of those seminaries of vice called alehouses that the poor are very burdensome. These houses are scattered all over the country and are daily increasing, which we owe either to the magistrates inattention or indulgence; or perhaps to a mistaken notice of serving the community by increasing the public revenue for licences; but they may be assured that nothing can compensate for depravity of morals and the loss of industry (p. 783).

### Wickwar

Leland says pretty clothing hamlet, now very little. Only one master who does little. Women employed spinning.

### Woodchester

Is famous for its fine broadcloths. Very extensive; 'the first napping mill in these parts was erected here by the late Sir Onesiphorus Paul. It is a machine for raising the nap upon the cloth in little knots at regular but very small distances that give it a singularly pleasing appearance. Near the same time another was set up by one Mr. Freame, and some years later a third by Mr. Richard Hawker, both of the neighbourhood, which later is still employed and yields a great profit to the proprietors.' (p. 841).

## The Journeys of Celia Fiennes
(ed. Morris, C., 1947, pp. 245–7)

There is very little about the South-west broadcloth trade. The only note of interest:

*Devizes*
'A very neat little town with a very good market house and town hall set on a stone pillars, it is a borough and a very rich trading place for the clothing trade'.
[Devizes specialised in druggetts.]

[The set piece in Celia Fiennes is, of course, the account of Exeter.]

There is an incredible quantity of serges made and sold in the town . . . the large Market House set on stone pillars which runs a great length on which they lay their packs of serges, just by it is a walk with pillars which is for the yarn; the whole town and country is employed for at least twenty miles round in spinning, weaving, dressing and scouring, fulling and drying of the serges, it turns the most money in a week of anything in England, one week with another there is £10,000 paid in ready money, sometimes £15,000, the weavers bring in their serges and must have their money which they employ to provide the yarn to go to work again.

The carriers I met going with it as thick all entering into town with their loaded horses, they bring them all just from the loom and so they are put into the fulling mills, but first they will clean and scour their rooms with them – which by the way gives no pleasing perfume to a room, the oil and grease, and I should think it would rather foul a room than cleanse it because of the oil – but I perceive its otherwise esteemed by them, which will send to their acquaintances that are tuckers the days the serges come in for a rowle to clean their house, this I was an eye-witness of; then they lay them in soak in urine then they soap them and so put them into fulling mills and so work them in the mills dry until they are thick enough, then they turn water into them and so scour them; the mill does draw out and gather in the serges, its a pretty diversion to see it, a sort of huge notched timbers like great teeth, one would think it should injure the serges but it does not, the mills draws in with such a great violence that if one stands near it and it catch a bit of your garment it would be ready to draw in the person even in a trice; when they are thus scoured they dry them in racks strained out, which are as thick set one by another as will permit the dresser to pass between, and huge large fields occupied this way almost all round the town which is to the river side; then when dry they burl them picking out all knots, then fold them with a paper between every fold and so set them on an iron plate and screw down the press on them, which has another iron plate on the top under which is the furnace of fire of coals, this is the hot press; then they fold them exceeding exact and then press them in a cold press; some they dye but the most are sent up for London white.

I saw the several vats they were a dyeing in, of black, yellow, blue and green – which two last colours are dipped in the same vat that which makes it differ is what they were dipped in before which makes either green or blue; they hang the serges on a great beam or great pole on the top of the vat and so keep turning it from one to another, as one turns it off into the vat the other rolls it out of it, so they do it backwards and forwards till its tinged deep enough of the colour; their furnace that keeps their dyepans boiling is all under the room made of coal fires; there was in a room by itself a vat for the scarlet, that being a very chargeable dye no waste must be allowed in that, indeed I think they make as fine a colour as their Bow dyes are in London; these rollers I spoke of; two men does continually roll on and off the pieces of serges till dipped enough the length of these pieces are, or should hold out, twenty six yards.

### The Revolt of the Shearmen

The five letters quoted below, a sample of many passing between the West of England and the Home Office officials in London illustrate the type of material that gives us such a detailed look at conditions in the West of England during the crucial first years of the nineteenth century.

An excellent selection has been printed by Aspinall in his *Early Trade Unions* (1949). See also Home Office papers especially 44/66.

Matthew Davies to Lord Pelham, dated Warminster, Tuesday evening, 15 June 1802

In addition to the many outrages committed in this town, I am sorry to be under the necessity of informing Your Lordship that this morning between 12 and 1 o'clock a rick of oats worth about £20 belonging to Mr Peter Warren, a clothier of this town, was maliciously set on fire and entirely consumed. A dog kennel at some distance therefrom, the property of the said Mr Warren and others was at the same time also set on fire and partly consumed.

That there is no doubt that this daring outrage was committed by some of the work men usually employed in the woollen manufactory who now, and have for many weeks past, refused to work on account of some machines being introduced which they consider as obnoxious, although the same have been used for many years in other parts of the Kingdom.

They have at present no visible means of any livelihood, and there is good reason to think they are supported and encouraged by contributions from many of the innkeepers and other inhabitants of the place. It is thought that some strong declaration on the part of the government of the illegality of this practice addressed to the neighbouring magistrates with orders that it may be printed and posted up in different places would be of great service.

(Aspinall, p. 41, Home Office Papers 42/65)

James Read to John King. Dated 3 October 1802

I have seen Richards, the agent of Messrs Wormald and Gott, and learn from him that their want of hands arises from the shearman refusing to work for those manufacturers who have taken apprentices after the age of fourteen and for a shorter period than is directed by the statute of Elizabeth, unless such apprentices are discharged; but he informed me that he did not expect to get many recruits.

(Aspinall, p. 64, Home Office Papers 42/66)

[Read enclosed the following printed handbill]:

Wanted immediately at Leeds in Yorkshire.
A number of journey-men and shearmen, sober, steady, good work-men. Who will meet with constant employ and good wages, by applying to Messrs Wormald, Gott & Wormald at their manufacturing near Leeds. Further particulars may be known by applying to Jacob Richards at The George Inn, Trowbridge, or to Mr Henry Richards, near the Market Place, Frome.
28th September, 1802.

(Aspinall, p. 65, Home Office Papers 42/66)

James Read to John King. (Dated Melksham, 4 October 1802)

Beaumont is a Bradford man. He was one amongst others that left Mr Jones's factory under a pretence that they had been threatened and forced to do it. I had Beaumont under examination about it, but he would not fix upon anyone; indeed he at first refused to give testimony and was committed, and after being in prison about three weeks he relented. Mr Jones after this conceiving that apprehension for the security of his person was the only cause (as Beaumont alleged it to be) why he did not go to work again offered to protect him within the walls of the factory and to give him constant work and a guinea a week instead of fourteen shillings, his former wages. Beaumont agreed to accept the offer but never went to work. I mentioned this merely to show what strict discipline they carry on.

I shall endeavour to learn when Beaumont returns and get hold of him if I can before he unloads himself. He has a wife close by Bradford. If she has any letters I think the post master at Bradford should intercept them.

(Aspinall p. 65, Home Office Papers 42/66)

John King to James Read. (Dated Whitehall 5 October 1802)

I gave the necessary orders yesterday for stopping the letters you suggested at Trowbridge or Bradford. If Beaumont could be met with on the road immediately on his arrival and thoroughly searched it might prove a great service.

(Aspinall, p. 65, Home Office Papers 42/66)

James Read to John King. (Dated Melksham, 18 October 1802)

I understand that a deputation from the Bath meeting of manufacturers are about to set off to London for the purpose of submitting a case to the Secretary of the Treasury for the repeal of some statutes which, as they imagine, cripple the present state of their trade, and I learn that their first visit is likely to be either to you or Lord Pelham upon the subject.

The shearmen continue to have meetings, particularly at Trowbridge, but I do not find there is at present any disposition to riot. In the town of Melksham where the usual manner of work does not provide sufficient employ I expect to influence some shearmen to cut cloths after the gig mills, and the combination once broken many others I dare say will follow.

The shearmen's wives begin to get impatient and complain that the clubs take away their husband's earnings, and there appears a disposition in some Warminster shearmen to go to work again. It cannot therefore be too strongly impressed upon the minds of the deputies who may come to you to recommend the body of manufacturers not to harbour any resentment against those who may be willing to return to their labour and to concert measures for their employment.

(Aspinall, p. 66, Home Office Papers 42/66)

## Hoare's History of Wiltshire

The monumental county histories that were published, mainly in the late eighteenth and early nineteenth centuries provide valuable topographical material. Naturally the interest of the writer affected the amount of space he gave to economic matters. Thus, for example, Rudder's information about the Gloucestershire trade is most valuable. Hoare's interest on the other hand, was mainly archaeological, and this is the only passage of real interest to the economic historian.

Comparatively little about cloth making, but has an interesting note on Warminster:

The clothing trade in woollen cloth was formerly carried on here to a considerable extent, but owing to the introduction of machinery and other causes it has dwindled away almost to nothing. (1831).

[Very interesting footnote to above]

'A petition was presented to the House of Commons in the session of 1830. The petitioner has represented that for many years he had been a manufacturer of broadcloth and Kerseymeres in the town of Warminster; and expressed his conviction that the evils which so grievously affected not only the manufacturers but the labouring population had arisen from the improvements made in machinery and had been greatly increased by the practice which had prevailed among the manufacturers and others in paying their work-men in goods instead of money at a profit of at least 100%; the consequences of which has been the ruin of the regular manufacturers. In proof of this the petitioners informed the House that forty years since the town had contained thirty prosperous manufacturers of woollen cloth, who gave employment to thousands of the town and neighbourhood; that there was at present but one manufacturer, who manufactured on an average four yards per week; that the poor rate of the parish, which at the above time amounted to £500 per annum in 1830 increased to upwards of £4,449. The petitioners prayed to the House to revise and amend the laws which relate to the payment of the wages of the operatives. (p. 13)

**Extracts from May on the West of England Woollen Manufacture, 1814**

The organisation of the manufacture of woollen cloths in Wiltshire, Somerset, and Gloucestershire is quite different (from that of Yorkshire). In this district only fine cloths and cashmeres are made. All the processes are carried out by the manufacturers in their own establishments. Many of their manufactories are very large and are to be found mainly in Bradford-on-Avon and the immediate vicinity. . . .

At Twerton, near Bath, I saw looms in Naish's factory for making fine woollen cloth. These looms are fitted with an appliance which stretches the cloth during the weaving process. I saw several women weavers at work in this factory.

. . . Gig mills and mechanical shears have been introduced throughout the Wiltshire, Somerset and Gloucestershire woollen region. Here, as in Holland, many types of mechanical cutters are in use. The best that I saw were in Saunder's factory in Bradford-on-Avon where fine cloths are made. In these machines the blades are fixed on moving runners and are drawn by cards which are gradually wound round a shaft. All the machines have two blades, each of which cuts half the breadth of a piece of cloth. The cutting action stops automatically as soon as the end of the length of cloth reaches the front blade. Then the cutting table is lowered a little and the blades are moved to the other side so that as soon as the table is raised again the cutting process is resumed. Compared with German and Dutch mechanical cutters the blades of English shears are fixed at a sharper angle – almost a right angle. I saw some excellent mechanical shears for cutting cashmere cloth at Twerton. They each had four blades which are in a fixed position. The cloth was drawn length ways across the blades by rollers.

**Marling, W. H. 'The Woollen Industry of Gloucestershire – A Retrospect'**
(Bristol, Gloucestershire Archaeological Society, Volume 36, 1913)

W. H. Marling, was one of the most successful nineteenth-century manufacturers and the account he wrote of the trade is of great interest.

[He considers decline largely due to fashion]

'The regular garb of clergymen, doctors and lawyers, and of all gentlemen is the evening dress.'

Today East Prussia, Silesia and Moravia produce wool of the very finest quality in this respect (though not in stable) superior to anything grown in Australia, and it is these continental wools exclusively that the best superfine broadcloth is comprised.

Some parishes, such as Uley, Bisley, borrowed money for the purpose of organising emigration, and Mr. Miles gives a detailed statement showing the cost of emigrating 68 persons from Bisley parish who on 31st August, 1837, were placed on board a steam vessel at Bristol to join the ships then lying in Kings Road.

Clothing – 68 persons at £1.10.8¾d. each, including bibles, prayer books, etc., £104.9.7d.
Cash paid for two wagons and a cart to take the 68 persons to Bristol, their victuals on leaving and on the road, and breakfast at Bristol. £24.13.6d.
Cash for one days victual, the first day put on board the steam packet. £2.
Cash paid Dr. Rogers the emigrant's surgeon for two men and their wives that were above age to go passage free. £15. each, = £60.
Total: £191.3.1d.

1839, hand loom weavers at home 6/10½d. per week.

    at Factory 11/9d.
    Wool sorters 30/-.
    White wool scourers 14/-.
    Women wool pickers 6/-.
    Women wool feeders 3/-.
    Mule spinners (men) 20/-.
    Women warpers 7/-.
    Miller men 20/-.
    Burlers (women) 6/-.
    Shearmen 13/-.
    Brushers 14/-.
    Drawers and markers (women) 9/-.
    Spinners (women) 6/-.

The Beer Act of 1830:
empowered any ratepayer to open his house as a beer shop, free from any justices licence or control merely on the payment of £2.2.0d. to the local office of

assize. Marling says they became in lonely districts great collectors of stolen property 'slinge'.

When I went into business 50 years ago, doeskins, venetians and kerseymeres were still hand woven in scores of cottages, and the click of the loom was a familiar sound as I drove down the village to the looms. I always felt sorry for the hand loom weaver as he brought his piece into the wool loft, for his earnings, even in the 50s, allowing for playtime, did not average I fancy much above 10/-. a week. A middle aged or elderly man, rather sad faced (at least looking as though he had never been young) and often quaintly dressed, sometimes in a blue frock coat with copper buttons once gilt, or in a swallow tail one, once black but grown green with age (presumably some gentleman's cast off garment) his pathetic figure now lives only in the memory of a few old clothiers like us.

## A. T. Playne, Minchinhampton and Avening (1915)

After Marling, Playne was the most successful Gloucestershire manufacturer of the nineteenth century. There is perhaps a difference in that the Playnes were more successful as a family clothing dynasty.

The Playnes came to Kent in the middle of the sixteenth century and to Gloucestershire c. 1650.

Trade declined, or rather profits became less 1836–48. A change of fashions brought in West of England finecloth, this lasted 40 years and then another fashion changed.

The great hand-loom weavers' strike of 1825. Playne says enforced by the leaders by strong parties demanding the surrender of the shuttle. Anybody showing signs of weakness had their cloth beams removed.

Riot Act read at Chalford.

Strike lasted three months.

Interesting account of how William Playne saved the bank at Tetbury by riding from London with a bag of gold.

Playne repeats Marling's point about the evil influence of beer house Act.

General adoption of power looms 1836. Playne pities the appeals of old hand-loom weavers, and has a good description of them. (See Ch. 16)

History of Playne's. Longford Mills. Land bought in 1759. Business had been at Frogmarsh in the parish of Woodchester. Part of the mill very Flemish looking, can still be seen. English wool, some to 1790 then all Spanish, which arrived sorted. Wool dried in round towers, still seen at Frogmarsh and Avening (now a cattle shed) rather like Martello Towers.

The early power looms 40 picks per minute.

Old fullers had gigantic wooden hammers weighing more than 1 cwt., replaced by fullers, that is the milling machines, older cloths often fulled for a week, now only a day. (Playne hardly appears to realise the difference in the type of cloth.)

All sorts of horrors used in milling and scouring, including pig's blood. Playne remembers a rougher (that is a dresser) who always wore gloves when gardening.

Cloths made at Longford's, were superior superfine black and blue, single buff cassimere, livery cloth, Spanish stripe, the latter for China. Later very big trade through East India Company. They each had to be 36 yards by 58½, weigh 34 lbs. One contract for 10,000 pieces. One payment £24,535.

First record of Spanish wool 1809. Big profit made by firm through holding large stocks when Napoleon tried his continental blockage. Prices went up to 20s 6d. Playne sold up to 18s, normal 3s to 3s 6d.

1806 great achievement. Building of lake. Many complaints from other mills.

During the machine riots, the dam was guarded day and night. Rioters had threatened to cut it through and wash away mills and machinery.

Steam engine 1815, cost £970. 20 hp Boulton and Watt.

German wool. First invoice of any size 24.1.1808. 235 bales of 4s to 6s 3d. Total £15,359 9s 6d. German wool superseded Spanish.

In 1824 William Playne, junior, made his first trip to Germany to buy wool, a pioneer in this. Very enjoyable. Most notably entertained by proprietors at their houses. Calais to Dresden 850 miles. Breslau, a further 200. Playne kept his carriage at Calais. Very annoyed by customs interruptions at each little German state.

One year father went too, interesting letters home.

Silesian wool was replacing Saxony. Great wool sale at Breslau.

In Breslau early in June wool was brought in by wagon from miles around and deposited in the streets and squares of the old city, or in the warehouses of the Jews who drove a very lucrative trade by lending money to the farmers and proprietors and taking wool as a security.

Fleece only 1½ to 2 lbs. clean.

## William Walker's Journal

This journal has not previously been published. William Walker owned the old established Trowbridge firm of Samual Salter and Company in the nineteenth century. Permission to publish comes from his grandson, Mr Lovel Mackie.

### (a) History of Trowbridge Families

From reports of old residents I have heard of former manufacturers in the town. One of the earliest was the Houlton family, they were amongst the founders of the Conigre Baptist Chapel, and in later years one of the family lived at Farley and owned the estate, and this remained in the hands of the family until recent years, when the last of the family, Sir Victor Houlton, died, the estate was sold and was lately bought by Earl Cairns.

Another old family was the Timbrells, one of these laid out Timbrell Street and built Timbrell Cottage in the Bradley Road, involving at the same time a lot of the roadside waste and made the road-way much too narrow.

Another family was the Mortimers, the builders of Mortimer Street. Another the Bythesea's, the family have lately taken down Bythesea building in Stallard Street and made a new road from Stallard Street to Mortimer Street and a new road is named after them, viz Bythesea Road. There were other families, such as the Harrisons, Dowdings, Temples Cottles, Sobers, Silverthorns, etc. There was also another manufacturer who built up the lately defunct business of Messrs J. H. Webb & Company, now Sainsbury's corn mill. This was the Revd William Waldron, the pastor for fifty years of The Conigre Baptist Church. Mr Webb was a boy in their counting house and grew up in the trade, and when the Waldron family gave up they handed the business over to him, but his sons did not keep pace with the times, and the business was closed and the mills sold. Coming to my own times, I remember the Edghills. They were located in Polebarn Lane and for Mr James Edghill my father worked when a boy. When this family gave up the business the mills were acquired by Mr Samuel Brown and are still in the hands of the successors of him. Formerly all the mill buildings were those behind the dwelling house in the field, and the only motive power to drive the carding engines and slubbing billeys (these were hand driven) was a horse wheel.

The Stancomb family. William Stancomb, the founder of the firm, was a shearman, but not like so many of his fellow work-men, he was of a thrifty turn, whereas shearmen as a rule were great drinkers.

I have heard of their drinking fifteen to twenty shillings worth of beer in a week. William Stancomb would lend these drinkers two shillings and on the Saturday receive two and six for the loan of the same. In this, and with saving up his earnings, he was enabled to start manufacturing, and with the introduction of machinery built the Cradle Bridge Mills. He was deacon at the Back Street Chapel, but a hard man. My father worked for him and he made him pay for the damage his own cow did on the cloth when it was drying in the rack in his own field. Also he made him pay damage for what the rats did on the cloths in the mill when he ought to have kept cats to keep the rats down. Old William Stancomb in his early days lived in Back Street in the house with the porch facing the entrance to the yard leading to the Conigre Chapel from Back Street. Most of his children were born there. I have never heard much about old William Stancomb's brother John as to his early history more than he built and worked Castle Mills, but after his death his eldest son John left the firm and joined William Stancomb's firm, he having married his Uncle William's daughter and when the firm of John Stancomb was given up Arthur and Edward, two brothers of John Stancomb, joined him at Cradle Bridge Mills, and William Stancomb junior, the only son of William Stancomb senior, left the firm to his three cousins, John retiring some years after in favour of his two aforementioned brothers. They continued in business until about 1906, when they gave up and the mills were sold to Mr Yates, a bedding manufacturer. William Stancomb senior died at The Limes, a fine house that stood on the site of the Town Hall, the grounds behind the said Town Hall and the people's park were the grounds belonging to this house. William Stancomb junior lived for many years at Springfield Hilperton Road; he then went to live at Farley Castle for some years until he built a house at Potterne in Devizes, and went there to live, and his son William still lives there. John Stancomb senior had several sons and daughters. Their mother was one of the three Miss Perkins. They were daughters of a baker who lived in Back Street in the shop and bake-house on the left hand corner opposite Ushers Brewery, leading into the Conigre from Back Street. Another daughter married Thomas Clark, and another the third, married Mr Norris Clark, a son of old parson Clark of The Tabernacle Chapel, and who lived at Polebarn House, and the parson Clark built that small square building in Polebarn Lane for studying in. It was then a quiet lane. These three families who married the Misses Perkins had children named after them, John Perkins Clark, William Perkins Clark, the son of Thomas Clark, and William

Perkins Clark, the son of Mr Norris Clark, hence the name of Mr Perkins Stancomb and Mr Perkins Clark etc. One of John Stancomb senior's daughters married Sir William Henry Wills of Bristol, now Lord Winterstoke. Another married the Revd Thomas Mann of The Tabernacle Chapel, and another to Mr Walter Mann of Highfield. John Stancomb junior had a son. He lived at Shaw, Melksham, and the only Stancombs living in the town are Arthur and his two sons, Graham and Fred, living in Hilperton Road.

The Salter family. Old Samuel Salter, founder of the firm, was also an old shearman. He had an only son Samuel, he lived a great many years at the house opposite Salter's Mill gate in Fore Street, and there he died. He had a partner, Mr Jesse Gouldsmith and a Mr John Hayward. These, with their sons, carried on the business until the fire in 1862, when they dissolved partnership, old Mr Gouldsmith and old John Hayward retiring from business, and Gouldsmith's sons taking a Mr Strachan into trade with them, built the Home Mills and worked them. The sons of Mr Hayward, John and Edward, going to The Courts and building Upper Mills. These they worked until they gave up business. They did not keep up to date in their machines, the same with the Stancomb's.

The Clarks. John and Thomas were native of Banbury in Berkshire. I have heard there is an entry in the life of old parson Clark that he had news that morning. His brother had died at Newbury leaving a wife and two orphan boys. He had them brought to Trowbridge, and they lived in the Tabernacle Yard; as the lads grew up they started cloth making in Yerbury Street. They started with one carding engine and a slubbing billey. My mother worked for them at this time. They had a blind man to turn the carding engine, named Shem Reed, and then they got another carding machine and got Ham Reed, the blind brother of Shem to turn that engine, and so they got on and left Yerbury Street for Duke Street Mills, and removed there until they built Studley Mills to which they removed and sold Duke Street mills to Messrs Blake. John Clark, when he got married, lived at Ching House, Yerbury Street, and Thomas lodged with him and his wife at that house. My mother's sister was a servant girl there. When Thomas got married he went to live at The Conigre Parsonage House, and all the family were born there. John went to live at Bellefield and died there, and Thomas then lived and died there, as also did his son Thomas, whose widow now lives there. The second son, Mr William Perkins Clark, lived for a great many years at the house at the corner of Quarterway Lane on the way to Hilperton.

He then re-built Wyke House at Marsh and lived there, and it is now occupied by his son. The third son, Bayfield Clark, lived and died at Wingfield, and his son now lives there.

The Kemps. The mother of John Kemp senior (the father of John Kemp of Kemp & Hewitt) kept a little shop in a cottage on the site where Marlborough Buildings now stands. She sold stays, laces and boot laces, cotton, worsted and such like small things. Her son John was a shearman in his youth, but taking his mother's shop he developed it into a general drapery business, and got on in life and became the owner of a lot of house property. He put his son John to learn the woollen manufacturing with Mr Abraham Laverton at Westbury, and when he left there he and his eldest brother, Edward, started cloth making, but they did not keep together long, Edward going to The Upper Mills with a partner, and John going to Innox Mill with Mr Hewitt of Upton Lovell, under the style of Hewitt and Kemp. Mr John Kemp and Mr Hewitt's son Lovell continued that business under the style of Kemp and Hewitt. Edward Kemp did not succeed in his business and it soon came to an end.

It is rather a noticeable feature that so many of the woollen firms in Trowbridge should have been founded by old shearmen. Mr Hewitt senior was a boy in Pocock's mill at Chippenham. Mr Pocock was also the worker and manufacturer at Upton Lovell Mills, and Mr Hewitt was sent to Upton and the trade gradually got into his hands, but being a warm liberal in politics he got into ill repute with the owners of the mill, the Everitt family, and therefore he left Upton Mills and came to Trowbridge and joined Mr Kemp and ran the Innox Mill.

The Gouldsmiths: Before they came to Trowbridge they were woollen cloth merchants in London, and were related to Mr Salter, and joined him in partnership in the firm called S. Salter & Company, which firm comprised then Mr Samuel Salter, Mr Jesse Gouldsmith and Mr John Hayward. Two sons of Gouldsmith and two sons of Hayward followed on in the business.

Mr Gouldsmith senior retired from business and the two sons, Jesse and William, in time became the sole partners of S. Salter and Company. William married Miss Devinish of Weymouth and when he died his brother Jesse married her, going to Germany I think to be married. She had a daughter and two sons by her first husband and one son by the last. Her daughter married Mr George Palmer, the only son of Mr Michael Palmer of the firm of Brown and Palmer, and now lives at Lackham near Lacock, and both being natives of Trowbridge take a great interest in the place of their birth. The sons of Mr Gould-smith two live in the district of Cirencester and one at Shanklin, Isle of Wight.

The Browns: Samuel Brown, the founder of the firm of woollen manufacture (Palmer & Mackay, formerly Brown & Palmer) was the son of a weaver, Roger Brown, who lived at Brick Platts. He went to London for some time, and returned to Trowbridge and kept a small shop, grocery and vegetables, on The Down. The shop still exists; it has two bow windows and is on the left hand side as you enter on the straight part of the road leading to the cemetery. He afterwards started cloth making, and after a time took Yerbury Street Mills, and on the Edghills giving up at Ashton Mill he left Yerbury Street Mills and took Ashton Mills, and lived in the house facing the mills. From here he moved to Rodney House, and I remember seeing the late Lady Brown and her eldest sister carrying a flat table up the Polebarn Road from one house to the other. He died there, I think, at the age of forty-eight, leaving seven daughters and his widow, who was a sister of Samuel Norris the carrier and Henry Norris, the sadler of Silver Street. Having no son he had introduced his nephew, William Roger Brown into his business, and he succeeded in the same, taking into his partnership Mr Michael Palmer, who was at that time head of the woollen department of Norris Ditton & Company, now the Fore Street Warehouse Company. Under the new firm the business grew, and the power looms coming into use at this time helped on the firm as they reaped a great advantage in wages, in cloths woven on the power loom, over the weaving on the old out-of-doors hand looms. The weaving, as well as the spinning, having now to be done at the mills, necessitated the building of mills, formerly the spinning was done away on spinning jennies as well as the weaving. After some years William R. Brown retired from the firm, having made enough I suppose to satisfy him, he having no family. He married his cousin, one of the daughters of his uncle Samuel Brown, and built Highfield on the Hilperton Road, and here both of them died, he leaving the property to his brother-in-law Mr William John Mann, a solicitor of Trowbridge. Some few years before they died, Mr Brown was knighted, which honour he deserved for his gift of the Town Hall to the town as a jubilee gift at the time of the jubilee. Some of the inhabitants of both parties wished for that honour to be given to him then, but a Tory Government being in power it was not done. So I resolved that I would see what I could do when a Liberal government came into power. Not waiting for this, I started quickly at once to bring the matter to the notice of Mr Fred Schnadhorst, the chief secretary of the Liberal Association, whom I had known for years in Birmingham before he went to London, and as a result Mr Brown was knighted. I was expecting the same, as I had a letter from Mr. Schnadhorst to say it would be all right. I do not know, but that others might have worked for the same end. I can only speak of what I did myself.

### (b) Early Recollections of the Woollen Trade

The woollen manufacturers of Trowbridge, when I was a boy, were Samuel Salter & Company at Home Mill with Dyehouse at Upper Mill; J. & T. Clark were at Duke Street Mills, and a Mr Cooper carried on at the top Mill, Duke Street, lately burnt down, and carried on for many years by Salters as their weaving department.

Mr J. W. Gabriel carried on the Yerbury Street Mill.

Mr Samuel Brown worked the mills originally Edghills in Polebarn Lane.

John Henry Webb carried on the mill at the bottom of Wicker Hill, now used as corn mills.

Samuel Parfitt carried on Studley Mills, which Messrs Clark pulled down, and built the present Studley Mills on this site. They then removed their plant from Duke Street and from Stone Mills, which they had rented off Mr Webber, and these remained empty for some time until I bought them and re-started them.

John Stancomb was at the Castle Mills, and for some years after his death his son ran them. After they gave up the Webbs ran there for some years.

Messrs Clark and Perkins ran the small mill next to the Castle Mill. This Mr Clark was not the same family as J. & T. Clark, although they were cousins, their mothers being sisters (Misses Perkins).

Cradle Bridge Mills were worked by William Stancomb, these were closed about three years ago, leaving no Stancombs in the woollen trade in the town.

The brick factory next to Stone Mills was mainly rented by James Cogswell the doeskin maker. After this was burnt he built the Innox Mills, and carried on there until burnt, and after re-building they were rented and worked by Mr Hewitt from Upton Lovell mills and Mr John Kemp junior, who had been apprenticed to Mr Laverton at Westbury. They comprised the new firm of Hewitt & Kemp (now Kemp & Hewitt).

The small mill in Silver Street was worked by Samuel Brown, and afterwards by Kemp & Hewitt.

These were all the mills worked in the town in my early days, but there were a number of small makers, including my father, a Samuel Norris, James Harper, John Dyer, James Watts, George Green, Jacob Cogswell, James & Edward Marchant and others.

who had their work put out to be spun, woven and dressed on commission.

In addition to the foregoing there was Mr James Wicks, who made all drab goods, he had a small mill at Cradle Bridge, now occupied by Mr Norris the builder. My father and brother Joseph worked at this mill for J. & E. Marchant when I was a small boy, and I used to carry their tea and often after went to sleep under the cutters they worked at. It was at this mill I saw the last two pairs of shears worked in Trowbridge. Joseph Gowen, the father I think of Mr. Gowen the painter, was one of the two men working at the shears. I bought these shears at Hayward's sale and have them now, for after Mr Wicks' death the Messrs Haywards, who had left Salter's, carried on Mr Wicks' business. They also on leaving Salter's, built the Upper Mills, now worked by McCalls.

In my early days few manufacturers did their own dyeing. This they put out to dyers, Mr Isaac Moore and Mr Webber. After the wool was brought back from the dyehouse it was opened and cleaned in a machine called a whaum or bumble, turned by hand, and then all the burrs were picked out by an army of women. They picked the wool on wire handles of small mesh; then picking machines came and did the work of picking. Then the wool was oiled and tucked and then carded and slubbed on a spinning machine called a billey. The carding machine turned out the wool on rollers the width of the engine, these were dropped on to a creeper cloth and picked up by boys called roller joiners and joined together by lapping the two ends and rubbing them together on the revolving cloth of the billey. These were then drawn through the rollers and reduced in size by the slubber, thus making the first process in spinning. The slubs or cops were taken off the spindles of the billey and taken to be spun smaller in the thread by hand in the spinning jenny and for smaller counts of yarn this had to be done in two spinnings, all yarn then spun had to be reeled off on a reel by women into hanks and then for warping it had to be wound off the hanks a thread at a time on to spools. These spools were simple lengths of the stalk of the hemlock and in the autumn people went into the field and cut the hemlock to make the spool. The weft or shool yarn was wound from the hanks on to small bobbins to go into the weaver's shuttle. This was the work of quite little boys and girls, and one had to keep two or three weavers supplied.

The warping was done on perpendicular bars and when the proper quantity was warped the warp was tied round at certain distances to keep all the warp threads together, and then the warp was taken off the bars and made into a coil and then tied up fit for the weavers to take away to weave. This was mostly done in the villages. Carts to convey these and the woven cloth with which the weavers used to come from Dilton Marsh, Bradford Leigh and Bromham, also other places. The nearer villages used trucks but each weaver used a large white bag to take his work home and bring the cloth back. The warp was put into a bag and the weft made up into a pad of what was called doublers. Each of these consisted of ten skeins of yarn, two of these were opened to take the other doublers and formed, when full, a round pad. This the weaver put into the mouth of his bag and tied the mouth up and then twisted the bag in the middle and threw it over his shoulder, the warp in front of him and the weft behind, or visa versa as the case might be, and carried the same to the carts etc., or if he lived in the district he would carry his work home in this way and thus he was handicapped and small boys sometimes teased him and going behind would give the bag a push sideways and running off a short distance would shout "blow weaver blow, put down your bag and fight". This the boys knew he could not do, for if he did he could not get his bag on to his shoulder again without help. These were good days for weavers. They lived in the country, were not tied to their work for fixed times, did their gardening when it suited or when they were playing for a change, and then the journey into town with other weavers, each time they filled or finished weaving their cloths, was a nice outing for them. The long windows in the villages around Trowbridge, seen now in so many of the cottages, were where the looms were worked, some of these are now partly walled up.

After the weaver had brought in his piece, and the passer had passed it, by measuring and perching it, the cloth was sent to the mill to be brayed. Many of these mills were in the country and did the braying and the milling. Only the old fashioned stocks were used for milling. After being brayed or scoured, they were brought back again into the towns, and after being dried they were knotted (that is all the knots were picked off) and burled, that is all broken and bad threads and neps or nibs picked out, and then mended that is all defects in warp and weft made good by the needle, then the piece was fit to be sent back to the mill to be milled. Then after milling and scouring to get all the mill soap out, it was brought back into the town again to be dressed. This was done by shearmen who dressed them on the timinogue, dried them on racks in the fields, and then cut off the wool or nap they had raised on them in dressing by the shears. The same men then pressed them and rolled them first to be sent to the cloth merchants, but just before and after my birth, gigs were invented which did the dressing and cutters which did the

cutting, then threw the old shearers out of work. My father was thus thrown out and he learnt to spin on a jenny. Other shearmen had also to turn their hands to other work. Some learnt to weave, but here again the power loom came into use and this necessitated the weaving being done in towns and consequently threw large numbers of the older weavers out of work. The younger men came into the town and worked at the power looms. So the old order changeth and this in my time also. The condenser did away entirely with the work of the slubbers and his four roller joiners, and the larks and self acting mules did away with the jenny and the old hand spinners, all tending to cheapen the production of the cloth to the benefit of the community at large, but doing a great injury to the old orders of workers as a body. This is the law of all inventions, but in the long run is for the greater good of all. If the old shearmen had not been superseded by machinery I do not suppose my father would have ever started manufacturing for himself, and then I should, I suppose, never have been a manufacturer. So out of seeming mis-fortunes at the time good resulted to my father and all of his family. The fullers, invented by an engineer of Trowbridge named Dyer, for the milling of cloth superseded the stocks so there was no necessity of sending the cloth to a country mill to be milled. Therefore the order of manufacturing cloth was quite revolutionised, large mills had to be built to take the long spinning mules and large sheds to take the power looms and with water and fullers manufacturers were able to do all the processess of cloth-making at home.

### (c) Business Career

About a year or so after I started courting in 1859, I began to think as to my future. My intended wife objected to my spinning, and as I could see no future here we talked the matter over and agreed that I should go to the U.S.A., where I had a brother, and she a sister. In view of this I had a large box (now in our bedroom) made so as to go – my intended promising to follow. When my people got to know of this they objected, and my cousin Jabez Walker backed my people up and suggested I should start selling the cloth my father made and what I could buy, and go out and try to sell it to the tailors. This I agreed to do, although I was only twenty years old. My first transaction was I bought a few short lengths of cloth as recorded in my bought book, and my first efforts at selling was I made a parcel of cloth and went to Bath. I could do no business there, and so went on to Bristol, and there I made my first sale to Mr Charles, a tailor of Stokes Croft, after this I got patterns of the stock of black doeskins and black broadcloths, which

Mr Wilkins kept and Mr Dunn ran a flock mill at Bradford which Mr Wilkins managed for them, and I had samples of the flocks they made, so with cloth and flocks I decided to start on a country journey. This I did, going to Burton then Wincanton and on to Sherborne the first day, but made no sales. This was not an encouraging start. I got to Yeovil in the evening, and stayed at John Perry's temperance hotel, there I met with a Mr Stead, travelling for Messrs Gardiner & Company, whole-sale grocers, etc., of Bristol. In conversation I told him my position and just starting in business etc. He said he was driving through Martock, Ilminster, Crewkerne, Chard and other towns and villages and back to Yeovil the end of the week, and offered me a seat in his trap and both share the cost of same. This I gladly accepted, as he said a number of his customers were tailors and he would introduce me to them. This he did, and with selling cloth and several large bales of flock I had a good weeks trade which was a great encouragement to me, and it was nice to have a driving journey through the country and have a friend to instruct me into the usage of the Commercial Room. I agreed to meet him at Yeovil again for the next journey in a months time. This I did, and got other patterns of cloth so as to have something new to show my customers. I went several journeys with Mr Stead in this way. One thing that greatly helped me was the railway between Yeovil and Exeter was making at the time and a lot of flocks for beds were required for the navies. On the flock I made 1d per pound profit, and had no stock to keep, and as a rule I got paid before I had to pay for the goods. I also took other journeys and gradually extended my ground so that during the time I was doing this class of business I opened all the ground south and west of a line drawn from Grimsby to Chester, and visited nearly all the towns of any size below the above named places, except North Wales. My business grew, so I thought it to be my duty to invite my brother Joseph in America to come home and join me. This I did and he returned. Soon after which we started making mattresses and palliasse beds etc. The business grew so fast we had to build a new place to make the goods in, and the business is now in the hands of Mr E. Taylor, my brother's son-in-law. In the year 1872 I expressed a wish to go cloth making again, and we went and looked over Stone Mills and bought them, and at once started fitting it up with machinery etc., and got it to work in the spring of 1873. I attended to the mill, my brother continuing at the mattress trade. We, having sold off our woollen merchanting business and stocks to two young men named Adey and Offer, but they did not agree and did not continue it very

long. I did not entirely give up travelling in the bedding trade, but only took near journeys, such as to the Isle of Wight, Weymouth and Reading districts. I did this as a little break from the mill work. We got Stone Mills in good working order, and were doing well, and then we bought Yerbury Street Mills, which were offered by auction. I had no intention of buying them, and had never mentioned such a thing to my father or brother, but on the evening of the sale I was near the sale room and looked in when the sale was on, and Mr S. Gauntlet, a rival of ours in the bedding trade, had just made a bid for the mills and the auctioneer was asking for a further bid and I gave the nod and Gauntlet, not knowing my presence in the room, did not bid again. I expect if he had known the last bid was mine he would have bid again, and tried to keep me out of the property. The machinery in the factory was sold afterwards and I bought some, and other people bought some. I thought it best to let the others do this, and buy it off them, rather than buy too much myself, in which case I feared they would have run the price up higher than what I bought back for. We worked Stone Mills and Yerbury Street Mills for a number of years, and about 1884 my brother left, taking the mattress business and leaving me the cloth mill. In 1885 Salter's Home and Duke Street Mills were in the market through the death of Mr. W. & J. Gouldsmith; they were offered by auction but drew no bid and I bought Home Mill buildings – Applegates Yard – the wool house and paddock between the back of the house in Applegates Yard and Home Mill buildings at the auction, after which I made an offer £13,000 for the Home and Duke Street Mills which was accepted. I afterwards bought the stock of wool yarns and cloth and machinery, as it stood, the total amount of this purchase was £48,888. Before my action the mills were likely to be stopped and sold, but my buying them they went on working without an hours stop. This was a great benefit to the work people and to the town at large. The next year, 1886, after the purchase of Salter's Mill, I bought the cloth mill at Upton Lovell, contents and most of the cottages and houses in the village, and I carried the mills on for about twelve years, when they were burnt out. Therefore, for a number of years I ran three firms. viz:

J. Walker & Company at Stone & Yerbury Street Mills.

S. Salter & Company at Home & Duke Street Mills.

The Upton Lovell Manufacturing Company at Upton Lovell.

Five mills in all. Later I concentrated the business, and after the destruction of Duke Street Mills by fire the trade continued at the three remaining mills under the style of Salter & Company and Walker & Company. I retired from business in September 1906, my eldest son taking my place.

About the time I bought Salter's Mills, Sir Samuel Marling of Stonehouse sent my wool broker – Mr J. R. Buckler – to me asking me to take over his two mills. I declined to entertain this offer, but he sent Mr Buckler to me again with an offer that if I would entertain the same he would leave me £100,000 in the business at a low rate of interest. I declined again, as I felt I had quite enough on my hands, but I told Mr Buckler to thank Sir Samuel Marling and that I took his offer to be a great compliment.

While I was in business as a woollen merchant and bedding manufacturer about twelve years, I was away from home nearly every week in a year and called at the towns in the part of England as before stated, opening out the West of England and South Wales first and then handing the old ground over to my brother and then I opened new ground. In this I was very successful, and frequently did as much business on a first journey as I did on many journeys afterwards. I did not dislike travelling when I could book orders, but it gave me a great opportunity of seeing the country and getting a knowledge of all the towns of any size in this half of the kingdom, not that I ever neglected the business to see any of the sights that were to be seen in any of the towns. If I had to wait for a train I would take the chance of seeing them. Cornwall and the eastern counties were my familiar grounds. I once remember being at Dover, and whether it was a mirage or not I cannot say but I could see the houses and the sun reflected from the glass in the windows of the houses and other buildings on the coast of France. I visited Dover often after, but never saw the like again. Once at Hastings I saw the tide out a great way, and exposed the stumps of trees for a large area in the bed of the sea. These were the remains of the submerged forest. I have noticed the same exposure of tree stumps in the fens of Lincolnshire, where the soil has been excavated to build up the railway embankments to raise them above the waters of the fens in wet weather. I had a great preference for working in the smaller towns in the country than the large towns; for I could do more business in the smaller places, competition being less keen. After starting cloth making again, I did all the cloth selling myself, except in London, where I had agents Messrs Clare and Walker. This took me to the large towns of England and Scotland, up to Aberdeen, but as business increased I had to employ other agents and travellers. I remember one time driving with my agent along the new embankment, seeing the

Thames River nearly frozen over; at another time I saw the river from the same embankment almost empty in fact, there was only a narrow stream of water flowing down in the centre, and hundreds of people on both sides were walking in the river bed seeking what articles they could find. In all the years since when visiting London and staying, as I have done for years, at the National Liberal Club, I have never seen the water so low as it was on this occasion, and on the occasion I refer to. I was, and am, an original member of the Club.

*(d) Early Recollections of the Town*
My earliest recollections of the town were connected with the Brickplatts and the Halve, where I was born April 19th, 1840, on an Easter Sunday, and it is rather interesting to note that my birthday did not come again on an Easter Sunday until 1908.

In the Halve, on the site of the Cottage Hospital, existed Paradise Road and they had gardens in front and the other side of these gardens another rank of cottages stood and, at the back, these other cottages stood back to back and their fronts came into another yard, entered at the end of Waterloo Buildings, then in front of these houses stood other houses, their front doors leading on to the pavement from the yard by the end of Waterloo Buildings, to the road at the corner of the Halve. So that on the site of the Cottage Hospital there formerly stood about 30 or more cottages.

I remember old Peter Millington, a Waterloo veteran, lived at the end house of Paradise Buildings. In Back Lane to Hilperton stood a Turn-pike stop bar which the children used to swing on, until the Keeper came out and drove them off. I remember just being able to toddle off playing about in the Halve, in the care of my brother Joe and his carrying me up Back Lane to see the ducks in the pond in the Farm yard and the Deer in Clark's park; there was no wall then only a hedge by the side of the footpath in the lane, the house where Mr Wiltshire now lives opposite the Hospital and next to the Fox Inn was a Public House in those days, called The Lancers. I remember the sign with soldiers on it.

At the Hilperton Road corner of the Halve and up to Clark's wall stood a row of cottages and there were no houses in the Furlong, it was only a narrow dirty lane leading down to a field called Four Acres, now the Ashton Street end of Harford Street and the upper part of Ashton Street. Ashton Street, itself, was also a narrow lane up to the same field, it was called Weaver's Lane and the whole of the ground on which Ashton Street, York Place and Alma Street now stand was allotment gardens and my father had an allotment on this site. He built his house in Ashton

53 *Edmund Cartwright, 1743-1823*

54 *Richard Arkwright, 1732-92*

Street; there was not a house in the whole of this area from the Hilperton Road to Polebarn Lane. The hill at the bottom of Ashton Street, leading to West Ashton, was narrow and when Mr Walter Long made the Lodge at the end of his new drive to his house, this narrow road was made wider. There was no house after the Turn-pike house at the bottom of this hill near the bridge on the West Ashton Road, all have been built since.

Coming to another part of the town there were no houses on the Frome or Bradley Road, except a few old ones at Middle Studley, the town end of the Barracks and all the land between the Frome and Wingfield Roads, now built over, was then all fields.

Trowbridge Fair on the 5th August each year was a great event to the young of the town – the fair lasted three days. The first day, in the morning, a cattle fair was held in the Innox – a Cheese fair on the Parade and a Horse fair in Timbrell Street and the Pleasure fair, I have known shows and stalls of various kinds standing from the town bridge up to the Cross Keys, now called the Market Tavern in the Market Place. On Saturdays, the market was held; Butchers' stalls were erected in the space between The Courts and The George and The Woolpack Hotels. Above those houses the vegetable market was held, the baskets being placed on the ground on the side of the pavements on each side of the road, at the bottom of Church Walk. Eggs and poultry were sold. The Saturdays market made the Market Place full of life on Saturdays and, in the evenings, the road was crowded with people. There were then no railways to take people out of the town.

I think I remember when the town bridge was widened. I remember the old Cradle Bridge, it was about 5 or 6 feet wide over the river there, it was built on piles, but across the land to the bottom of Mortimer Street the planks or beams carrying the footpath rested on dwarf walls so that the water, in flood times, could pass under the footbridge or footway between the two streams. The cause of the new bridge being built was the horse soldiers at the Barracks used to use this bridge sometimes, and one day the bridge surface gave way in one place, under the weight of horse and rider. I remember the present bridge being built and a school-mate of mine, living in Longfield, died and I remember planks were laid over the wood arches that the stones of the bridge were to be built on for his funeral to be able to go that way to the Conigre Chapel burying ground.

I remember, before the railway was made, and seeing them driving the piles in the river at the Innox to bridge the river. I also remember the building of the railway bridge in Mortimer Street and seeing a navvy tipping a wheel barrow of bricks over

the side of the cutting and he fell over with the barrow, but I don't think he was hurt much. The new road named the Bythesea Road has only been made recently, before then, there was only the foundry footpath entering opposite Longfield House gates and coming out into Stallard Street by the side of the Rose & Crown Public House.

The public footway leading to the fields behind the British School formerly ran by the side of the British School, but the late Mr Burchall Rodway got the way diverted, by granting a way to the fields lower down towards Conigre. The old footway by the side of the British School was a part of an old footpath leading from Trowbridge to Bradford, so I have heard old inhabitants say, it started at Silverthorne Yard, Trowbridge, crossed Duke Street through late Clark's Factory Yard into Union Street (I remember when the public used the Duke Street to Union Street way) it then crossed through the Rectory grounds to the path by the side of the British School. The path then crossed the lane into the fields and ran down to the River Biss which was crossed by a footbridge. The path from the lane to the river can now be traced, for it is raised down under the hedge higher than the field. After crossing the river the path was continued to the Bradford Road.

I remember the ford across the river at the Town Bridge, it went straight under what is now Clark's wall and came out into Stallard Street and was the only way into the town before the bridge was built. On the site of the Town Bridge Gardens, stood some cottages and Norris's Wagon Yard. These were bought by the Old Local Board for £800, and the site turned into gardens as at present. The water from Stone Factory Mill Water wheel came out into the river under the arch, now to be seen in the wall near the entrance to what is now Sainsbury's Corn Mill. At that time, the water of the river spread out nearly up to the gates of this mill, then, when it was desired to confine the river within banks at the Town Bridge, I, being the owner of Stone Mill, came to an agreement with Messrs Clark and Messrs Webb to turn the mill tail water into the river nearer to Stone Mill, as at present, not for it to flow down through Clark's land to the town ford. The right of way to Stone Mills was up this ford in former times, right up the mill stream.

I remember the Parish Church being restored about the year 1846 when a good length of the steeple was re-built, and people were drawn up in a basket; the weather-cock was put on by a son of Mr William Wilkins. I think he was the architect of the Upper Studley Church and died young and is buried there.

M

At this date, 6th May, 1910, ladders are put up the Parish Church Steeple in order to fix a lightning conductor to the Steeple. I remember the Stocks. They were inside of the iron railings and exactly opposite the door of the Blind-house. I don't remember seeing anyone in the Stocks, but remember plenty of people being locked up in the Blind-house and their friends used to gather out side and talk to the prisoner inside. I heard of one man talking to a prisoner inside and asking him what he had done to be locked up. The man inside told him, and the out-side man replied;

'Jack, they can't lock thee up for that!'
The prisoner replied:
'You fool I am here.'

After the new Police Station was built, the Blind-house was not used.

Opposite the Conigre Chapel there existed two cottages and a nasty stable, so there was only just room for a cart to pass. I bought this property and pulled down the two houses and the stable and gave the site to the town, keeping the other portion of the property. This greatly improved the Chapel and the Liberal Club.

I remember the Market House being built and Mr Stancomb, the builder, was promised at that time that the authorities of the town would make the road through into the Courts. This was not done but, remembering the promise, when the Foundry and dwelling house on the site of what is now Market Street was for sale, I bought the property and held it until the Local Board took it over to make the promised street, although the day after I bought it, the late Mr Geo. Snailum came to me and asked if I would sell at a profit? I replied:

'No, it is to make the new road through to the Courts and I should not sell.'

On this site stood work shops, where Mr Pitman, the father of Sir Isaac Pitman, started making cloth before he removed to Bradford-on-Avon. Sir Isaac Pitman was born down a yard in Hill Street.

Manvers Street was formerly only a drive, leading from Fore Street to Back Street, but a fire having taken place there, other buildings were pulled down and Manvers Street made.

# Sites of Historical Interest

## I. GLOUCESTERSHIRE

### CHURCHES

*Northleach*
The woolman's church *par excellence*, by which all others are judged. The church was, of course, built by rich woolmen, particularly by John Fortney, who raised the nave to make it more 'light-some' and splendid in 1458. He asked to be buried in the aisle and his brass is probably the best of the outstanding collection in the church.

*Chipping Camden*
An equally important centre, with excellent brasses, William Greville, described as the flower of the wool merchants of all England, is buried there, and his house, one of the finest medieval buildings in England, stands in the village street.

*Minchinhampton*
A Gloucestershire hill town with a good church and excellent stone houses. One of the oldest of the Gloucestershire mills (Playne and Company) still 'drape' as Leland would say, on the outskirts.

*Sevenhampton*
A hidden-away village church, mainly Perpendicular, and built by John Cambrey, a rich wool stapler. His brass is in the church.

*Cirencester*
The church is one of the finest parish churches in the country with an outstanding south porch. It is a fine monument to the prosperity of the town which rested on wool. The later architecture, in particular the fine seventeenth- and eighteenth-century houses, belongs to the days of the Gloucestershire cloth trade prosperity.

*Fairford*
This is where John Tame, a merchant dealing in both wool and cloth, placed stained glass from Flanders in the church, perhaps the finest late medieval stained glass in the whole of England.

**169**

### Painswick

The famous church with its clipped yews is but one of the many monuments that make this the most beautiful small town in Gloucestershire, just as Bradford-on-Avon is in Wiltshire. Visitors should explore the village streets, and in particular the Court House and the Falcon Inn, with its famous bowling green where Shakespeare may have played.

### Wotton-under-Edge

It is easy today to forget that during the Tudor dynasty and later, the southern Cotswold or edge country was just as much a clothing centre as the Stroud Valley. Unfortunately the church here has been rather badly restored, but the town itself should be visited.

### FACTORIES

### Ebley

An impressive building, still used as a wool-spinning factory.

### Kings Stanley

Now Marling and Evans and still a woollen mill. An outstanding example of iron-framed mill building.

### Longfords

As Dr Jennifer Tann so rightly says in her book *Gloucestershire Woollen Mills,* 'a complex and fascinating site. Many of the buildings shown on the 1813 map can still be seen, among these the eighteenth-century four-storey stone mill which housed the yarn and fulling mill belonging to William Playne.' Much interesting information about the site can be obtained from A. T. Playne's *Minchinhampton and Avening*, already quoted. And it is perhaps permissible to mention here that the mill continues to be one of the most successful in the trade, and makes, besides superfine flannels, the best tennis ball coverings in the world.

### Dunkirk Mill

Architecturally perhaps the finest mill in the Stroud Valley, built between 1800 and 1821.

### Lodgemoor

Architecturally very different to the other Stroud mills, mainly because of its date. The older mill was destroyed by fire in 1871, and the present brick building was erected in 1875. Fortunately the very fine eighteenth-century mill house escaped the fire. It is now the offices of Strachan & Company, who still make the finest woollen cloths (including billiards) at Lodgemoor, and also of Winterbotham, Strachan & Playne who control most of the woollen mills still operating in Gloucestershire and Wiltshire.

### Cam

Varied architecturally, but interesting because cloth is still made there, indeed the fabrics made by Hunt and Winterbotham are world famous. The main mill building was probably built in 1815.

### MISCELLANEOUS

### Woodchester Round Tower

The best of several in Gloucestershire, whose use is still in dispute. Probably intended either for drying or stoving (that is bleaching) wool.

*Chedworth Roman Manor*
Loveliest of all Cotswold sights, and included here because it was for so long considered to be a Roman fulling mill. Alas they were simply Roman baths.

*Greville's House*
See Chipping Camden.

## 1a. BRISTOL
### CHURCHES

*Church of St Mary's, Redcliffe*
Called by Queen Elizabeth the fairest, goodliest and most famous parish church in England, and the main memorial of the wealth of Bristol's cloth trade. The famous merchant, Canynge, gave much of his wealth to the church, and is buried there with a good memorial, c. 1465. Even better, the slightly later monument of him as Dean of Westbury, 1467, an alabaster effigy of good quality with the features, as Mr Bryan Little rightly says, of a Quaker businessman.

*Temple Church*
This had a weaver's chapel, now destroyed. The leaning tower is distinctive.

## 2. WILTSHIRE
### CHURCHES

*Steeple Ashton*
One of the great architectural glories of Wiltshire, and the finest clothier's church in the West. The only one, in fact, that can really be compared with the great churches of East Anglia (Lavenham and Long Melford). Originally possessed a steeple, giving a total height of 186 ft., hence the name of the village. We know that two clothiers, Robert Long and Walter Lucas, paid for the aisle and Long's will, dated 1501, says the work is begun but not completed.

*St Mary's, Calne*
The proud church of a prosperous clothiers' town, nearly all Perpendicular outside; this was the great age of Calne. Actually clothing ceased in Calne relatively early.

*Trowbridge*
With Bradford, this is the Wiltshire clothing town *par excellence*, but the church, unfortunately, was much restored in 1847–48. Originally built in 1460, when John Wykes left goods and money to help construct it; and later James Terumber, who died in 1483, left more.

*Salisbury: St Edmunds*
Completely Perpendicular, begun in 1407 when clothing at Salisbury was at its most prosperous stage.

*Salisbury: St Thomas*
The older church collapsed in 1447, and rebuilding began almost immediately, financed by the rich merchants of the town, above all William Swayne, who was responsible for the south chapel dated 1450. His name and merchant's mark are in the two beams of the fine roof. There is also a monument to the Godmanstone family, who were also famous merchants. There is some glass with the merchant's mark of Swayne and also Webb.

*Westwood*
See under Westwood Manor.

*Seend: Holy Cross*
The fine new aisle was built by John Stokes, a clothier, in the fifteenth century. There are cloth shears in the west window moulding.

*Bradford-on-Avon: Holy Trinity*
Naturally full of clothing remains. The eastern aisle was built by the Horton family. There are brasses to Thomas Horton and his wife, and then, from the later coloured cloth days, a monument to Antony Methuen by the distinguished eighteenth-century sculptor J. M. Rysbrack. Pevsner describes it as 'a noble standing monument with a grey sarcophagus framed by ionic columns carrying a pedant.' Also, about the same date, a monument to another clothier John Thresher, father and son.

### HOUSES

Architecturally speaking the clothiers' houses of Wiltshire are outstanding. They can be divided into two groups, medieval, that is white broadcloth trade; and eighteenth century, that is coloured broadcloth trade.

### *Medieval*

*Westwood*
Once again the house and church must be considered together. Here, however, the church is less changed, and the fine Perpendicular tower of Somerset style was built by Thomas Horton (see Bradford). He died in 1530. The house, another gem, is rather complex, and what we see today was built over four periods: (1) c. 1400, (2) c. 1480, (3) c. 1515–30, (4) early seventeenth century, and only the third was the work of Horton.
   Westwood belongs to the National Trust and can therefore be visited.

*South Wraxall*
Probably the grandest of the three medieval houses that so excellently illustrate the wealth of the Wiltshire Tudor cloth trade. It is a successful mixture of the fifteenth century and later Elizabethan and Jacobean styles. The owners throughout (until the last few years) have been the Long family, one of the principal clothing families of the area around Trowbridge for so long.

*Salisbury: the Hall of John Hall*
The finest city clothier's house of the period, today most incongruously disguised as a cinema, but behind the façade, if that is the right word, the very substantial remains of the house of John Hall, woollen cloth merchant of Salisbury, four times mayor, can be found.

*Salisbury: the House of John à Port*
c. 1450 and very fine.

*Stockton House*
A fine square Elizabethan house, built by the clothier John Topp, faced with bands of flint and stone so typical of the area. Also Topp Alms-Houses, built c. 1657.

*Eighteenth Century*

*Trowbridge: Lloyds Bank*
An outstanding piece of domestic architecture, built c. 1720 for John Cooper, a clothier, and, as Pevsner says, so stately as to call to mind Genoa.

*Trowbridge: Midland Bank*
Comparable with Lloyds, but lacking a little the delicacy of the former. Of these two houses and the group comprising The Parade (see below) Pevsner says, in his introduction to his *Buildings of Wiltshire,* 'the houses of the eighteenth century at Bradford and Trowbridge are up to the best in Bristol, and at least two at Trowbridge (that is Lloyds Bank and the Midland Bank) are grander than any and would make quite notable additions to the palazzo architecture of say Verona'. Might one suggest Vicenza rather than Verona?

*Trowbridge: The Parade*
Best group of clothiers' houses in Wiltshire. Not equal to Lloyds Bank individually, but as a group unique and kept in an outstanding condition by the present owners, Ushers Brewery.

*Warminster: Byne House*
Built for a clothier named Wansey. Finished 1755.

*Bradford-on-Avon: The Hall*
Really belongs to the earlier period of the white broadcloth trade. Built by John Hall, a clothier of about 1610, and very typical of the period.

*Bradford-on-Avon: Druces Hill House*
Almost an archetype of the early Georgian clothier's house.

*Bradford-on-Avon: Westbury House*
Early Georgian with palladian garden.

*Bradford-on-Avon: Belcombe Court*
A surprise. Belcombe Court belongs, architecturally speaking, to Bath. Frances Yerbury of the famous clothing family called in John Wood to adapt an older house. And the architect thought it was one of the best jobs that he had ever done. There is also fine interior decoration.

### FACTORIES

*Bradford-on-Avon: Kingston Mill*
Early and large. Thomas Divett bought the ground in 1802 and presumably built shortly afterwards.

*Bradford-on-Avon: Abbey Mills*
Much later, indeed the last woollen mill to be built in this part of the West Country. The architect was Richard Gane, an interesting figure, and the building probably dates from 1875, perhaps a little earlier.

*Trowbridge: Stone Mills*
Typical early mill, c. 1814.

*Trowbridge: Home Mills*
Later (further up: The Courts, 1865). Built following the great fire of 1862.

*Malmesbury: Avon Mill*
Architecturally the best in Wiltshire.

MISCELLANEOUS

*Bradford-on-Avon: Middle Rank and Tory*
Terraces of three-storied houses, obviously built during Bradford's great days as a clothing town, but I do not think they were weavers' houses as is sometimes stated.

*Avoncliff Weir*
One of the many that show how the late medieval and Tudor cloth trade changed rivers to get the power needed for their fulling mills. A very attractive site. Was the Old Court Hotel a workshop for weavers? There is also a fine aqueduct by John Rennie.

*Trowbridge: Weavers' Cottages*
Many scattered through the town; see, for example, Mortimer Street and Timbrell Street, also Newtown. They are being quickly destroyed.

*Trowbridge Workshops*
In the eighteenth century clothiers frequently built workshops behind their houses – deplorable from an architectural point of view – but perhaps necessary.

3. EAST SOMERSET

CHURCHES

*Shepton Mallet: St Peter and St Paul*
Comparatively little known about who was responsible, but a great clothing town. The church has a wonderful roof.

HOUSES

Not as many outstanding examples, and one looks at townscapes rather than individual buildings: see especially Frome, Shepton Mallet.

FACTORIES

*Bath: Mill at Twerton*
Typical early nineteenth century; clothing continued there until the late 1940s.

*Freshford: Dunkirk Mills*
Typical early nineteenth-century country mill, with clothier's house next door. A wonderful growth of ivy covers the building.

*Telisford Mill*
A small country mill. The sites of the workers' houses can still be seen. Very attractive site.

MISCELLANEOUS

*George Inn, Norton St Philip*
Certainly one of the most remarkable medieval inns in England. Built, it is said, by Hinton Priory as a staple for their produce, and according to tradition the woolmen met in the upper rooms there.

*Weirs at Stowford and Farleigh Hungerford*
Two excellent examples of the type of work the builders of the early mills did in the twelfth and thirteenth centuries.

## 4. DEVON AND WEST SOMERSET
### CHURCHES

*Tiverton: St Peter*
Well displaying the richness, even the ostentation, of the Devon serge merchants. Showpiece is the south porch for which John Greenways was responsible, and one is inevitably reminded of the church at Long Melford.

*Taunton: St Mary*
Dominated by the 163 ft. tower, actually rebuilt 1862, but said to be a faithful copy.

*Cullompton: The Lane Chapel*
The famous Lane chapel, or more correctly speaking, aisle, was built c. 1525 by John Lane, often called a wool merchant but actually a cloth merchant. Typically flamboyant without any modesty and with the usual emblems of merchant marks and shears and teasels. Probably the finest monument to the trade in the area.

### FACTORIES

*Tiverton: John Heathcoats*
Unfortunately (from an architectural point of view) the old factory to which John Heathcoat brought his machine lace manufacture in 1816, after his Loughborough factory had been destroyed by the Luddites, was itself destroyed by fire a few years ago. Most of what one now sees is modern, and most interesting: the finest modern textile factory in the West of England. A more detailed examination, however, shows that a great deal remains from the earlier period, for example the gate lodges, the terraced workers' cottages and the schoolhouse, which Heathcoat built in 1841; a delightful place.

*Wellington: The Mills of the Fox Family*
The industrial buildings of this long-established and famous firm are a little outside the town at Tonedale. Not as important architecturally speaking as their literary documentary material.

*North Tawton*
A worsted manufacturing industry lingered on in various Devon centres into the twentieth century, and North Tawton can be taken as a representative example. The buildings are well preserved, and are in fact the collecting and storage depot for the British Wool Board. Although not very exciting architecturally, they do give a good impression of the nineteenth-century mill.

*Ottery St Mary*
Comparatively little-known town lying a few miles off the much crowded summer route to Devon. It is very attractive and well worth a detour for those interested in architecture. The serge factory, built 1788–90, is a dramatic piece of work. The church is also good, but it does not dominate the town, which is itself full of many good things.

### MISCELLANEOUS

*Exeter: Tuckers' Hall*
Time and the bombing raids of 1939–45 destroyed most of medieval and Tudor Exeter, and with

it what textile remains there were—not in fact very many. Tuckers' Hall in Fore Street is well worth a visit. It was the former chapel and after the Reformation the hall of the Guilds of Weavers, Tuckers and Shearmen. Built in 1471, but unfortunately has been very much restored.

### Tiverton: Blundell's School
A delightful building of 1604, built by the clothier Peter Blundell. The school, of course, still exists in newer buildings, 1880–82, on the outskirts of the town. Perhaps a school foundation is the best way for a wealthy businessman to be remembered.

## 5. BERKSHIRE

The textile trade of the Kennet valley awaits its historian. Newbury was the main centre and for the most part had little connection with the broadcloth trade described in this book. According to Leland it was, with Reading and Abingdon, the most important cloth-making town in Berkshire. Judging by what remains, it was the chief town. The history of the clothier Jack of Newbury (actually John Smallwood) is well known from Deloney's writings, although the two hundred looms, two hundred pretty boys, two hundred maidens and one hundred women who worked for him are, to a considerable extent, a product of the imagination. However, Newbury does have two memorable buildings listed below.

### Museum in Wharf Road
Pevsner describes this as the most interesting house in Newbury. Often called the Cloth Hall, but was actually built as a cloth-weaving, municipal run workshop to give occupation to the poor, and as such almost unique in Great Britain.

### Shaw House
On the outskirts of the town, one of the loveliest Tudor houses in existence. Built by Thomas Dolman, a wealthy clothier, in 1581.

## 5b. WORCESTERSHIRE

Worcester was, in Tudor times, an important broadcloth town, specialising in white broadcloth. There was a Worcester Hall at Blackwell Hall in London, but unlike the industry farther south it did not survive into the coloured cloth trade, and there are few remains, with none that can really be included in such a brief survey as has been given here.

\*     \*     \*

This survey of the architectural remains of the West Country wool textile trade is admittedly superficial, but has been added because the author feels that even today the value, and in the case of this industry, the beauty of what remains, is not always appreciated. For example, the number of people who are in the trade today and interested in its future and who have not wandered through such clothing towns as Bradford-on-Avon, Painswick, Minchinhampton and Trowbridge, never fails to surprise. If this note encourages them to do this then its object will have been completely fulfilled. Such wanderers will have with them the Pevsner volumes in the *Buildings of England* series. All who know and have used them know how they have contributed to our knowledge of English architecture. They will also realise how much the present writer has depended on them.

In addition to the buildings that relate to the trade described in this gazetteer, there are several other towns which are essentially textile towns, and in this respect one can mention Witney, with its blankets, Bridport and its rope industry, Axminster and Wilton with their carpets.

# Textile Glossary

*Abb:*
1. Alternative name for weft.
2. Skirtings of poor wool kept separate when classing after shearing.

*Abb Wool:*
Wool for weft yarn.

*Acid Dye:*
A class of coal-tar colours, usually themselves colourless salts, but having the property of combining with acids to form colour bases or dyes and widely used in the wool textile trade.

*Ageing:*
Really the process of oxidising the bleaching agent in the cloths, which are taken from the chlorine bath and left exposed to the air; but sometimes used more generally to denote the practice of allowing material to rest between one stage of processing and another.

*Alizarin:*
The colouring principle of the important old natural dye, madder, now of course produced synthetically and the basis of a wide range of dyes.

*Alpaca:*
The hair of the alpaca, a type of llama found in South America; very soft handling and used alone or mixed with worsted for superfine lightweight cloths. The use of alpaca was the great achievement of Sir Titus Salt.

*Alum:*
A complex salt of great antiquity. Has been very important in the history of the wool textile trade as a mordant. See an excellent account of the alum trade in Singer: *The Earliest Chemical Industry.*

*Angola:*
Yarn made of a mixture of wool and cotton. For example, the wool–cotton khaki shirting was known

as the angola shirting. But how was the word derived? The *Oxford English Dictionary* suggests that it is a corruption of angora.

*Angora:*
The hair of the angora rabbit which has a very soft handle, and is used for making soft fabrics for children's wear and for dresses. Should be distinguished from the angora goat, which produces mohair, quite a different fibre.

*Anthrax:*
A disease caught, in the past, from handling certain types of wool, particularly from India. Now very rare, at least in this country, due to the stringent precautions taken.

*Astrakan:*
Wool taken from the skins of the Karakul sheep of South Africa. Very black and curly, the lambs are killed very shortly after birth. Often called Persian Lamb.

*Backed Cloths:*
Cloths which are made heavy by using an extra warp or weft.

*Backing off:*
The process in mule spinning whereby the slack yarn on the spindle is unwound.

*Back Roller:*
The roller in a drawing or spinning frame that delivers the sliver to the drafting zone.

*Backwashing:*
In worsted yarn manufacture the washing of the wool between carding and combing.

*Baize:*
A heavy woollen cloth, well felted, and usually raised on both sides.

*Bale:*
Wool pack, the weight varies with the country of origin, usually 200–300 lb. from Australasia and 500–600 lb. from South America.

*Ballooning:*
The flight of the yarn between the front rollers and the ring on the ring spinning system.

*Barathea:*
The twilled hopsack weave widely used for men's worsted suitings.

*Bartrees (or Bars):*
The frame upon which the warp was prepared.

*Barwood:*
A widely used natural dye.

*Batt:*
A sample of wool felted together and made to match a shade before sending the main lot forward to the production line.

*Batten:*
The bar which forms the base of the loom sleigh.

*Bays:*
Cloth made of worsted warp and woollen weft, first manufactured in England in the sixteenth century, especially in Essex and particularly at Bocking. Bocking Bays were famous. Later widely manufactured in the West Country.

*Beam:*
Several meanings:
1. The warp beam upon which the warp yarn is wound.
2. The cloth beam upon which the woven cloth is wound.
3. The breast beam which is the front part of the loom and guides the cloth on to the cloth beam.
4. The back beam which guides the warp from the warp beam to the healds. Sometimes called the backrest.

*Beaming:*
The process of winding the warp from the warping bar to the weaver's beam.

*Beating up:*
The action by which the reed in the loom beats up the pick of weft into the fell or edge of the cloth.

*Beaver:*
A heavy milled woollen cloth with a raised finish, resulting in a nap like a beaver's skin.

*Bedford Cord:*
A distinctive weave giving a well-defined rib in the cloth.

*Beer:*
A term denoting a definite number of warp threads – usually 40. The warp is then said to consist of so many beers. For example, 2,400 ends would be 60 beers. Not so widely used as formerly. Sometimes spelt bier.

*Bellies:*
The wool from the belly of the sheep. Can be good quality but usually very dirty.

*Berlins:*
The name given to torn up knitwear which is used again in cheap cloths. The derivation of the word is mysterious.

*Bichromate of Soda (or Potash):*
Today the most widely used mordant in the wool textile trade. A compound, of course, of chrome and soda (or potash). Known in the trade simply as chrome.

*Billy:*
The slubbing billy, an important machine during the first half of the nineteenth century. The slubbings taken off the carding machine were drafted and given a modicum of twist on the billy before being properly spun on the jenny.

*Bird's Eye:*
A distinctive design which gives, with a two and two colouring, a neat spot effect. Widely used in the worsted trade.

*Blackface:*
The native sheep of the hills of Scotland. The wool is used for the well-known Harris Tweed, for carpets, and in Italy for stuffing mattresses.

*Bleaching:*
The process of improving the whiteness of textile materials.

*Blending:*
The mixing of different qualities and colours and types of textile raw materials together previous to spinning.

*Block Printing:*
The printing of cloth by hand blocks. The original method of printing now largely replaced by roller and screen printing.

*Blowing:*
A process in wool cloth finishing whereby the fabric is set and further shrinking avoided. Also known as decatising. In the cotton trade the word is applied to the opening or scutching operation.

*Bobbin:*
A round spool used for holding the yarn. The word is also used more widely, and the weft pirn is in some areas called the weft bobbin.

*Bombazine:*
A fabric, usually black, made of worsted warp and silk weft. Originally a speciality of Norwich. Not made today.

*Botany:*
A generic term covering the best wool and the yarns and fabrics made therefrom. The word derives from Botany Bay, New South Wales, and emphasises the superfine nature of these wools.

*Boucle:*
Fancy yarn with loops and curls. Also cloth made therefrom.

*Box Cloth:*
A very heavy milled woollen fabric.

*Bradford System:*
The method of drawing and spinning worsted yarn used in the Yorkshire (that is Bradford) worsted trade.

*Brazilwood:*
A good natural dye, much used for rich browns. The dye was known before the discovery of South America and in fact gave the name to the country not vice versa.

*Britch:*
The rough wool grown around the tail. Sometimes called breech.

*Broadcloth:*
Originally any cloth made on the broad loom, but later a fine cloth, woven in the plain weave, but heavily milled. Yorkshire broadcloths were sometimes called Leeds Cloths where they were chiefly made, but West of England broadcloths were the finest and the best.

*Buckskin:*
Fine woollen cloths with a milled and dressed finish showing a distinctive twill. A West of England speciality.

*Bulked Yarn:*
Yarn given special treatment to increase the bulk – a word much used at present in the man-made fibre trade, where yarn bulking is an important and prosperous industry.

*Bunting:*
Plain worsted cloth.

*Burling:*
Removal of vegetable matter and the rectification of certain cloth faults in woollen and worsted fabrics. The meaning of the word varies from district to district. For example, sometimes includes knotting, that is the removal of knots on the yarn. Does not include mending (sometimes called drawing) which puts right the faults caused by broken ends and other weaving mistakes.

*Burling Irons:*
The implements used for carrying out the above operation.

*Burrs:*
The spiney seed which contaminates so much wool. Removed either by mechanical action, or more often by carbonising.

*Callimancoes:*
A worsted cloth made originally in Norwich and then in the West Riding.

*Camblets:*
Cheap coarse worsted (or stuffs) often made with brilliant warp stripes. Was supposed to be rain resistant, and consequently used for cloaks and wraps, and for cheap coatings. Made in Norwich and exported by the East India Company. Not to be confused with Camlets.

*Camlets:*
Fine plain weave fabric, originally made from camel hair hence the name.

*Cap Spinning:*
A method of spinning worsted yarn popular for producing yarn for the hosiery trade. Technically, the important point is that the hollow metal cap plays the same part in winding on as the ring and flyer, with the important difference that the cap is stationary.

*Carbonising:*
A method of removing burrs and other vegetable matter from wool by means of sulphuric acid. Can be done either in the wool, which is usual when heavily contaminated, or in the piece.

*Carding:*
A preliminary treatment before spinning to open and mix the wool. Originally done by hand cards which were covered with teasels and later wire. The word derives from the latin name for teasels.

*Card Wire (or Card Clothing):*
The covering, now leather or other suitable material, into which staples or wires are inserted, and then used for covering the carding set.

*Carriage:*
The front part of the mule, that is the part that moves backwards and forwards.

*Cashmere:*
The wool of the Tibet goat. Probably the finest and loveliest of all fibres. The word has occasionally been badly corrupted to denote torn up knitwear.

*Cassimere:*
A fine woollen cloth made in the two and two twill weave, deriving from Francis Yerbury's patent of 1766. The word is sometimes misspelt kerseymere, but this is misleading as it comes from the French casimir, that is fine cloth, and has nothing to do with kersey. It should be pointed out that the common twill is very much older, and was certainly not Yerbury's invention.

*Cavalry Twill:*
A fine distinctive cloth with a kind of double twill (technically caused by a faulty stitch in a double weft cloth), but best known as the correct habit for riding. Sometimes called a tautz twill.

*Chain:*
Alternative name for warp, widely used in the West of England.

*Cheese:*
A package of yarn similar in form to a truckel cheese so presumably the name.

*Cheviot:*
The breed of sheep native to the Cheviot hills. A good dual purpose sheep, giving crisp wool, hence the name for the distinctive cheviot suiting. It should perhaps be pointed out that the best Cheviot suitings were not often made from pure cheviot wool; a mixture of this wool with New Zealand Halfbred and English Southdown being the most usual.

 The word Cheviot is now used in a wider sense to cover fabrics made from any type of wool other than Merino quality.

*Chlorination:*
The treatment given to wool with chlorine to remove the surface scales and so prevent shrinking.

*Classing:*
The classing of wool after shearing. Not be be confused with sorting. Classing, as the name infers, classes the fleeces, sorting divides different qualities of wool in the same fleece.

*Cochineal:*
The scarlet dye obtained from the dried bodies of insects which gave the brightest of all natural dyes, especially when used with a tin mordant.

*Cockled:*
Cloths that, for one reason or another, have become puckered up in manufacture.

*Colonial Wools:*
Wools from Australia, New Zealand and South Africa. Surprising that the word is still used.

*Combing:*
The preparatory process for long wools. The short fibre, the noil, is removed and the product, the top, is spun into worsted yarn.

*Combing Wool:*
Long wool that is suitable for combing.

*Comeback:*
Wool produced by crossing the Merino sheep with a Crossbred sheep and then crossing back with Merino. In other words three-quarter Merino.

*Condenser:*
The final part of a complete carding set, where the carded web of wool is divided into strips which are rubbed into a kind of twistless sliver.

*Cones:*
A package of yarn in conical form. For some purposes more convenient to handle than a cheese.

*Cop:*
The yarn package obtained on the mule.

*Cord:*
Cloth woven in a weave which gives a cord effect, either down or across the fabric. Obtained by extending the plain weave either in warp or weft.

*Cotty Wool:*
Wool which, due usually to malnutrition, has become felted and matted together.

*Count:*
The system used for measuring the size of yarn. Usually the number of hanks of unit length that weigh 1 lb. For example, in the standard West of England areas the number of hanks of 320 yards that weigh 1 lb. The South Devon serge trade uses a different system. Most woollen districts have their own numbering system, but the worsted basis (hank of 560 yards to weigh 1 lb.) was and is fairly generally used, and has in fact led to the most common method of judging wool fineness. Thus a 60s wool is one that would spin to yarn of such a fineness that 60 hanks of 560 yards would weigh 1 lb. All these traditional numbering systems of yarn sizes are to be replaced by the new Tex system.

*Crabbing:*
A worsted finishing process; the fabric is treated in boiling water or steam while wound on a perforated roller, and this sets and defines the fabric so that variations will not occur in the following processes. Rather similar to blowing for woollens. Also called decatising.

*Creel:*
The stand for holding the yarn package, cop, cone, etc., for warping.

*Crimp:*
The distinctive waviness of wool, a most important and distinctive property.

*Cropping:*
The cutting of the surface fibres from the cloth. Also called shearing or simply cutting.

*Crossband:*
Yarn where the twist direction is from right to left. Compare with openband. The word derives from the nature of the driving band on the spinning machine, whether crossed or not. This im-

portant property of the yarn is often now indicated by the word S or Z twist, the main line in the letter indicating the direction of the twist.

*Crossbred:*
The result of crossing two distinct breeds of sheep. In wool terms crossbred wool has come to mean any wool below 60s quality (that is other than Merino); but this is really a misuse of the word as it would mean that wool from, say, the Romney sheep, would be classed as crossbred.

*Crutching:*
The wool obtained when sheep, particularly in hot countries, are taken to the shearing sheds half way through the year and there have their backsides clipped. Also often their faces, but this wool should strictly be called wiggings. The two are often put together and sold as crutchings.

*Cut:*
When a warp was long enough to make two or three pieces, each one as cut out and taken to the clothier was called a cut, that is a piece. In manufacturing today warps are known as one, two, three cuts, etc.

*Cuttling:*
Folding of cloth backwards and forwards. An alternative to wrapping or rolling. Sometimes called in cuttle.

*Daggings:*
The name given to wool that is heavily contaminated with dirt, and the natural grease of the animal. Hence daggy wool.

*Darning:*
An alternative name for mending.

*Dead Wool:*
Wool removed from sheep that have died from natural causes, *not* if killed for meat.

*Decatising:*
An alternative name for blowing or crabbing.

*Degreasing:*
Removal of the wool fat, etc., by means of a solvent.

*Delaine:*
Light worsted cloth in plain weave.

*Dent:*
The space between the wires on a loom reed.

*Design:*
The plan of a weave, usually made out on squared paper with crosses to indicate where the warp goes over the weft.

*Devil:*
A machine by which wool rags are torn up by the shoddy or mungo manufacturer.

*Devil's Dust:*
The waste made during the tearing of wool rags.

*Discharge:*
A method of printing whereby the fabric is dyed a solid colour and then printed with a substance that removes the dye, thence producing a pattern.

*Distaff:*
The cleft stick that holds the carded fibre on the hand spinning wheel.

*Dobby:*
An arrangement for raising and lowering the harnesses on a loom, hence the dobby loom.

*Doeskin:*
A fine woollen cloth made in a five-end weave and dress finished. The traditional dress for naval officers.

*Doffer:*
Last roller on a carding set.

*Doffing:*
Removing the cops from the mule or any other similar process.

*Dolly:*
The piece-scouring machine where the fabric is treated in rope as opposed to open width form.

*Donegal:*
Characteristic Irish tweed, made in the plain weave, with specially prepared fancy yarn.

*Double Cloth:*
When two cloths are woven together and stitched by intertwining one of the warp (or weft) with the other weft (or warp).

*Doubling:*
The twisting together of two yarns, very common in the worsted yarn trade. Also the name given to the combination of slubbing or slivers in worsted drawing, so done to produce evenness or rather to obviate unevenness that would arise if a single sliver was drawn out into yarn.

*Drafting:*
The attenuations of slubbings, slivers or rolling in drawing and/or spinning. There are really two types of drafting, (1) roller drafting where the fibres are pulled away from each other by passing between pairs of rollers running at different surface speeds, (2) spindle drafting where the attenuation takes place between a pair of rollers and a spindle that is both revolving and moving away from the rollers, thus inserting twist during the drafting.

*Draft:*
The measurement of attenuation given in drafting, for example 1 : 2 would mean that the size of the sliver had been halved; also, quite differently, the way in which the treads of the warp are arranged in the loom so as to give the necessary pattern.

*Drawing:*

The process, particularly with reference to worsted spinning, by which the combed top is drawn out to a finer sliver ready for spinning. Also, very differently, the alternative name for mending.

*Drawing In:*

The drawing of the warp threads through the heddles ready for weaving.

*Drawloom:*

The old form of loom for fancy weaving, where the weaver had control of each warp end.

*Dressing:*

The process of raising and then cutting the nap of the woven cloth, thereby giving the traditional dress finish. Sometimes the preparation of the warp for the loom.

*Drop Box:*

The type of shuttle box, invented by Robert Kay, which made changing shuttles simpler and ultimately automatic.

*Dry Combing:*

Combing without the addition of oil, more common on the Continent than in England.

*Duffel:*

A thick woollen cloth raised on both sides, obviously popular for duffle coats. Originally known as a flushing.

*Dumping:*

Compressing the wool when in bale form so as to reduce cargo space.

*Ell:*

The old standard length for measuring cloth. It varies in different countries. Scotch ell 37·2". English 45". Flemish 27". French 54".

*End:*

An individual thread of yarn either in spinning or in weaving with special reference to the warp.

*Extract:*

Waste (that is shoddy) that has been obtained by carbonising wool-cotton rags. About the lowest type of waste that can be reused.

*Face cloth:*

A fabric where either warp or weft predominates on the surface, usually the warp. Also an alternative name for the dress finish. Incidentally today, warp usually predominates rather than weft in dress finished cloths.

*Fag End:*

The end of a cut of warp, particularly if woven up with odd weft.

*Faller:*

The wire arm on a mule that controls the building of the cop.

*Fancy:*

The important roller on the carding set that lifts the material to the surface of the wire so that it can be removed by the doffer.

*Fearnought:*
A machine fitted with spiked rollers used for mixing the wool before carding. The same as the willey.

*Fell:*
The edge of the cloth during weaving. The word also has another meaning, namely the completion of the weaving of a cut or piece of cloth. In other words, one fells a piece.

*Fellmongering:*
The removal of wool from the skin of sheep that have been killed for mutton.

*Felt:*
A fabric made by matting or felting together the fibres, there being no separate warp or weft. Sometimes woven cloths that have been heavily felted are called woven felts, which is really a misnomer.

*Felting:*
The matting together of wool fibres. Once highly valued, now often regarded as a nuisance.

*Fent:*
Short, sometimes damaged, lengths of cloth. In some areas known as bribes.

*Fettling:*
Cleaning of the carding set.

*Flannel:*
A woollen or worsted cloth in a plain colour, usually if a woollen fairly well milled. Often, but not necessarily, grey in colour.

*Fleece:*
The wool shorn from one sheep.

*Flock:*
Very short lengths of wool obtained during processing, particularly during cutting or cropping, but also from rag pulling, where it is really an alternative name for devil's dust.

*Flushing:*
See duffel.

*Flyer:*
Once the attachment on the hand spinning-wheel that enabled winding and twisting to be done simultaneously. Now the little ring on the rim of the ring spinning-frame.

*Fly Shuttle:*
Kay's method of driving the shuttle across the loom.

*Fork:*
Two-pronged feeler that acts as a stop motion in the loom if the weft is missing.

*French Comb:*
Heilmann's system used for short wool.

*French Drawing:*
A system of drawing where porcupine rollers replace gills. In addition, no twist is inserted until the final stages.

*Frieze:*
Heavy woollen cloth.

*Fuller's Earth:*
A clay once very popular for cleaning cloth. The name, of course, derived from the great use that the fullers made of this material.

*Fulling:*
The shrinking and thickening of woollen cloths, now often called milling.

*Fustic:*
Probably the best of the natural yellow dyes.

*Gabardine:*
Closely woven twilled cloth, widely used for raincoats.

*Garnet Machine:*
A machine used for tearing old yarn and occasionally rags. Less severe in action than the devil.

*Gig:*
The teasel-covered raising machine.

*Gilling:*
The early stages of worsted drawing.

*Glauber's Salts:*
Sodium sulphate widely used in dyeing.

*Going Part:*
The moving part, that is the ley-sword of the loom.

*Grey Cloth:*
Pieces of cloth just off the loom, especially if intended for piece dyeing.

*Hair:*
Fibres from other animals than the sheep.

*Handle:*
The feel of wool, or the fabric. The outstanding handle of wool is very important, it varies greatly with different types, for example Geelong wools, particularly the lambs, give the softest handle, and for this reason are widely used for mixing with Cashmere for knitwear.

*Hank:*
A length of reeled yarn. Yarn for hand knitting is often sold in hanks. And the standard yarn measurement is usually so called.

*Harris Tweed:*
Genuine Harris must be 100 per cent. Scottish, and have been spun, dyed, woven and finished in the islands of the Outer Hebrides.

*Headstock:*
The controlling machinery of the mule.

*Healds:*
The cords or wires that the warp threads pass through in the loom and thereby very much a controlling mechanism of the loom. Also called heddles.

*Heilmann's Comb:*
The comb used for short wools, mainly on the Continent. It was invented by a Frenchman, Heilmann, living in Alsace and operates on a quite different principle to the Noble or circular comb.

*Herringbone:*
The weave effect obtained by reversing the direction of the twill.

*Hogg:*
A wool term – others with the same meaning are hoggett and teg, and in Australia weaner – it means wool from a sheep that has not been shorn as a lamb. Can be very choice.

*Hopsack:*
A weave based on the plain weave but with every end and pick duplicated. Also known as the matt and the celtic.

*Hosiery:*
Knitted fabrics.

*Indigo:*
The most famous of all dyes. Was originally a natural dye but now, of course, made synthetically. The synthesis of indigo by the great German dyestuff chemist Bayer was one of the key events in the development of the synthetic dyestuff trade.

*In the Grease:*
Wool in its natural state.

*Jack:*
The levers in the loom that control the harnesses.

*Jacquard:*
Loom used for weaving very fancy cloths. It was invented by the Frenchman of that name and replaced the old draw loom.

*Jenny:*
Hargreaves' famous spinning invention. It was essentially a multiple spinning-wheel using spindle, that is twist, drafting.

*Jersey:*
Now any knitted piece goods. Originally presumably referred to knitted fabrics made on the island of Jersey.

*Kemp:*
Dead wool. Kemps in wool are a serious fault. They are mainly found in the coarser types.

*Kendal:*
The famous green cloth of the Lake District. Made from Herdwick wool.

*Keratin:*
The substance from which wool is made.

*Kersey:*
An important coarse woolled cloth originally made in the East Anglian town of that name. Later the main product of the Yorkshire woollen trade, where it was sometimes known as Northern Dozens.

*Knop Yarn:*
Fancy yarn, that is yarns with some distinguishing feature other than the normal colour, fineness, etc. Strictly speaking, knop yarns are that type of yarn where a knop (that is a small lump of fibre or yarn) distinguishes the structure. Perhaps the best example of all is the Donegal Tweed where knops of material are added late in the carding process and these give the well-known spotted effect.

*Lambswool:*
Wool shorn from sheep under six to eight months old. Can be very soft handling, but sometimes liable to coarse hair and even kemps.

*Laps:*
Waste from the worsted drawing process.

*Lasting:*
A hard-wearing tightly woven fabric, usually made in a five-end weave.

*Lease:*
The weaving plan of the warp. The word has slightly changed its meaning, and now usually simply means the division of the warp between odd and even threads that is made at the time of warping. Therefore such words as lease rods.

*Leaves:*
Alternative name for loom shafts.

*Ley-sword:*
The beating up apparatus on the loom.

*Linsey Wolsey:*
Coarse cloth traditionally made with a mixture of linen warp and woollen weft.

*List:*
Same as selvidge.

*Llama:*
The Peruvian goat, which gives an interesting fibre, similar in some ways but not the same as mohair. Compares very closely to alpaca.

*Lock:*
The short wool from a fleece, normally separated from the main part during the skirting operation, which is really part of classing.

*Lofty:*
Full handling wool.

*London Shrinking:*
The finishing process whereby the cloth is damped and then allowed to resume its relaxed state so as to avoid shrinking later, especially during such making-up processes as Hoffmann pressing.

*Looming:*
Alternative name for drawing in.

*Madder:*
Very important red natural dye. Really alizarine.

*Matching:*
The varying sorts of wool, etc., into which the fleece is divided during sorting. In the past the wool merchants or staplers would sell matchings. Also the word is used for the matching, that is correct copying of colours.

*Medulla:*
Central cellular space in many types of wool.

*Melange:*
A mixture. Now especially applied to melange printing (vigoureux printing) whereby colour is printed along the slubbing. For example, white and black so as to obtain a better grey mixture shade.

*Melton:*
Heavy woollen cloth, until recently widely used for overcoatings.

*Mending:*
The repairing of faults in cloth that arise due to trouble in weaving, (that is broken ends), off shoots (that is missing picks), runches (that is collections of ends at the edge of the piece), etc.

*Merino:*
Merino wool.

*Milling:*
The fulling process; the word probably came into general use with the development of the rotary milling machine.

*Mohair:*
The hair of the angora goat, produced mainly in Turkey, South Africa and the United States of America.

*Moquette:*
A pile cloth used for furnishing fabrics and carpets.

*Mordant:*
The chemical agent used for fixing dyestuffs.

*Moreen:*
A stout woollen cloth used for curtains. Word is now almost, if not completely, obsolete.

*Moser:*
Meaning varies from district to district. In Yorkshire a brushing machine. In West of England the name for the raising machine when fitted with wire instead of teasels.

*Mule:*
Woollen spinning machine. The word, of course, derives from Crompton's famous machine which combined roller and spindle drafting, hence the name. It is, however, worth noting that the woollen mule, the main form in which it remains in the industry, uses spindle drafting only.

*Mungo:*
The name of the material obtained from tearing felted woollen cloths. Consequently shorter than shoddy. The name traditionally arose because the Yorkshire manufacturer attempted to use this very short material and was told by his spinner that it would not go (that is would not spin) and he replied, 'It mungo'.

*Nail:*
An old yarn measure, equals $2\frac{1}{4}''$, now very rarely used.

*Nap:*
Fibrous surface of cloth. One raises the nap and (or) cuts it down. Hence the word napping. In the West of England the word has acquired a specialised meaning, and a cloth is produced in which the nap after being raised up, is rubbed in a special napping (sometimes spelt knapping) machine to give a kind of ribbed or rubbed-up surface.

*Narrow Width:*
Cloth under 44" wide, usually 27" to 30". Now only common for riding tweeds and occasionally vestings.

*Needle Loom:*
A new machine used for making needle fabrics. A number of layers of fibres are taken and a needling machine pulls fibres from one layer through to another thereby producing a kind of fabric. This is one of the several techniques of fabric making producing non-woven cloths.

*Nep:*
Small knots of entangled fibre, a great curse with certain types of wool.

*Neppy Cloth*
A cloth containing neps which have to be picked out, sometimes at very great expense, indeed sometimes impossible to do at all.

*Noble Comb:*
The favourite combing machine of the Bradford worsted trade.

*Noil:*
The short fibre from the worsted combing process. An important material for the woollen trade.

*Nun's Veiling:*
A very light woollen cloth, usually black.

*Oil Combed Top:*
As name implies, tops that have been combed in oil.

*Olein:*
Oil, consisting mainly of oleic acid, used for woollen spinning. It is later removed in a saponification scour. Soda ash is added, and with the oil produces a soap.

*Open Band:*
Indicating twist direction, the opposite to Cross Band.

*Optical Bleach:*
Term sometimes used to cover a fluorescent brightening agent. In other words where an attempt is made to improve the brightness of wool without performing a real bleaching operation. Compare with the traditional blue bag of the family household.

*Papermakers' Felt:*
Fabric widely used in paper making, and an important section of the woven felt trade.

*Paramatta:*
An imitation of Merino, woven with cotton and worsted. Now very rare, but the word has a possible interesting derivation: Paramatta was the town in New South Wales where John McArthur first began his work that led to the founding of the Australian Merino sheep trade and the arrival of fine Merino wools, suitable for combing, on the British market.

*Pastel:*
Originally a blue dye, based on woad, now means any light colour.

*Pattern Chain:*
The chain that controls the interlacing of the warp and weft in weaving.

*Pegging Plan:*
The paper plan that indicates how the pattern change should be made up.

*Perching:*
Examination of cloth, particularly after coming from the loom, to find what faults need mending, and secondly after finishing has been completed, in order to see that everything has been put right and that the ultimate customer will be satisfied.

*Perpetuanas:*
The alternative name for serges, widely met with in the Devon serge trade.

*Persian Lamb:*
The alternative name for Astrakan. The pelt, that is the skin and wool complete, is taken from the Karakul lamb which has been slaughtered within a few days of birth and as a result a very attractive skin with tight curls is obtained.

*Petersham:*
Heavy woollen cloth, the hairy surface of which is usually rolled into little knots. It would seem to approximate to a West of England knap.

*ph:*
Scale for expressing the acidity or alkalinity of a solution.

*Pick:*
The thread carried across the warp during one passage of the shuttle or other container.

*Picker:*
The block of leather that hits the shuttle across the loom.

*Picklock:*
English term, not now common, indicating the best part of the fleece.

*Piece:*
Length of finished cloth. Often with wool textile fabrics about 70 yards, but would have been much shorter, say 25 yards, in days of hand-weaving.

*Piecer:*
The operator who attends the mule. Derives from the verb to piece, that is to twist or knot together the slubbings.

*Pieces:*
The rather inferior part of the fleece, poorer than the main part but better than the locks.

*Pilling:*
Accumulation of small clusters of entangled fibres on surface of fabric, especially liable to happen with certain synthetic fabrics.

*Pirn:*
Alternative name for weft spool, used in both Scotland and the West of England. Could be defined as the wooden, plastic, paper or metal spool on which weft yarn is wound for weaving.

*Plain weave:*
The design or cloth pattern in which each thread of weft passes alternately over and under a thread of weft.

*Ply:*
Twist of a yarn where two or more threads are put together. The number indicated by 2-ply, 3-ply, etc.

*Potting or Roll Boiling:*
A finishing process. The piece is rolled on a roller and boiled in water. This provides a very serious test for dye fastness and gives a very lovely finish. Used for traditional West of England fabrics.

*Pressing:*
Final finishing process.

*Prunelle:*
Name of two and one, or one and two twill. A familiar weave in the West of England.

*Pulling:*
Has two quite distinct meanings: (1) the process of reducing rags to a fibrous state, (2) the process by which wool is pulled off the skins of sheep.

*Quadrant:*
Important control mechanism on the mule.

*Quality:*
The properties of wool, especially applied to the fineness of the fibre. Traditionally the fineness,

that is the diameter of the fibre, is indicated by a series of numbers going from 28s to 100s. These numbers represent the limit in the size of yarn to which the wool can be spun. Yarn sizes in worsteds are indicated by the number of hanks of 560 yards that weigh one pound. In other words, 48s worsted yarn is yarn of such a size that 48 hanks of 560 yards make 1 lb. And a 48s wool indicates that a 48s worsted yarn is the limit of fineness to which such a wool could be spun. In practice today, a 48s wool would never be spun as fine as that. Gradually this numbering system is being replaced by an exact micron measurement of the size of the fibre. Today, for example, a 64s wool (a particularly common type of Merino wool) would be approximately 22 microns.

*Quill:*
Alternative name for the weft pirn, widely used in the West of England. Also quilly winding, the process of winding these quills.

*Rack:*
Alternative name for the tenter frame.

*Raddle:*
Rows of pegs used in beaming the warp in order to keep the threads straight and avoid them becoming tangled.

*Rags:*
Are called new rags where they have not been turned into fabric; old rags where they have come from made-up garments. Waste nomenclature is today rather involved. Some indication is given under the various sub-headings, for example Berlins and the mis-use of the word Cashmere. New worsteds indicate worsted rags that have not been made into garments, and which usually have come straight from the tailor.

*Raising:*
The production of the nap on the cloth.

*Reaching in:*
Drawing of warp threads through the heald, sometimes simply called drawing, but the word drawing is also used in some areas an an alternative to mending.

*Reed:*
The name given to the loom part (where it is removable) which consists of wires set between slats. Used to control the set of the warp. An important part of the loom.

*Reel:*
Revolving frame upon which hanks of yarn are wound.

*Reeling:*
The process of unwinding the yarn from the cops on which it has been spun on to bobbins or other containers ready for it to go to the next process, or, in the case of knitting yarn, to go for sale.

*Regain:*
The weight of water in a sample of wool expressed as a percentage of the dried weight. Usually around 16 per cent., but rather strangely the figure officially differs with varying states of the material, that is whether raw wool, combed top or yarn, etc.

*Relative Humidity:*
A measure of the amount of moisture in the atmosphere of a mill. Particularly important in cotton spinning, as this fibre will not spin unless the atmosphere is damp, hence its success in Lancashire. Wool is not so sensitive in this respect.

*Rep:*
A corded fabric, usually weft wise, made by putting two picks in the same shed.

*Reprocessed Wool:*
Alternative name for shoddy and mungo. According to Lemon in his *Wool Textile Industry* the word is sometimes limited to wool recovered from new cloths, but the present author's experience is that it is used in a much wider way.

*Resist Printing:*
One of the methods of printing patterns on to a cloth, a substance that resists the dye is printed on and then, as this stays white in dyeing, the pattern is formed.

*Reused Wool:*
Usually an alternative name to reprocessed wool, but Lemon (op. cit.) considers it applies to waste made from old cloth, or in other words from torn up garments.

*Ring Spinning:*
Method of worsted spinning where drawing, twisting and winding on is done simultaneously. It was an American invention, and is the most common type of worsted spinning today. The twist is inserted by a flyer revolving around a ring.

*Rock:*
An alternative name for the distaff.

*Roving:*
The name usually given to the sliver in its last stage of worsted drawing, that is immediately before it goes to the spinning.

*Russel:*
A worsted cord usually of a fine type and made in Norwich. Not in any wide use today.

*Saxony:*
A high grade of wool originally obtained from Saxony in Germany, and consequently fine yarn made therefrom, and more particularly cloth. In fabric form it is always a woollen as opposed to a worsted fabric, probably because when these Saxony wools first came from Germany in the early years of the nineteenth century they were used entirely in the woollen trade.

*Say:*
A relatively cheap worsted cloth.

*Scouring:*
There are two processes: (1) the washing of the wool, that is wool scouring, and (2) the washing of the pieces, that is piece scouring.

*Scribbler:*
The first part of a carding set. There is also the word scribbling which is the process done on a

scribbler. The word was more widely used in the past, where the scribbling was regarded as a quite separate process from the carding.

*Self-acting Mule:*
The fully developed mule. The change from the hand mule invented by Crompton was made by the important Manchester engineer Roberts.

*Selvidge:*
Sometimes selvage, another name for the list, that is the edge of a piece of cloth. It is perhaps worth noting that selvidges in certain modern types of loom are quite different in structure from the traditional selvidge, as each pick of weft is inserted as a separate entity.

*Serge:*
Originally a worsted warp, woollen weft cloth, widely made in Exeter. Now an all-worsted cloth, usually, but not necessarily, dark blue (that is navy). Thirty to forty years ago a navy botany serge was the most fashionable wear for men.

*Shalloon:*
Worsted cloth, one of the first types of worsted fabrics to be made in the West Riding.

*Shearling:*
A sheep one to two years old that has only been shorn once.

*Shed:*
The opening of the warp threads so that the weft can pass through.

*Shepherd Check:*
The four and four colouring on the two and two twill. The name originated in Scotland.

*Shetland Wool:*
Particularly soft-handling wool coming, of course, from the Shetland sheep found on the islands of that name. Unfortunately the word is now applied to a great many garments that do not have any Shetland wool in them.

*Shives:*
The vegetable matter in wool. There is a differentiation with burr. The latter is a big round seed, while a shive refers to the smaller type of grass-like vegetable matter.

*Shoddy:*
The material obtained by pulling unmilled cloth. There has been a tendency recently to use the word to cover all types of pulled material.

*Shoot:*
Alternative name for weft.

*Shrink Resistant:*
Name given to fabrics which have been given a treatment that means they will either not shrink or only within certain limited standards.

*Shuttle:*
The carrier of the weft across the loom.

*Skein:*

The length of yarn made up into a hank or similar type of container. It often refers to the measurement of yarn sizes, for example the standard hank for measuring the size of yarn in Yorkshire is the number of hanks of 256 yards that weigh 1 lb. and the resulting answer is described as 16s skeins, etc.

*Skin Wool:*

Wool removed from the skin of sheep that have been killed for meat production. Compare with dead wool.

*Skirtings:*

Stained and inferior pieces of the wool fleece removed during the skirting process, which takes place at the shearing station when classing is done. The fleece, after being sheared from the sheep, is placed on the table, the classer removes the odd bits around the edges and these are the skirtings. The name is also used to describe the process itself. The resulting materials are the locks, the pieces and the bellies.

*Sley:*

Alternative word for the reed.

*Slipe:*

Skin wool removed from skin by steeping in lime. But now also used to cover other methods, including removal by the sweating process or by the new slipe master.

*Sliver:*

The name given to the loose strands of fibre which come from the carding condenser, or from the drawing frames in the worsted process. The important point to remember is that they do not contain any twist.

*Slub:*

Defects in yarn caused by thick places. Occasionally these are obtained purposely to give special effects. But most slubs are certainly not deliberately made.

*Slubbing:*

Now used as an alternative name for sliver or even roller. The application of the word has become even wider, and in one sense is an alternative for tops because those people who dye tops are now called slubbing dyers. In the woollen trade it is definitely an alternative name for the sliver or roller (roller is more commonly used in the woollen trade than sliver). The word was more important in the past than now. The slubbing then was the result of piecing together the cardings on the billy, sometimes called the slubbing billy, ready for the jenny.

*Spindle:*

The key to the spinning process. In all earlier forms used both to insert the twist into the yarn and as a container for the spun yarn.

*Spindle Whorl:*

The small solid whorl with ground edges fixed on the base of the spindle, around which the driving band is held.

*Spinning:*
The manufacture of the yarn.

*Spool:*
Name used to cover almost any yarn container; all woollen manufacturers will have met the phrase 'we are short of spools'.

*Standard Condition:*
The natural condition of the material, especially with reference to the moisture content of the wool.

*Staple:*
A collection of wool fibres.

*Stenter:*
Alternative name for tenter.

*Suint:*
The excrement from the sweat glands of sheep. Compare with yolk.

*Tammy:*
The worsted weft cotton warp cloth in fancy colours and usually highly glazed.

*Tappet:*
A cam which controls the harnesses and is thereby used to describe the type of loom where the shedding is done by means of tappets. Compare with dobby looms, and Jacquard looms.

*Tartan:*
Special type of check, of course, deriving from Scotland. They may be compared with district checks.

*Tear:*
The weight of top relative to noil obtained by combing wool.

*Teasel Gig:*
The gig set up with teasels.

*Tegg:*
See Hogg.

*Temples:*
These keep the cloth the correct width during weaving.

*Tender Wool:*
Wool which has less than the normal strength.

*Tenter:*
A machine used for drying cloth and also for removing any creases and straightening it before further processing. Originally, of course, done on tenter racks which were such a common sight in all cloth-making areas. Also used in conjunction with other names, for example tenter hooks.

*Tex:*
The new system of yarn measurement based on metric units, and recommended by the Internation-

al Organisation for Standardisation to be universally used so as to do away with the many local systems that have been common for so long.

*Throstle:*
The name given to the bobbin and fly-spinning frame which uses the drag of the bobbin for winding on and derives direct from the fly system of the final hand-wheel.

*Thrum:*
The surplus ends of cloth, particularly of warp only coming from the loom.

*Tippy Wool:*
Wool where the tips of the fibre have been damaged by weathering while on the sheep, so much so that dyeing is affected.

*Tops:*
The slivers of fibre produced by the comb during worsted processing. Could also be defined as the raw material of the worsted spinner.

*Traveller:*
The small steel ring that runs on the flange of the ring in the ring-spinning frame, acting as the winding-on drag.

*Tucker:*
Originally, and indeed in most areas today, the alternative name for the fuller. Tucking, of course, describes the process. But in the West of England the name has come to be used to describe the early blending or willeying process.

*Tuner:*
The engineer who keeps the loom in working order.

*Tweed:*
Originally a cloth made in the lowland area of Scotland, but the term is now used for a wide variety of woollen cloths having effects produced by colour and design combinations. It is worth noting that the word itself did not come from the river Tweed but from the misreading of the word twill.

*Twill:*
The common type of weave which shows a line running across the cloth.

*Twisting in:*
Joining a new warp to the ends of an old one, sometimes also done by tying-on and then described in that way. Today often done by machines, which do in fact tie-on rather than twist-on.

*Twitty:*
A name given to yarn with a number of small irregularities in it, usually caused by faults in spinning.

*Union:*
The fabric made by mixing wool and cotton, either as raw material or yarn.

*Velour:*
The word has several meanings; as far as the wool textile trade is concerned it is used for any soft-handling fabric usually light in weight.

*Velvet:*
The warp pile fabric woven of silk or with a ground of worsted or cotton and usually with the pile cut to give the pile appearance.

*Venetian:*
A distinctive twill widely made in the West of England.

*Vicuna:*
The undercoat, that is the fine part of the fleece of a vicuna, a kind of llama. It produces a remarkably soft and fine fibre, indeed the most expensive in the world, although probably not any better than cashmere. The name is also given to the type of fabric made from this fibre.

*Vigoureux Printing.*
See melange printing.

*Virgin Wool:*
New and unused wool.

*Walk Mill:*
An old alternative name for a fulling mill.

*Warp:*
The threads that run lengthwise in the cloth.

*Warping:*
The arranging of the warp yarns on the warp bar and then their winding on to the warp beam ready for the loom.

*Warp Knitting:*
The usual and older type of knitting is usually called weft knitting, a misleading phrase but meaning that only one thread is used in the knitting process. With warp knitting there are two series of threads hence the name. A very progressive section of the textile trade today.

*Washing Off:*
The treatment of the fabric in water or some detergent solution to remove substances – more often than not the soap used in the milling process.

*Weaving:*
The forming of the fabric by the crossing of the warp and the weft.

*Weft:*
The threads that run across the cloth.

*Weft Fork:*
The small pronged fork which indicates when the weft is missing.

*Weft Knitting:*
The method of knitting with a single thread, in which the loops are formed across the width of the fabric. This is, of course, the traditional method of knitting and the one used in hand-knitting.

*Willey (sometimes Willow):*
There are many types of willey machines with alternative and localised names, all are used for

opening wool either in its greasy state before scouring, also probably more commonly, the blending process.

*Woad:*
The ancient blue dye. The colouring principle is the same as indigo.

*Woof:*
The alternative name for weft.

*Wool Classing:*
The dividing of the whole fleece into separate classes. The process is usually done on the sheep station if it is big enough, or almost always in the producing country. See note on skirting.

*Wool Scouring:*
The cleansing of raw or loose wool before any other processes are done.

*Wool Sorting:*
The separation and grading of the wool in individual fleeces into various qualities. Note difference compared with classing. The various sorts of wool made during the sorting process are known as matchings.

*Worsted:*
Now used to define that type of fabric that is made from yarn spun on the worsted as opposed to the woollen principle; in other words, where the short wool has been removed and the yarn spun from tops. The name derives from the Norfolk village of that name, but it is important to remember that worsted cloths, that is cloths made from combed wool, were made long before the use of this name.

*Yolk:*
The grease of the wool.

# Select Bibliography

| | |
|---|---|
| Alfred (S. Kydd) | *History of the Factory Movement from the Year 1802 to the Enactment of the Ten-Hour Bill in 1847.* (London 1847.) |
| Ashley, M. P. | *Financial and Commercial Policies under the Cromwellian Protectorate.* (1934.) |
| Ashley, W. J. | *The Early History of the Woollen Trade in England.* (1887.) |
| Ashley, W. J. | *An Introduction to English Economic History and Theory.* (1909.) |
| Aspin, C. | 'New Evidence on James Hargreaves and the Spinning Jenny.' (*Textile History*, Vol. I, No. 1.) |
| Aspin, C. and Chapman, S. D. | *James Hargreaves and the Spinning Jenny.* (1964.) |
| Aspinall, A. E. | *Early English Trade Unions.* (1949.) |
| Aubrey, J. | *Brief Lives* (various editions). |
| Aubrey, J. (ed. Britton) | *The Natural History of Wiltshire.* (1847.) |
| Aubrey, J. (ed. Jackson) | *Wiltshire Collections.* (1862.) |
| Baines, E. | *Account of the Woollen Manufacture of England.* (1970.) |
| Barford, K. E. | 'The West of England Cloth Industry: A Seventeenth Century Experiment in State Control.' *Wilts. Arch. Soc.* Vol. XLII, No. 141. |
| Bateson, M. | Review of Beverly Town Documents. (In *English Historical Review*, Vol. XVI.) |
| Beardwood, A. | *Alien Merchants in England 1350–77.* (1931.) |
| Beckensale, R. (ed.) | *Trowbridge Woollen Industry as Illustrated by the Stock Books of J. & T. Clark, 1804–1824.* (1951.) |
| Bickley, F. (ed.) | *The Little Red Book of Bristol.* 2 vols. (1900.) |

Bischoff, J.      *A Comprehensive History of the Woollen and Worsted Manufacturers,* 2 Vols. (1842.)

Bowden, P. J.      'The Wool Supply and the Woollen Industry.' (In *Economic History Review,* 2nd series. Vol. IX. 1956.)

Bradford, G.      'Somerset Social and Economic History.' (In *Victoria County History of Somerset,* Vol. II.)

Bland, A. E.
Brown, P. A. and
  Tawney, R. H.      *English Economic History, Selected Documents.*

Burnley, J.      *The History of Wool and Wool Combing.*

Butler, R. F.      'Gloucestershire Social and Economic History.' (In *Victoria County History of Gloucestershire,* Vol. II).

Cartwright, E.      *Memoirs of Edmund Cartwright.* (New Edition, 1971.)

Carus-Wilson, E. M.      'Cloth Production and International Competition in the Seventeenth Century.' (In *Economic History Review,* 2nd series, Vol. XIII, No. 2.)
'The Woollen Industry.' (In *The Cambridge Economic History of Europe,* Vol. II. 1952.)
'*Medieval Merchant Venturers.*' (1954.)
'An Industrial Revolution of the Thirteenth Century.' (*Economic History Review,* Vol. XI, also in Medieval Merchant Venturers.)
'Evidence of Industrial Growth in some Fifteenth Century Manors.' (In *Economic History Review,* 2nd series, Vol. XII, No. 2.)
'The Aulnage Accounts.' (In *Economic History Review,* Vol. II.)
'The English Cloth Industry in the Twelfth and Thirteenth Centuries.' (In *Economic History Review,* Vol. XIV.)
'The Overseas Trade of Bristol.' (In *Studies in English Trade in the Fifteenth Century,* ed. Power and Postan 1933.)
*The Overseas Trade of Bristol in the Fourteenth and Fifteenth Century.* (1937.)
'Trends in the Export of English Woollens in the Fourteenth Century.' (In *Economic History Review,* 2nd series, Vol. III. No. 2.)
*The Merchant Adventurers of Bristol in the Fifteenth Century.* (1962.)

Carus-Wilson, E. M.
  and Coleman, Olive      *England's Export Trade, 1274–1547.* (1963.)

Chaloner, W. H.      'The Cartwright Brothers.' (In *Wool Through The Ages,* I.W.S.)

Clapham, J. H.      *The Woollen and Worsted Industries.* (1907.)
'The Industrial Organisation of the Woollen and Worsted Industries of Yorkshire.' (In *Economic Journal,* Vol. XVI.)
*An Economic History of Modern Britain.* (1930–38. 3 vols.)
'The Transference of the Worsted Industry of Norfolk to the West Riding.' (In *Economic Journal.* Vol. XX.)

Clark, C. O.      'Ancient and Modern in Scouring and Dyeing.' (In *Journal of Society of Dyers and Colourists,* Vol. 66. No. 3.)

Clark, G. N.      *Science and Social Welfare in the Age of Newton.* (1937.)

Crabbe's Life, by his son.

Crabbe's poems.

Crump, W. C.                *The Leeds Woollen Industry 1780–1820.* (1931.)

Crump, W. C. and
  Ghorbal, G.              *The Huddersfield Woollen Industry.* (1935.)

Collinson, J.               *History of the County of Somersetshire.* 3 Vols. (1791.)

Cunningham, W.              *The Growth of English Industry and Commerce.* 3 Vols. (1910.)

Cunnington, B. H.           *Records of the County of Wiltshire* (1932.)
                            *Some Annals of the Borough of Devizes.* (1926.)

Curwen, E. Cecil            'The Problem of the Early Water Wheel.' *Antiquity.* Vol. 18.

Daniels, G. W.              *The Early English Cotton Trade.* (1920.)

Davis, R.                   'English Foreign Trade 1660–1700.' (In *Economic History Review,* 2nd series, Vol. VII, No. 2.)
                            'The Rise of Protection in England.' (In *Economic History Review,* 2nd series, Vol. XIV, No. 2.)

Defoe, D.                   *A Tour Through England and Wales.* 2 Vols. (Everyman.)

Dyer, John                  'The Fleece.' *Minor Poets of the Eighteenth Century.* (Everyman.)

Fiennes, Celia
  (ed. Morris)             *The Journeys of Celia Fiennes.* (1947 edition.)

Fisher, F. J.               'London's Export Trade in the Early Seventeenth Century.' (In *Economic History Review,* 2nd series, Vol. III, No. 2.)
                            'Commercial Trends and Policy in Sixteenth Century England.' (In *Economic History Review.* Vol. X.

Fox, J. H.                  *Quaker Homespun.* (1958.)

Fox, J. H.                  *The Woollen Manufacture at Wellington, Somerset.* (1914.)

French, G. J.               *The Life and Times of Samuel Crompton.* (1875.) New edition with an introduction by S. D. Chapman. (1970.)

Friis, A.                   *Alderman Cockayne's Project and the Cloth Trade.* (1927.)

Fuller, T.                  *The Worthies of England.*

Gray, H. L.                 'The Production and Exportation of English Woollens in the Fourteenth Century.' (In *English Historical Review,* Vol. XXIX.)
                            'English Foreign Trade from 1446–1482.' (In *Studies in English Trade in the Fifteenth Century.*)

Guest, R.                   *A Compendious History of the British Cotton Manufacturer.* (1823.)

Hammond, J. L. & B.         *The Skilled Labourer.* (1920.)
                            *The Town Labourer.* (1920.)
                            *The Village Labourer.* (1924.)

Hammond, J. L.              'The Movement of Population during the Industrial Revolution.' (In *History.* Vol. XII.)

Haskins, C.                 *The Ancient Trade Guilds and Companies of Salisbury.*

Hatcher, H.                 *History of Salisbury.*

Heaton, H.            'Yorkshire Cloth Traders in the United States 1770–1800.' (In *Thoresby Soc. Publications*. Vol. XXXVII.)
'Benjamin Gott and the Anglo-American Cloth Trade.' (In *Journal of Economic and Business History*. Vol. II.)
'Benjamin Gott and the Industrial Revolution.' (In *Economic History Review*, Vol. III,)
'Leeds White Cloth Hall.' (In *Thoresby Soc. Publications Misc.* Vol. XXII.)
*The Yorkshire Woollen and Worsted Industries*. (1920.) 2nd edition 1966 new preface.
*The Letter Books of J. Holroyd and S. Hill* (1914.)

Hirst, W.       *History of the Woollen Trade for the Past Sixty Years.* (1844.)

Historical MSS
  Commission:      Various Collections. Vol. I. (1901.)

Hobsbawn, E. J.     'The British Standard of Living 1790–1850.' (In *Economic History Review*, 2nd series, Vol. X, No. 1.)

Hobsbawn, E. J.     'The Travelling Artisan.' (In *Economic History Review*, 2nd series, Vol. III, No. 3.)

Hoskins, W. G.      *Industry, Trade and People of Exeter, 1688–1800.* (1935.)

Hunt, W. H.       *Bristol.* (1887.)

Hunter, D. M.      *The West of England Woollen Industry.* (1910.)

Hyett, F. A.       *Glimpses of the History of Painswick.* (1928.)

James, J.        *The History of the Worsted Manufacturers.* (1857.)
*The History and Topography of Bradford.* (1841.)

Jones, W. H.
  (ed. Beddoe)     *Bradford-on-Avon.*

Kitchen, G. W.     *Winchester.* (1890.)

Klein, J.         *The Mesta. A Study in Spanish Economic History, 1273–1836.* (1920.)

Leach, A. F. (ed.)    *Beverley Town Documents.* (1900.)

Lemon, H.       'Some Aspects of the Early History of Spinning, With Special Reference to Wool.' (*Journal of the Textile Institute*, August 1951.)

Lestocquiz, I.      'The Tenth Century.' (In *Economic History Review*. 2nd series, Vol. 1.)

Lipson, E.       *Woollen and Worsted Industries.* (1953.)
*The Economic History of England* (1943–45) 3 Vols.

Lloyd Pritchard, M. F.   'The Decline of Norwich.' (In *Economic History Review*, 2nd series, Vol. III, No. 3.)

Manley, Canon F. H.   'William Stumpe and His Family'. (*Wilts., Notes and Queries*, Vol. VIII.)

Mann, J. de L. and
  Wadsworth, A. P.   *The Cotton Trade and Industrial Lancashire, 1600–1780.* (1931.)

Mann, J. de L. (ed.)  'Documents illustrating the Wiltshire Textile Trade in the Eighteenth Century.' (Wiltshire Records Society, Devizes, 1964.)
'Wiltshire Woollen Industry.' (In *Victoria County History of Wiltshire*, Vol. 4.)
'Wiltshire Family of Clothiers.' (In *Economic History Review*, 2nd series, Vol. IX, No. 2.)
'The Textile Industry: Machinery for Cotton, Flax, Wool, 1760–1850.' (In *History of Technology*, Vol. IV, ed. Singer.)
*'Clothiers and Weavers in Wiltshire during the Eighteenth Century.'* (Studies on the Industrial Revolution presented to T. S. Ashton, ed. L. S. Pressnell, 1960.)

Mantoux, P.  *The Industrial Revolution.*

Marling, W. H.  'The Woollen Trade of Gloucestershire'. (In *Bristol and Gloucestershire Arch. Soc.*, Vol. 36.)

Miller, E.  See *Victoria County History of Yorkshire*, Vol. IV. (1961.)

Moir, E.  'Gentlemen Clothiers.' (In *Gloucestershire Studies*. ed. Finberg.)

Parliamentary Papers  'Minutes of Evidence taken before the Committee to whom the Bill respecting the laws relating to the Woollen Trade is committed.' In *Accounts and Papers (1), 1802–3*. Vol. 7.
'Report from the Committee on Woollen Clothiers Petition 1803.' Report (3), 1802–3, Vol. 5.
'Reports from the Committee on the Woollen Manufacture of England'. Reports of Committee (2), 1806. Vol. 3.
Hand Loom Weavers – Reports of the Assistant Commissioner, 1840.
Hand Loom Weavers – Reports of the Assistant Commissioner, 1841.
Report of Select Commission on Factory Children. (1831.)
Report of House of Lords Committee on Wool Trade. (1828.)

Pattern books and documents of Messrs S. Salter & Co. Ltd., of Trowbridge.
Pattern books and documents of Messrs J. &. T. Clark Ltd., of Trowbridge.
Pattern books and documents in possession of Messrs Abraham Laverton Ltd., Westbury. (All these documents are now deposited at the Wilts. County Record Office, Trowbridge).

Peel, F.  *The Rising of the Luddites.* (1885.) Reprint 1969 with an Introduction by E. P. Thompson.)

Pelham, R. A.  'Fourteenth Century England', *Historical Geography* (ed. Darby).

Perry, R.  'The Gloucester Woollen Industry, 1100–1690.' (In *Transactions Bristol and Gloucestershire. Arch. Soc.* Vol. 66.)

Pevsner, N.  *The Buildings of Britain: Somerset* (2. Vols). *Wiltshire*, (1 Vol.) *Devon*, (2 Vols.). *Berkshire*, (1 Vol.), *Gloucestershire* (2 Vols.).

Pilgrim, J. E.  'The Rise of the New Draperies in Essex.' (In *University of Birmingham Historical Journal*. Vol. VII, No. 1. 1955.)

Pirenne, H.  *The Economic and Social History of Mediaeval Europe.* (English translation 1941.)

Playne, A. T.  *Minchinhampton and Avening.*

Ponting, K. G.        'The Fullers of Marlborough.' *Wilts.* (In *Arch. Soc. Magazine.* Vol. LIII.)
                      *The West of England Cloth Industry.* (1957.)
                      *The Wool Trade Past and Present.* (1961.)
                      'Old Fulling Methods.' (In *Journal of the Society of Dyers and Colourists.* Vol. 67. No. 11.)

Postan, M.           'Economic Relations between England and The Hanse 1400–75.' (In *Studies in English Trade in the Fifteenth Century.*)
                      'The Fifteenth Century.' (In *Economic History Review.* Vol. IV.)
                      'Some Social Consequences of the Hundred Years War.' (In *Economic History Review.* Vol. XII.)

Power, E.            *The Wool Trade in English Mediaeval History* (1941).
                      'The Wool Trade in the Fifteenth Century.' (In *Studies in English Trade in the Fifteenth Century.*)

Prothero, R. E.
  (Lord Ernle)       *English Farming Past and Present, 1066–1900.* (1912.)

Ramsay, G. D.        *The Wiltshire Woollen Industry in the Sixteenth and Seventeenth Centuries.* (1943.)

Roth, H. L.          'Hand Card Making.' (In *Bankfield Museum Notes, Halifax*, No. 11.)
                      'Hand Wool Combing.' (In *Bankfield Museum Notes, Halifax*, No. 6.)
                      'Primitive Looms.' (In *Bankfield Museum Notes, Halifax*, Series 2, 8–11.)

Rudder, S.           *History of Gloucestershire.* (1779.)
Ruddock, A. A.       *Italian Merchants and Shipping in Southampton 1270–1600.* (1951.)

Salzman, L. F.       *English Industries in the Middle Ages.* (1913.)
Sellers, M.          'Chapters on Economic History and Textile Industry.' (In *Victoria County History of Yorkshire*, Vols. II and III. 1913.)
                      *The Merchant Adventurers of York.*

Sigsworth, E. M.     'The West Riding Wool Textile Industry.' (In *Wool Through the Ages*, I.W.S.)
                      *Black Dyke Mills.*

Singer, C.           *The Earliest Chemical Industry.* (1948.) (The Industry referred to in the title is the alum industry, which was closely linked with the dyeing.)

Smith, J.            *Chronicum Rusticum – Memoirs of Wool.* (1747.)
Smith, L. T. (ed.)   *Leland's Itinerary.* (1907–10.)
State Papers
  Domestic:          Elizabeth.
Stephens, W. B.      *Seventeenth Century Exeter.* (1958.)
Stone, L.            'Elizabethan Overseas Trade.' (In *Economic History Review*, 2nd series, Vol. II. No. 1.)

Tann, Jennifer       *Gloucestershire Woollen Mills.* (1967.)
                      'The Bleaching of Woollen and Worsted goods 1740–1860.' (In *Textile History.* Vol. 1. No. 2.)

| | |
|---|---|
| Tawney, R. H. | *The Agrarian Problem in the Sixteenth Century.* (1912.) |
| Tawney, R. H. and Power, E. (ed.) | *Tudor Economic Documents.* (1924.) 3 Vols. |
| Toynbee, A. J. | *The Industrial Revolution.* |
| Unwin, G. | *Industrial Organisation in the Sixteenth and Seventeenth Centuries.* (1904.) |
| Unwin, G. (ed.) | *Finance and Trade under Edward III.* (1918.) |
| Unwin, G. | *Studies in Economic History.* (1927.) |
| Unwin, G. (ed.) | *Samuel Oldknow and the Arkwrights.* |
| Ure, A. | *Philosophy of Manufacture.* |
| Veale (ed.) | *The Great Red Book of Bristol* (1913). 4 Vols. |
| Waylen, J. | *History of Marlborough.* (1854.) |
| Webb, S. & B. | *History of Trade Unionism.* (1920.) |
| Westerfield, R. B. | *Middlemen in English Business.* (1915.) |
| Wilkinson, J. | 'Broughton Gifford.' (In *Wilts. Arch. Magazine.* Vols. 15–16.) |
| Willcox, W. B. | *Gloucestershire 1590–1640.* (1940.) |
| Wood, A. C. | *A History of the Levant Company.* (1935.) |
| Wool Industries Research Association | Wool Research, Vol. 4. Carding. |
| | Wool Research, Vol. 6. Drawing and Spinning. |

# Index

*References to illustration numbers are in bold type*